Patriot Hearts:

World War I Passion and Prejudice in a Minnesota County

Frederick L. Johnson

First Printing
June 2017

Published by:
Goodhue County Historical Society
1166 Oak Street
Red Wing, MN 55066
651-388-6024
www.goodhuecountyhistory.org

Editing: Diane Johnson

Layout and Design: David Thofern and Diane Johnson

Proofreader: Ruth Nerhaugen

Indexing: Char Henn

☆   ☆   ☆

Goodhue County Historical Society and the author
would like to thank the Philip S. Duff, Jr. Endowment Fund
for its generous financial support of this project.

☆   ☆   ☆

ISBN-13: 978-1546563556
ISBN-10: 1546563555

Also by Frederick L. Johnson

The Sea Wing Disaster

Goodhue County, Minnesota: A Narrative History

Sky Crashers: A History of the Aurora Ski Club

Uncertain Lives:
African Americuns and Their First 150 Years
in the Red Wing, Minnesota Area

Red Wing: A Portable History

Richfield: Minnesota's Oldest Suburb

Suburban Dawn: The Emergence of Richfield, Edina and Bloomington

The Big Water: Lake Minnetonka and Its Place in Minnesota History

The Sea Wing Disaster: Tragedy on Lake Pepin

Shadows of Time: Minnesota's Surviving Railroad Depots
(with Bill Schrankler)

With love to all: The World War I Letters and Photographs of
Minnesota Brothers Marland and Stanley Williams
(with Elizabeth Williams Gomoll)

Table of Contents

Women workers from Boxrud Dry Goods Company march in an April 1917 Red Wing Loyalty Day parade.

CHAPTER 463—House File No. 1270.   **[Minnesota Sedition Act]**

An act making it unlawful, to interfere with or discourage the enlistment of men in the military or naval forces of the United States or of the of Minnesota, and providing punishment therefor.

Be it enacted by the Legislature of the State of Minnesota:

463]   p. 765

Section 1. Interfering with enlistment unlawful.—It shall be unlawful from and after the passage of this act for any person to print, publish or circulate in any manner whatsoever any book, pamphlet, or written or printed matter that advocates or attempts to advocate that men should not enlist in the military or naval forces of the United States or the state of Minnesota.

Sec. 2. Speaking by word of mouth against enlistment unlawful.—It shall be unlawful for any person in any public place, or at any meeting where more than five persons are assembled, to advocate or teach by word of mouth or otherwise that men should not enlist in the military or naval forces of the United States or the state of Minnesota.

Sec. 3. Teaching or advocating by written or printed matters against enlistment unlawful.—It shall be unlawful for any person to teach or advocate by any written or printed matter whatsoever, or by oral speech, that the citizens of this state should not aid or assist the United States in prosecuting or carrying on war with the public enemies of the United States.

Sec. 4. "Citizen" defined.—A citizen of this state for the purposes of this act is hereby defined to be any person within the confines of the state.

Sec. 5. Violating a gross misdemeanor.—Any person violating any provisions of this act is hereby declared to be guilty of gross misdemeanor and shall be punished therefor by a fine of not less than one hundred dollars, ($100.00) nor more than five hundred dollars, ($500.00), or by imprisonment in the county jail for not less than three months nor more than one year, or by both.

Sec. 6- Officers given right to arrest.—Any police or peace officer of this state, or any regularly commissioned officer in the army or navy of the United States or of the national guard or organized militia of the state of Minnesota is hereby authorized to summarily arrest any person violating any provisions of this act.

Sec. 7. This act shall take effect and be in force from and after, its passage.

Approved April 20, 1917.

Author's Note

In this narrative I document a disturbingly large number of individuals who, in apparent reaction to persistent and alarming home front pressures of the Great War years, pushed toward and eventually over the line of lawful behavior. The overarching issue most worrying to all Americans at this time was the horrific war—the most deadly in human history—raging in Europe. It was a struggle that the United States and its allies had to win. Nonetheless, as the war abroad progressed, reports from across America told of a divided nation. Those worried about the loyalty of German Americans and organizations suspected of disloyalty looked with suspicion upon ethnic and political minorities. A significant number of citizens, unaffected by the headline-making events produced by this American rift, cautiously hoped for a resolution.

There is much to criticize in the Minnesota of 1917–18. I join other historians in pointing to a fundamental failure of government that left unprotected the constitutional rights of citizens. Research from this study and other similar works indicts some individuals for extralegal actions that deprived fellow citizens of their freedoms of speech and liberty.

It also appears that, in all but the most egregious cases of unlawful behavior, there were signs that fallible people were trying to do the right thing. Indeed, we see that patriot hearts beat in the chests of intolerant superpatriots and war skeptics alike.

Distinguished Minnesota scholar Rhoda Gilman offered us all wise advice in the conclusion of her biography of Henry Sibley, Minnesota's first governor. She cautioned against judging, through the murky prism of time, the motivations and actions of our distant predecessors. "If any lesson can be learned," wrote Gilman, "it is the inseparability of individuals from their times and from the assumptions and pressures of the society in which they have lived. Some swim with the current, some struggle against it, and some have divided hearts."

Frederick L. Johnson
April 2017

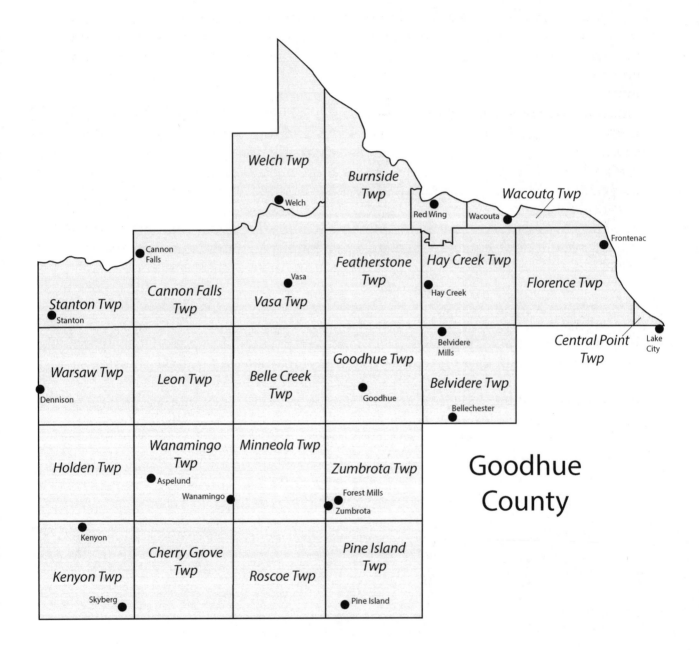

Welch Twp

Burnside Twp

Wacouta Twp

Welch

Red Wing

Wacouta

Cannon Falls

Frontenac

Featherstone Twp

Hay Creek Twp

Florence Twp

Vasa

Stanton Twp

Cannon Falls Twp

Vasa Twp

Hay Creek

Stanton

Central Point Twp

Lake City

Warsaw Twp

Leon Twp

Belle Creek Twp

Goodhue Twp

Belvidere Mills

Dennison

Goodhue

Belvidere Twp

Bellechester

Wanamingo Twp

Minneola Twp

Goodhue County

Holden Twp

Zumbrota Twp

Aspelund

Wanamingo

Forest Mills

Zumbrota

Kenyon

Cherry Grove Twp

Pine Island Twp

Kenyon Twp

Roscoe Twp

Skyberg

Pine Island

Choosing Sides

If Nonpartisan League (NPL) supporters of Charles A. Lindbergh Sr. and his 1918 candidacy for Minnesota governor harbored any doubt about which way the political winds were blowing in Goodhue County, effigies of their candidate swinging from nooses in Red Wing and Stanton provided disturbing indicators. Bitter animosity toward the Nonpartisan League—a growing pro-farmer group led by socialists and radicals—and suspect pro-German elements in the area were on display across the county. Months of negative newspaper coverage leveled against the NPL and its alleged skepticism regarding America's entry into Europe's Great War had created deep anti-League sentiment.[1] A prolonged and highly publicized legal assault against Nonpartisan League speakers, spearheaded by Goodhue County Attorney Thomas A. Mohn, only added to the hostility. Goodhue County juries became Minnesota leaders in indicting and convicting citizens for sedition. And, in a significant decision eventually confirmed by the United States Supreme Court, a Red Wing jury ordered the imprisonment of Nonpartisan League strategist and speaker Joseph Gilbert.

Goodhue County officials did not act alone in prosecuting citizens unenthusiastic about American involvement in the European conflict. Just one week after Congress issued an April 6, 1917, declaration of war against Germany, state legislators created the Minnesota Commission of Public Safety (MCPS). Its far-reaching mandate: Take all measures necessary to suppress anti-war movements and pro-German activity in Minnesota.[2]

An effigy of Nonpartisan League gubernatorial candidate Charles Lindbergh Sr. hangs from a lamppost near the State Bank of Stanton in western Goodhue County.

William Watts Folwell, first president of the University of Minnesota, a professor and historian, looked on in amazement as the Commission of Public Safety was empaneled. Folwell later commented, "Thus composed, armed with extraordinary powers, and granted an ample appropriation by a practically unanimous Legislature, the commission proceeded to exercise functions the like of which the history of American law had never disclosed."[3]

On April 20 the Legislature passed the Minnesota Sedition Act, a law with which a number of Goodhue County citizens would become intimately familiar. The new statute made it illegal to interfere with enlistments in the nation's armed forces or persuade other Minnesotans to refuse to support the American war effort [see page viii for a copy of this act].⁴ Nonpartisan League leaders were foremost among those questioning the new legislative measure and its limits to free speech. Following stunning triumphs in North Dakota's 1916 elections, the NPL had dispatched organizers to Minnesota. The League advocated socialist-styled governmental reforms—a fundamental and controversial change in how the state functioned. Minnesota's Republican Party and its influential supporters in business and industrial sectors, fiercely opposed philosophically to the NPL's ideas, monitored the group for evidence of disloyalty. Proof of such treachery would brand the League and its members as un-American.

Goodhue County's economy in 1917 provided a less than perfect target for the Nonpartisan League. In North Dakota, the League capitalized on the burning anger of spring wheat growers frustrated by what they believed to be rigged grain prices and transport costs. Goodhue County farmsteads were diversified in their operations, and owners tended to be financially more secure. In 1917 the county had a network of prosperous modest sized towns and cities—Cannon Falls, Zumbrota, Kenyon, Pine Island and Red Wing, the larger county seat. Middle-class business owners and entrepreneurs, professionals and modestly wealthy capitalists in these communities were literally and figuratively invested in the prevailing socioeconomic order. They wanted no part of a farmer rebellion, particularly one led by NPL socialists. Nonetheless, the League received backing from residents in the state's vast agricultural districts, including some who owned Goodhue County farms.

As the summer of 1917 wore on, the Nonpartisan League endured heavy criticism for what opponents labeled its radical proposals. Persistent reports that NPL

Joseph Gilbert, Nonpartisan League leader and a central figure in a Goodhue County sedition trial

organizers opposed the war and were treasonously pro-German plagued the farmer faction. In response, Joseph Gilbert, part of the League's leadership circle, authored a proclamation of principles. The declaration supported the nation's participation in the fighting: "…we declare unequivocally that we stand for our country, right or wrong, as against foreign governments with whom we are actually engaged in war." The Gilbert manifesto also asserted, "We declare the freedom of speech to be the bulwark of human liberty." He added what appeared to be a direct challenge to the Minnesota Commission of Public Safety: "A declaration of war does not repeal the Constitution of the United States, and the unwarranted interference of military and other authorities with the rights of individuals must cease." The NPL leader also criticized profiteering by "bloodstained wealth," noting, "the ugly incitings [sic] of an economic system based on exploitation" was a cause of the war.⁵

Gilbert's widely distributed statement outraged NPL opponents for its suggestion that the nation's military would take "unwarranted" actions against the people. His message intensified feelings of contempt for the League held by Minnesota's business community and Republican Party leadership. By mid-summer 1917, avid supporters of the government's wartime policies were using the phrase "100% American," popularized by former president Theodore Roosevelt to describe "superpatriots" completely committed to the war effort. Gilbert's language proved anathema for 100-Percenters.[6]

Incumbent Republican governor Joseph A. A. Burnquist possessed remarkable wartime political power and, by summer 1917, was beginning to wield it. Now, besides performing the duties of his office, the 38-year-old Burnquist chaired the Commission of Public Safety with its Legislature-endowed wartime dominion over the Minnesota populace. Burnquist appointed five of the seven commission members; the governor and Attorney General Lyndon A. Smith also served. MCPS member John F. McGee, a prominent Minneapolis corporate lawyer and former judge, emerged as a driving force on the committee. McGee would prove a relentless, resolute enemy of the Nonpartisan League, labor unions, socialists and others the MCPS perceived to be anti-war, anti-business.[7]

THE MAP GROWS

"One by one the states are realizing their common interest and are being sewed into a one-piece blanket that will cover when finished, the whole United States. Since this cartoon was made sewing has extended much farther, Kansas, Washington, Colorado, Wisconsin, being among the pieces added by the patient stitching of the National Nonpartisan League."
Cartoon and caption from *Nonpartisan Leader*

In October 1917, John McGee publicly compared the Nonpartisan League to the International Workers of the World (IWW), a militant working class labor union. He attacked the IWW and then the NPL in the same sentence, claiming the union was "…un-American and against all government but not as dangerous as the Nonpartisan League or the Red Socialists."[8] McGee's loathing of the NPL drifted toward the violent six months later. Addressing the U.S. Senate Military Affairs Committee, Judge McGee declared, "A Non-Partisan League lecturer is a traitor every time…no matter what he says or does, a League worker is a traitor. Where we made a mistake was in not establishing a firing squad in the first days of the war."[9]

Minnesota Governor
Joseph A. A. Burnquist

The Nonpartisan League's March 1918 St. Paul convention supported ex-Congressman Charles A. Lindbergh Sr., a Republican with Nonpartisan League ties, as its challenger to incumbent Burnquist in the state's June Republican gubernatorial primary. Lindbergh's nomination upped the political stakes in the widening struggle between pro-war elements and those with reservations about the conflict. Already on the defensive against accusations of being disloyal and pro-German, NPL leadership, its candidates and allies dealt with a renewed barrage of criticism. In this "you're either for us or against us" atmosphere, Lindbergh, Joe Gilbert, NPL supporters and their associates became targets of the Commission of Public Safety and its eager confederates—hawkish newspaper editors, watchful government agents and aggressive county attorneys.[10]

With the United States declaration of war against Germany, Goodhue County's elected officials and political establishment emerged as 100-Percenters determined to follow the MCPS lead. Displaying equal amounts of fervor and efficiency, county superpatriots sharpened their attacks against the NPL and its followers. A county grand jury meeting in Red Wing in March 1918 captured the spirit of repression when it issued a warning to the public: "…[W]e must all be boosters for the war and 100% American."[11]

In May 1918 a Goodhue County jury convicted Nonpartisan League manager Joseph Gilbert of sedition. An appeals process eventually brought Gilbert before the United States Supreme Court where, once again, he lost. Associate Justice Louis Brandeis produced a memorable dissent in *Gilbert v. Minnesota* that included a significant conclusion. In referring to Minnesota's "policy of repression," he wrote: "…the most serious cases of alleged interference with civil liberty were reported to the federal government *from that state [Minnesota]* [emphasis added]."[12]

Nearly a century later Brandeis's words resound with questions for the present day: Why, during the First World War years, did Minnesota prove more aggressive than the other 47 states in repressing the civil liberties of its citizens? And, for the purposes of this study, why, in this category of rights repression, did Goodhue County lead Minnesota?

Goodhue County, Minnesota

Seeds of Discord

Angry voices reverberated through the chamber as members of the Minnesota House of Representatives shouted epithets and accusations at each other during a debate showing no sign of conclusion. Combative legislators had been arguing for two hours over a provision in a proposed law that required the registration of all aliens—immigrants without U.S. citizenship—residing in Minnesota. Foes of the bill, particularly those foreign born or having parents who were, believed the measure was an insult to their loyalty; its supporters claimed only aliens opposed it. The raucous showdown was described as among the most bitter in the Legislature's history. The debate took place on April 5, 1917, the day prior to the decision by the United States to declare war against Germany.[13]

State legislator Oscar Seebach, the prominent Spanish-American War hero from Red Wing and first-generation German American, surprised some with his strong support of alien registration. Many Minnesotans believed the Act to be anti-immigrant. He is pictured in 1917 shortly after his appointment to organize the Minnesota Home Guard.

Both Goodhue County House members involved themselves in the dispute. Oscar Seebach, a hero of the Spanish-American War and an American-born son of German-born parents, surprised listeners when he thundered his support of the alien registration law: "I am German to the backbone, but I am for this bill." Anton V. Anderson, born of immigrant parents in Vasa, Goodhue County's largest Swedish colony, observed the ongoing fracas in dismay. Anderson, a "scientific" farmer, manager-president of Belle Creek Cooperative Creamery, and supporter of the Nonpartisan League, proposed a halt to the squabbling with a motion to continue the discussion after an upcoming three-day recess. The angry lawmakers consented by a 59–51 vote, but not before exchanging more insults.[14]

Anton V. Anderson, state legislator from Goodhue County, managed to quiet the chaotic April 5, 1917, Minnesota Legislature debate on alien registration with a successful motion to continue the talks.

Jens Kristian Grondahl came to Minnesota from his native Norway at age 11, and later built a successful career in publishing. He edited the *Red Wing Daily Republican* and ran Red Wing Printing Company. As the U.S. entered the Great War, he became Goodhue County's most voluble superpatriot, advocating "100% Americanism" in his newspaper.

Words flew in the U.S. House of Representatives the following day as members debated President Wilson's call for war. Another Goodhue County man, Jens K. Grondahl of Red Wing, editor of its *Daily Republican* newspaper, helped cool tempers by some indirect intervention. In the midst of the bitter discussions, Rep. Isaac Siegel, New York, rose to defend the loyalty of his German American constituents and to remind his colleagues that duty to country was "paramount." Siegel then read into the record Grondahl's patriotic poem, "America, My Country." House members greeted it with enthusiastic applause. A *Minneapolis Tribune* reporter on the scene wrote, two days later, the poem "has attained unusual popularity in Washington during the last few days."[15]

Back in Red Wing, Grondahl seized the moment, ordered music added to his verse, and assigned his Red Wing Printing Company to publish the resulting song. Its sheet music featured a bold subtitle: "The New National Anthem." Grondahl commenced an aggressive campaign to get his song made the official national anthem of the United States (President Wilson recognized "The Star-Spangled Banner" for ceremonial use in 1916, but it would not become the official national anthem until 1931). The Red Wing newspaper editor faced a challenge. Patriotic wartime music was now flowing from the pens of other American songwriters—the Parker World War I Sheet Music Collection has 753 such pieces—although no other composition was known to have been touted as a possible American national anthem.[16]

A resourceful song salesman, Grondahl mailed the sheet music to troops in France, schools, national magazines, social organizations and individuals [see pp. 138–9], along with his description of how the U.S. House came to praise his words. The National Council of Women and National Editorial [newspaper] Association became important boosters. NEA members sang the tune at meetings in Minneapolis and Red Wing. In a novel October 1917 promotion, some 500 "school men" meeting at the University of Minnesota sang "America, My Country" with Grondahl listening on a telephone in Red Wing. The *Minneapolis Tribune* headline read, "Singing of New Anthem is Heard 50 Miles Away."[17]

America, My Country (first verse)
America, my country, I come at thy call;
I plight thee my troth and I give thee my all;
In peace or in war I am wed to thy weal —
I'll carry thy flag through the fire and steel.
Unsullied it floats o'er our peace-loving race,
On sea, nor land shall it suffer disgrace;
In rev'rence I kneel at sweet liberty's shrine:
America, my country, command, I am thine!

In an overt sales pitch to the influential Alice Winter, chair of the Minnesota Commission of Public Safety's Women's Auxiliary, Grondahl immodestly asserted, "[W]e feel that a vast number of copies [of his music] should be used in view of the extraordinary favor with which this song has been received." He urged Winter to create support for his anthem within her organization and other similar groups to purchase enough of his music "to supply army and other patriotic needs." Grondahl offered to sell his anthem "in large quantities for commercial purposes at the cost of manufacture."[18]

Continuing, Grondahl informed Winter that he had received "perhaps 250 unsolicited orders from High school and county superintendents," and noted "laudatory letters from governors of states…and patriots [that] will show the nation wide interest in this song." He boasted of one correspondent "who said he wished he was rich so that he might give a copy of this song to every person in America." Included with his letter were 100 copies of the song and 500 copies of a postcard order form.

The patriotic hymn never caught fire. Nevertheless, issues of Grondahl's newspaper printed during the war carried the first verse of *America, My Country* directly below the *Daily Republican* masthead and an engraving of the American flag.

Clearly Grondahl, at age 47, wouldn't be carrying the American flag in combat anywhere, much less through "fire and steel." Nationalistic sentiments, like those of the Red Wing editor, drew fire from critics—Nonpartisan Leaguers and their allies would be among them—who attacked business and community leaders for brandishing

After his poem "America, My Country" was read to acclaim in the U.S. Congress, Jens Grondahl, editor of the *Red Wing Daily Republican*, had music added. He then began a campaign to make his composition the national anthem.

their support of war while being too old or well-connected to fight in it. His activities during the 1917–1918 war amply demonstrated that the diminutive Grondahl was not one to shy away from confronting those he believed to be unpatriotic.

From its outset, Jens Grondahl wholeheartedly embraced the nation's war effort. He clearly loved his adoptive country and city, regularly proclaiming his feelings in the *Daily Republican* during the 1917–1918 war years. He became, without question, Goodhue County's most visible "100% American," a person who would do far more in support of the war than write poems.

Through use of his newspaper and his leadership activities on the home front, Grondahl's influence was to be deeply, and sometimes painfully, experienced. The Red Wing editor emerged as a superpatriot and ultra-nationalist, a caustic and relentless critic of any group or individual that, in his view, lacked sufficient patriotism.

☆ ☆ ☆

A diversifying economy extended Goodhue County's remarkable decades of growth, leaving it well balanced and healthy in 1917 as the United States contemplated entering Europe's Great War. Its advantageous geographic position featured thriving farms resting on rich prairie loam, southern sections watered by the Zumbro River and districts to the north and west by the Cannon River. The Mississippi River formed the county's irregular northeastern boundary. Red Wing served as its governmental center and river port. Widely settled prior to Minnesota statehood in 1858, Goodhue County was an early and important agricultural center and transportation hub. As the new twentieth century progressed, an expanding industrial base and broad railroad network kept the county economy both stable and strong.

Goodhue County had emerged as the state's wheat capital when the 1870s King Wheat Era burst upon the state. Southeastern Minnesota blossomed in a vast "wheat field"—the state's western regions were still being settled—accounting for 61 percent of its cultivated acres. In 1872 the county ranked first in Minnesota wheat acreage (116,977), bushels produced (2.3 million) and bushels per acre (19.76).[19]

Entrepreneurs in Red Wing hustled to buy, store and ship wheat at its riverside facilities. In 1873 the Mississippi River port shipped 1.8 million bushels valued at more than two million dollars and ranked as the world's largest primary wheat market. In 1874 Goodhue County earned the *Illustrated Atlas of the State of Minnesota* label "the banner wheat county in America."

Wheat growers in Goodhue County and other nearby districts profited during the King Wheat years despite farmer complaints that grain-buying middlemen and their grading and weighing processes were rigged against them. Wheat producers had a point. In

A portion of Red Wing's riverfront and industrial district is shown around 1905. Settled in the early 1850s and seat of government for Goodhue County, the city also served as a rail and shipping center.

Red Wing, agile far-sighted merchants, professionals, factory and business owners became grain buyers, storage facility owners and shippers. For some, the profits were enormous.[20]

To the west, the Little Cannon and Cannon rivers supplied waterpower for the flourishing Goodhue County flour milling centers at Cannon Falls and Stanton. In the county's southwest sector, Gunderson Brothers flour mill and elevator at Kenyon proved successful. Zumbrota thrived, as did neighboring Forest Mills, a flour mill venture backed in part by future Minnesota governor Lucius Hubbard of Red Wing, even before railroad connections added to their success. Rail links stirred additional growth in Pine Island and Wanamingo.

When stem rust threatened wheat production in the late 1870s, county farmers, along with leaders in industry and business, deftly sidestepped disaster. Wheat money cushioned the setback and helped bankroll further industrialization. Railroad baron James J. Hill later complimented the foresight of county residents in an 1897 speech, "…Red Wing…for a few years was considered the champion wheat market, the largest primary wheat market in the world…but the wheat market of Red Wing has passed away and the farmers there are doing other and better things."[21]

As war approached in 1917, Goodhue County's economy had surfaced as an example of an agricultural-industrial mix. Farmers continued to enjoy a gratifying surge in total value of farm property, starting at $18 million in 1900 and moving past the $50 million mark in 1917. Total county farm values would reach $70 million by 1920.[22]

Goodhue County's industrial sector in 1917 proved diverse and strong. County clay pits supplied busy stoneware, sewer pipe and silo tile operations; quarries produced lime and stone; the shoe and boot industry was expanding. County manufactories made, among other products: flour, malt, linseed oil, beer, boat motors, auto tires, tanned leather, boilers, rope and twine, furniture, hats, and buttons. Cheesemakers centered in Pine Island led the state in production, while dairy farmers throughout the county supported proliferating "co-op" creameries.

A large hydroelectric dam at Cannon Falls became a major regional supplier of electricity; all county towns were linked to an electrical grid and a telephone system. Modern hospitals and a new tuberculosis sanatorium provided improved medical care; earlier, the county built the state's first facility for the poor. Goodhue County included four cities with around 1,000 residents each, Cannon Falls, Kenyon, Zumbrota and Pine Island, and the city of Red Wing with 9,068. Red Wing's High Wagon Bridge spanned the Mississippi, linking Goodhue County to bordering Wisconsin. Major railroads, Chicago Milwaukee and St. Paul, Chicago Great Western, and Chicago North Western, crisscrossed the county.

Members of Goodhue County's varied ethnic groups found themselves under scrutiny as America moved to intervene in the Great War, later known as World War I. Americans had looked on as millions of European soldiers mobilized for war in August 1914. After nearly three years of catastrophic losses, the war was nearing stalemate. Germany, France, Russia, England and Austria-Hungary each sustained more than two million killed, wounded and missing, and smaller nations suffered proportionally. Although America was not yet involved in the conflict, residents from Goodhue County's largest ethnic groups, Norwegians, Swedes and Germans, followed the fighting with interest and concern. German Americans naturally tended to favor the forces of Germany and its allies.

Norwegian and Swedish Americans assumed a more neutral stance since their homelands weren't directly involved in the conflict. Then, in April 1917, the United States

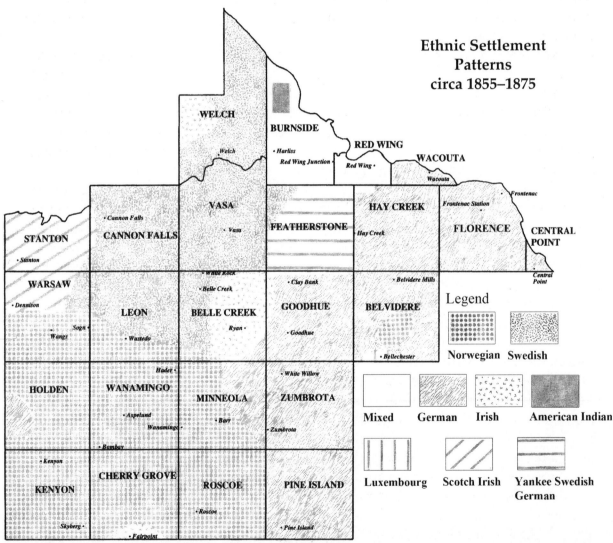

Ethnic Settlement Patterns circa 1855–1875

Legend

Norwegian | Swedish

Mixed | German | Irish | American Indian

Luxembourg | Scotch Irish | Yankee Swedish German

One of Minnesota's first settled counties, Goodhue gradually filled with immigrants from northern Europe. As they entered the New World, the newcomers tended to form ethnic enclaves by claiming land in the same districts. Assimilation was an ongoing process. When the U.S. entered the World War in 1917, vague yet distinguishable borders separating these groups were still visible. Note: The original Kunau map mistakenly labeled Florence Township "Frontenac" and showed Welch on the south side of the Cannon River. Map by G. J. Kunau declared war on Germany. As Americans began to unite in support of the war effort, the loyalty of the nation's foreign born and their families came into question. Would these citizens get behind their adopted nation or align with their European homelands?

Europeans who first settled in rural Goodhue County chose to live in ethnic enclaves with their immigrant Norwegian, German, Swedish, Irish or Scots Irish brethren. They maintained differing levels of attachment to the European nations of their ancestors. The foreign-born carried memories of life in the "Old Country," while the American-born generations that followed tended to view themselves as Americans first. Members of each generation typically stayed connected to American and European branches of the family, observed Old World religious customs, continued traditional food preparation and maintained some fluency in the language of their forebears.

Olaf Stageberg, a politically active professor at the Red Wing Seminary, later reported that by 1870, Goodhue County had no more land available for settlement. Norwegian immigrants had snapped up some of the last available acreage. Stageberg had been born in 1868 at Wanamingo in the midst of the county's sprawling Norwegian settlement: the southwest townships of Holden, Kenyon, Cherry Grove, Roscoe, Minneola, and the southern half of Warsaw. An 1874 visitor to that region described it as "a compact mass of Norwegians."[23]

The earliest Swedish immigrants established a colony eight miles south and west of Red Wing that they called Vasa after the powerful monarch who established an independent Sweden in the 1520s. Townships with Swedish majorities included Vasa, known locally as Swede Prairie, Cannon Falls, Welch, northern Leon and western Belle Creek. Vague yet distinguishable borders separated Swedish settlements from the Scots Irish in Stanton and northern Warsaw townships, Norwegians south and west of them, and Irish to their east in Belle Creek Township.[24]

Relatively few Irish traveled to Minnesota and Goodhue County, preferring America's North Atlantic states where they first settled. Exceptions to that rule were railroad workers Walter Doyle and James O'Neill. They left jobs in north central Illinois, headed to Minnesota Territory and staked claims in Belle Creek in July 1854. Their wives, Johanna Doyle and Margaret O'Neill, and children followed. The greatest growth in this Irish community occurred after the Civil War. Irish Americans built St. Columbkill Church, named for a well-known Irish saint, and also served German and Luxembourg Catholics from the area.[25]

Across Minnesota, German speakers made up the state's largest ethnic group until 1905 when Swedes surpassed them. Norwegians were a strong third. That order was different in Goodhue County. Norwegians were first in population (10,198), Swedes second (9,549) and Germans third (7,016). German Minnesotans gained ground in the early twentieth century, however, and soon held a commanding lead.[26]

Hay Creek Township, south of Red Wing, became the heart of Goodhue County's New Germany, with German immigrants making up 80 percent of the population by

1860. Germans were also in the majority in the neighboring townships of Frontenac, Goodhue, Zumbrota, Pine Island, Wacouta and Belvidere.

☆   ☆   ☆

German American immigrants in Minnesota continued to use the language of their former country for religious activities, in school and at home, as did Irish, Swedes, Norwegians and other European immigrants. But such traditions came into question in April 1917 when the United States entered the Great War.

For the members of the nation's many ethnic groups, assimilation into the greater society, the "Americanization" process—former President Theodore Roosevelt called it becoming "hundred percent American"—was more unpredictable. Roosevelt believed a person using a hyphen to identify himself, German-American, Irish-American or French-American for example, was "not an American at all." He asserted, "Americanism is a matter of the spirit and the soul. Our allegiance must be purely to the United States." He condemned "unsparingly…any man who holds any other allegiance."[27]

There could be no method certain to determine if residents from Minnesota's various ethnic factions had been instilled with enough values and beliefs to be considered truly "American." It was equally true that no foolproof system existed guaranteeing that Minnesotans with family lines stretching to the founding fathers were the real thing.[28]

AMERICANIZATION
MEANS

The use of a common language for the entire nation.

The desire of all peoples in America to unite in a common citizenship under one flag.

The combatting of anti-American propaganda, activities and schemes, and the stamping out of sedition and disloyalty wherever found.

The elimination of causes of disorder and unrest, which make fruitful soil for the propaganda of enemies of America.

The abolition of racial prejudices, barriers, and discriminations, and of immigrant colonies and sections, which keep peoples in America apart.

The maintenance of an American standard of living through the proper use of American foods, care of children, and new world homes.

The discontinuance of discriminations in the housing, care, protection, and treatment of aliens.

The creation of an understanding of and love for America, and of the desire of immigrants to remain in America, to have a home here and to support American institutions and laws.

With the United States at war with Germany, questions arose regarding the loyalty of Americans of German birth or ancestry. Defining what makes a person American was a topic for debate.

At this same time, American Catholics quietly continued a simmering debate among the church's "Americanists." The argument was between those who believed it wise to embrace American culture, thus reducing anti-Catholic hostility, and those wanting to remain more ethnically-centered—for example, preserving foreign language parochial schools. Minnesota's leading Catholic prelate, Archbishop John Ireland, was a prominent Americanist. An 1899 decree by Pope Leo XIII created a temporary truce, but, to the adversaries, the matter was not settled. The religious dimension in the Americanizing process could hold as much importance as political and economic considerations.[29]

In the study *Ethnic Encounters: Identities and Contexts*, George L. Hicks writes, "The characteristics and symbols that set off one category of people from another are not relics from the past but result from the creative process involved when people take on different, or reaffirm the same, ethnic attributes."[30]

To Minnesota's German Americans in April 1917 and the months following, the "creative process" of assimilation to which Hicks refers would become increasingly complicated. It seemed that nearly all those of German ancestry, even individuals born in the United States and saw themselves as Americans, could be suspect. As America went to war, one needed to not only display their patriotism, they needed to act on it.

Loyalty Already Proven

In Goodhue County's German American-dominated areas and other such ethnic districts around the state, teachers taught for most of the day using the German language. Before the war, use of German in public and private schools was not a major issue. With the onset of the conflict, however, Minnesota's Commission of Public Safety made its position on language use clear: "One Country, One Flag, One People and One Speech." By such direct statements and other more subtle suggestions, German Americans were warned to discard any lingering devotion to their fatherland.[31]

Minnesotans had not forgotten the Spanish-American War heroics of Red Wing's Oscar Seebach, shown in a circa 1898 photo.

Goodhue County's "100% Americans" believed there were those in their midst who would serve as examples for Minnesotans with German roots. Prominent among them was Oscar Seebach of Red Wing who supported alien registration as a member of the Minnesota Legislature, even though critics saw the law as anti-immigrant.[32]

After the declaration of war, the state Commission of Public Safety chose 50-year-old Seebach to organize the new Minnesota Home Guard. Major Seebach's brother Fred, meanwhile, was selected to be commander of the Red Wing Home Guard. No one doubted the loyalty of the Seebach brothers.

And Oscar Seebach held an even stronger proof of patriotism. As commander of Red Wing's Company G and stationed in the Philippines during the Spanish-American War, then-Captain Seebach was wounded while leading his men during a Manila firefight. Shot through the lungs, he nearly died.

Before the waves of European immigration reached Minnesota and Goodhue County, Old Stock Americans—descendants of European immigrants whose families had lived in North America for generations—had begun new lives on the northwest frontier. They left New England, the Mid-Atlantic region, and the newer Midwestern states in the knowledge that first choosers moving into new federal domains—Minnesota became a U.S. territory in 1849—got the best land. Unlike the comparatively poor Europeans who would follow them, these established Americans often carried money to invest. Old stock merchants operated businesses in scattered towns and trading points throughout the county.

Settled Americans dominated the business class in Goodhue County's largest towns, including Zumbrota, Cannon Falls, Kenyon, Pine Island and Red Wing. Storekeepers, business owners, grain dealers and professionals held an advantage over the new European-born Americans. Newcomers were forced to rely upon little or no English and minimal familiarity with American commercial practices. With limited competition in larger communities and almost none in the smaller towns, some Yankees would make the most of their edge. Bitter feelings resulted and continued to fester into the 1900s, playing a part in the county's rural-urban divide as entry into the Great War neared. The Nonpartisan League would attempt to take political advantage of such ill will when its recruiters arrived in the county in 1916.

Onset of the Temperance movement, a remarkably powerful national social phenomena that banned the making and selling of alcoholic beverages, illustrated another division between Old Stock Yankees and the county's rural ethnic groups. Townsfolk with New England religious backgrounds in Protestant Christianity (Episcopal, Presbyterian, Congregational, Methodist) led the effort to restrict alcohol use. Zumbrotans claimed none of their citizens used alcohol; Pine Island and Kenyon formed the county's first Woman's Christian Temperance Union chapters; Central Point became home to Rest Island, Minnesota's first refuge for "inebriates and drunkards;" Red Wing's Harriet Hobart served the WCTU as its state president for thirteen years (1881–1894); and Olaf Stageberg became the National Prohibition Party candidate for governor in 1918.[33]

German, Swedish, Irish and Norwegian immigrants, with some notable exceptions, did not view alcohol use as sinful. Red Wing, despite its strong WCTU presence, had more than a dozen saloons and four German-owned breweries during the nineteenth century's last decade. Hay Creek's German community had its own brewery. Residents in Goodhue, the county's newest village, split over Prohibition, with those in town largely anti-liquor and rural residents supporting its use. Many Norwegian followers of Hans Hauge, founder of a rural pietistic movement, favored temperance; WCTU activists in the Belle Creek Irish community earned strongly anti-liquor "Dry" status.

Goodhue County's battle over alcohol usage would never be more in evidence than during the 1918 national vote on Prohibition. By a paltry 34-ballot margin,

2,842–2,808, the county voted to go Dry. Voters in the towns of Pine Island, Cannon Falls, Zumbrota and Red Wing, all with higher numbers of Dry New Englanders, opted for Prohibition, along with rural Norwegian Americans. Residents in nearly all the other rural townships preferred to keep alcohol use legal.

☆   ☆   ☆

Goodhue County wielded considerable economic and political power in Minnesota during the twentieth century's first two decades. Its leadership maintained an influential presence in the state Legislature, banking sector, industry, agriculture, education, women's issues, and the Prohibition movement. County notables would be certain to assume consequential state roles with America's involvement in the Great War.

Minnesota political insiders viewed Zumbrota attorney, newspaperman and politician Anton J. Rockne as perhaps the state's most powerful legislator. Rockne captured a Goodhue County seat in the House of Representatives in 1903 and emerged, in his fourth term, as Speaker of the House. The Zumbrota Republican moved to the state Senate in 1913, and became chair of the Senate's influential finance committee in his second term (1915–1916). Approaching his fortieth birthday in 1917, Rockne was earning the nickname bestowed by his colleagues and the press: Minnesota's "Watchdog of the State Treasury." He would hold his Senate seat for a record 36 years. And, as co-owner of the *Zumbrota News*, Anton Rockne was important in affecting attitudes of its Goodhue County readers.[34]

Influential state senator from Zumbrota Anton J. Rockne is pictured in the 1917 *Minnesota Legislative Manual*. As he neared a fortieth birthday that year, Rockne had chaired the Senate Finance Committee for two years. Over the next three-plus decades, he earned the title "Watchdog of the State Treasury." He was also co-owner of the *Zumbrota News*.

John Stone Pardee, a well-known Duluth and Red Wing newspaperman and writer, accepted an offer to become Minnesota Commission of Public Safety's secretary as it started operations in spring 1917. Pardee had moved to Red Wing in September 1897, assuming operational control of the Times Printing Company, the purchaser of two former weeklies, *Red Wing Argus* and the Cannon Falls-based *Goodhue County News*. A Yale graduate, Pardee was an excellent writer and editor who failed to surpass Red Wing rival Jens Grondahl of the widely read *Daily Republican*. Pardee joined the *St. Paul Pioneer Press* in 1905. The departed editor did get to know Goodhue County well during his eight-year stay, and brought to the MCPS insights about his former home.[35]

Banking practices in the United States and Minnesota underwent fundamental change in 1913. Red Wing manufacturing magnate and banker John H. Rich assumed a key Minnesota role at the forefront in this evolution. The United States organized twelve Federal Reserve Districts, including District 9, based in Minneapolis. John Rich assisted in incorporating the Minneapolis Federal Reserve Bank. On October 1, 1914, Rich was selected to be the first Federal Reserve Agent and Chairman of the Ninth

District Bank's Board of Directors. Rich still held that position in 1917. An early leader in the Goodhue County clay industry, Rich parlayed ownership of a stoneware and sewer pipe factory into the presidency of Red Wing's Goodhue County National Bank. Rich also assumed a large financial stake in the Minneapolis Steel & Machinery Co. and Minneapolis Electric Elevator Co.[36]

Minnesota bankers also knew William H. Putnam, a skilled and experienced Red Wing bank executive with legislative experience. Putnam began his career in 1873, joining the Bank of Pierce & Simmons Company and later becoming president of that King Wheat Era institution. Elected to the state Legislature in 1907, Putnam put his years of banking experience to use in House committees, the Appropriations and the Board of Control (chair), and the Banks and Banking Committees among them. With business and political connections across the state, Putnam was considered an expert on

Red Wing industrialist and banker John H. Rich added investments in Minneapolis manufactories to his portfolio, gaining influence in the Twin Cities. In October 1914 he became the first board chairman for the Minneapolis Federal Reserve Bank. He still held that position in 1917.

Minnesota money dealing practices. Putnam, 69 years old in 1918, also invested in Red Wing manufacturing firms and was twice elected mayor.

William H. Putnam, a leading Red Wing banker for four decades and former state legislator, would become chairman of the Goodhue County division of the state Commission of Public Safety. That role made him, in 1917, the most powerful person in Goodhue County. He would wield that power.

Modern agricultural science was coming to Minnesota in 1900, and Arthur W. Parkin of Pine Island matured into a leading figure in that advance. Parkin trained under pioneering American agricultural chemist Stephen M. Babcock at the University of Wisconsin before bringing his knowledge to the southeast corner of Goodhue County. Thanks to Parkin's expertise, the Pine Island area became the state's top cheese producer by 1906. His success convinced state agriculture officials to name him Minnesota's first dairy and food inspector. He spent six years in that office, 1907 to 1913. Parkin served as Pine Island mayor at war's outbreak in 1917.[37]

Goodhue County possessed ties to former Minnesota Governor John Lind, a member of the mighty Minnesota Commission of Public Safety. Lind was a native of Sweden who, at age 14, immigrated with his family to Vasa Township. He grew up there. Sporting a University of Minnesota law degree, Lind moved to New Ulm. In 1886, at age 32, he

Innovative Arthur W. Parkin gained prominence in Minnesota dairying circles as the state's first dairy and food inspector. He also made Goodhue County's southeast sections the state's top cheese producing area. As mayor of Pine Island, he confronted Nonpartisan League organizers who wanted to hold a rally in the town.

became the first Swedish American elected to the United States Congress. A turn-of-the-century progressive, "Honest John Lind" (a title bestowed by his followers) remained close to his Burnside Township cousin Alexander P. Anderson. Professor Anderson, the inventor of "puffed cereals," lived with his family at their new Tower View research farm west of Red Wing.[38]

Goodhue County supplied the Minnesota Woman's Christian Temperance Movement with two of its most important leaders, Julia Bullard Nelson and Olaf Stageberg. Nelson, of Belvidere Township and Red Wing, had become a charismatic star whose forceful, fiery speeches led the WCTU to employ her as a Minnesota organizer. Nelson also managed and edited *Minnesota White Ribbon*, the WCTU's official newspaper, and found time to represent the group at the state Legislature. The Minnesota Woman Suffrage Association elected her president in 1890, and she held that office for eight years.[39]

Stageberg, a Red Wing Seminary professor, became the Prohibition Party candidate for Minnesota governor in 1918, thanks in part to the efforts of his activist wife.

Susie Stageberg would come forth as the campaign's most important beneficiary. The Goodhue County woman broadened her political base and, in two years, developed into that era's most rare kind of Minnesota politician—a female in a leadership position. For her role in founding a Minnesota political alliance between farmers and organized labor, Susie Stageberg earned the title "Mother of the Farmer-Labor Party," a forerunner of the more powerful Democratic Farmer Labor Party (DFL).[40]

Susie Stageberg learned politics while supporting her husband Olaf's political ambitions—he ran for governor on the Prohibition Party ticket in 1918. She stayed in Minnesota politics for decades, earning, along the way, the title "Mother of the Farmer-Labor Party."

Other Goodhue County politicians with state office aspirations appeared in 1917. Frederick A. Scherf, the county treasurer who, along with his older brother Albert, ran a Red Wing hardware and farm implement store, decided to run for the state Legislature. Albert Scherf served in the 32nd Legislature's House of Representatives (1901–1902). The Scherfs of Hay Creek Township were among the most prominent German American families in the county.[41]

Fred Scherf emerged as Goodhue County's leading defender of German Americans—their heritage and loyalty. A member of a Hay Creek family proud of its German heritage, Scherf, a successful businessman and county treasurer, confronted anti-German sentiment wherever he found it. Photo: *Minnesota Legislative Manual*, 1919.

Scherf hoped to replace the well-known Oscar Seebach, a member of another notable German American family, who had rejoined the military. But, unlike Oscar Seebach, Fred Scherf had yet to prove his 100-Percent loyalty to the United States that the times seemed to require.[42]

Grondahl and Gates: Republican Rivals

Kenyon physician Joseph Gates suffered bitter disappointment when Republican regulars turned against him and his 1916 candidacy for lieutenant governor. His loss was brought on in large part by Goodhue County's one-time "boy candidate" of the state Legislature, Jens Grondahl. In 1895, the boyish-appearing 25-year-old Grondahl captured a seat in the Legislature and served three terms. By 1916, the Norwegian-born Grondahl ran the *Red Wing Daily Republican* and was among the state's most influential Republicans.[43]

Kenyon physician and businessman Joseph A. Gates rated as a leading figure in the community. He served in the state Legislature, but his unsuccessful run for lieutenant governor ended his time in office. He was a central figure as a witness in several Goodhue County sedition cases.
Photo: *Minnesota Legislative Manual*, 1907

In a stinging June 10, 1916, editorial broadside, the Red Wing editor attacked Dr. Gates's "fitness, sincerity of purpose and past political record as well as ability," and questioned the Kenyon doctor's "reliability, tact, judgment [and] principles." Grondahl asserted Gates was "simply a politician forever seeking office and will trim his sails to get the benefit of any change of the political wind." Grondahl's destructive commentary regarding a leading Kenyon citizen and fellow Republican was surprising in its passion.

The Grondahl-Gates rivalry appears related to a 1914 Wanamingo speech during which, according to Grondahl's *Daily Republican*, Gates gave Red Wing and its residents a "lambasting." The doctor also allegedly uttered words to the effect, "he thanked his lucky stars that he wasn't a citizen of Red Wing." Other county newspapers rallied to Gates and his 1916 campaign. E. F. Davis of the *Zumbrota News* was typical, endorsing Gates while reporting broad support for him in Goodhue and Rice counties. Davis wrote that the doctor was a strong candidate who "needs no defense" from critics. On the contrary, Dr. Gates appeared to need defense from the attacks of Jens Grondahl.[44]

Grondahl also quoted a history of the 1909 state Legislature of which Gates was a member: "Gates was very active and usually reactionary." In 1918, Dr. Gates would become the government's star witness in three of the Goodhue County sedition trials. If defense attorneys in those court cases had known of Grondahl's condemnation of Gates, they might well have used those words against the Kenyon physician.

The 1916 Republican primary race to become the lieutenant governor nominee grew competitive, developing into "the hottest contest on the Republican ticket." Dr. Gates's early advantage vanished, and he finished a distant third behind winner Thomas Frankson and James A. Peterson. Gates did get recognition when, in 1917, the Minnesota Republican Party rewarded him with a position on its Central Committee.

In 1915, Minnesota native Arthur C. Townley, a 35-year-old failed North Dakota flax grower, took advantage of long simmering farmer unrest in his adoptive state and organized the Nonpartisan League (NPL), a union of spring wheat farmers. NPL members pledged to free themselves from what they saw as the remorseless grip of a Minneapolis-based flour milling monopoly and St. Paul-operated railroads. NPLers believed these Twin Cities cartels had secured a stranglehold on the regional grain trade. In a breathtaking 1916 political coup, the League captured near total control of North Dakota's government. They pulled off the triumph in little more than a year's time. Results from that election showed the NPL had seized 81 of the 113 seats in the state's House of Representatives—holdovers kept Senate NPL sympathizers in the minority—and, from the governorship on down, took control of all but one of its constitutional offices. Emboldened by this success and the entreaties of angry agriculturalists in neighboring Minnesota, Townley promptly dispatched League organizers across the Red River border. NPL promoters would soon appear in ten other midwestern and northwestern states.[45]

Nonpartisan League emissaries piloting a fleet of "Tin Henrys" (Model T Fords) surged onto rugged Minnesota rural roads in spring 1917, joining advance men who already were enrolling foot soldiers in the NPL farmer army. Representatives drove from farm to farm, selling League memberships while preaching the gospel of farmer unity. They promised to bring to heel the Money Trust controlled by Twin Cities-based industrialists. Carefully schooled League recruiters energized farmers with new ideas: government ownership and control of grain storage terminals, flour mills and packing houses; state inspection of the grain grading process; establishment of rural credit banks that operated at cost. And farm wives learned they became Nonpartisan League members when their husbands did and were thus "entitled to participate in all League caucuses and to vote." The NPL vowed to give farm families a square deal.[46]

A. C. Townley needed dues-paying League members to strengthen the organization and fund its efforts. He had demonstrated in North Dakota how not to take "no" for an answer. One of his directives illustrated that policy for his sales force: "Make the rubes pay their god-damn money to join and they'll stick—stick 'til hell freezes over…talk anything he'll [the farmer] listen to but talk, talk, talk, until you get his god-damn John Hancock to a check for six dollars." Townley would later say, "An idea, a Ford, and six dollars" built the Nonpartisan League. In February 1917 Townley relocated the headquarters of what was now officially known as the National Nonpartisan League from Fargo, North Dakota, to St. Paul. At the same time, he established a separate alliance, the Minnesota Farmers' Nonpartisan League. Minnesota capitalists cringed.[47]

The NPL's North Dakota-based leadership triad, Townley, along with William Lemke and F. B. Wood, drafted Joseph Gilbert into the League during a 1917 New Year's Day meeting. The St. Paul interview brought Townley and Gilbert, a 52-year-old socialist, together for the first time. The NPL was establishing its new base in the Minnesota capital when Joe Gilbert agreed to come on board. A gifted writer, experienced orator and able organizer, Gilbert ran a Seattle-based Social Democrat newspaper, *The Socialist Herald*, and was prominent in Washington State socialist circles.[48]

Gilbert proudly advocated American socialism, a new political movement emerging from labor union roots at the twentieth century's turn. Socialists contended that a comparatively small ultra-rich clique ("Big Biz" in the NPL lexicon) controlled the nation's wealth by exploiting its workforce. Socialists and the Nonpartisan Leaguers advocated government ownership of American industry, with workers dividing profits derived from their labor. In 1900 the Socialist Democratic Party nominated for the U.S. presidency Eugene V. Debs, a founder of the American Railway Union. Debs and the Socialists managed just 0.63% of the nation's vote; in Goodhue County he gained only 26 of 6,231 votes cast. By 1916, however, the Socialist presidential candidate garnered 3.18% nationally, making the organization a small yet viable political party.[49]

In November 1916, Socialists proved they could win big in Minnesota when Minneapolis voters elected Thomas Van Lear, an avowed socialist and labor leader as mayor. Residents from blue collar, immigrant-dominated neighborhoods also sent four Socialist Party members to the city council, creating another headache

Please Bear In Mind

What is found here in the way of interesting reading matter for Minnesota Voters does not come from "BIG BUSINESS" OR THE "KEPT PRESS" It comes from the records which the leaders of the Non-Partisan League have made themselves—it clearly shows that the

Non-Partisan League is only another name for "Socialism"

Mr. Farmer, Business Man, Worker:

Do you want your government controlled by Socialists?

Read this—do your own thinking—note the statements which come from the Socialist leaders at the head of the Non-Partisan League who are co-operating with their comrades—the Bentalls and Van Lears—and you will realize how Socialism proposes to gain control of your state government through the aid of the loyal Minnesota farmer and laboring man.

Many farmers who are not Socialists have joined the Non-Partisan League believing it was a farmer's organization to further the interests of the farmer, when, as a matter of fact, the organizers, officers and leaders—the men who have absolute control of the league, its wealth and its newspapers, and who map out its policy are not farmers but Socialist agitators.

The farmers had no voice in the selection of these Socialist leaders as officers of the league—they have no power to remove them. When Socialism gets control of the government, the farm is to be taken over the same as the mine and the factory under collective ownership of all the means of producing wealth, as will appear from the following:

The Minnesota State Convention of the Socialist Party in 1918 nominated J. O. Bentall for Governor.

That convention also adopted a platform for the party, the interesting part of which, to the Minnesota farmer is as follows: From the Minneapolis Times (Socialist) April 6, 1918:

The Socialist Party recognizes that present day society is fundamentally divided into two great economic groups—

(Which group do you belong to, Mr. Farmer?)

"The working class, which obtains its living by working for wages, and the upper capitalistic class, which obtains its enormous incomes by reason of its ownership of lands, mines, factories, railroads, food, clothing, supplies, etc."

Socialism divides society into two groups—the property-owning class on the one hand and the non-owing class of workers on the other. The farmer as a land and property owner in one class The property-less worker in the other—

This message, used in newspapers or handed out, warned readers that socialists running the Nonpartisan League are trying "to gain control of your state government...."

for the Minneapolis establishment. City business interests were accustomed to dictating to labor unions through the Civic and Commerce Association (CCA). The CCA had evolved from the Commercial Club, formed in 1903, and had torpedoed every labor strike in Minneapolis since. But the specter of a Socialist Party alliance with union activists and the still-organizing, socialist-leaning Nonpartisan League deeply concerned Twin City and other Minnesota business communities.[50]

Corporate interests and the Republican Party with which they traditionally aligned also worried about defections from their ranks. The 1912 presidential campaign had fractured Republican unity, and memories from the infighting remained fresh. They split when former president Theodore Roosevelt challenged his friend, incumbent President William Howard Taft, for the White House. "Old Guard" conservatives and insiders controlled the party and backed Taft; insurgent progressives were for Roosevelt. A rancorous campaign destroyed party solidarity and the Roosevelt–Taft friendship with it. With the Republican vote divided, Democratic Party choice Woodrow Wilson became president.[51]

Minnesotans had been voting for progressives in growing numbers since 1896. Small wonder they rallied to the reformist Roosevelt, giving him 125,999 votes to Taft's 64,342. Goodhue County Republicans provided Roosevelt nearly three times more votes than Taft (2,844-1,052). It was the same across the nation. The two Republicans would share their party's votes. Roosevelt won six states, Minnesota among them, delivering to him a total of 88 electoral votes. Taft claimed two states and eight electoral votes, while Wilson, the winner, garnered 435.[52]

Minnesota's Old Guard Republicans lamented renegade Roosevelt's triumph over Taft. Democrat Wilson also outpolled Taft, while Socialist candidate Eugene Debs nearly doubled his 1908 ballot total. Although the Old Guard eyed with suspicion the progressives who abandoned Taft for Roosevelt, they cast few aspersions at the party's still potent liberal wing. State Republican regulars settled for celebrating victories in nine of the ten U.S. House races and placing their candidate in the governor's office.

Joseph Gilbert openly admitted, during a 1954 interview, to being a socialist. "First of all it [the Nonpartisan League] was a socialist organization," he stated, "so that the enemies of the league were correct in saying it was a socialist set-up." NPL operatives spread socialist ideology among their Minnesota recruits, but upon entering the state in 1916, they avoided the socialist label. The Nonpartisan League leadership team, however, was not made up of the Bolshevik-styled revolutionaries who triggered civil war in Russia, despite efforts by Governor Joseph Burnquist and others to portray the NPLers as "Red socialists."[53] The vast majority of farmers joining or supporting the league did not see themselves as socialists. They retained their old party ties, mainly Republican and Democratic, but promoted NPL-affiliated candidates within those organizations.

Socialists in Hennepin and Ramsey counties, the state's most urban areas, along with Iron Range union supporters found in St. Louis, Itasca and Carlton counties, produced Minnesota's largest percentages of Socialist Party votes for president in 1916. The Socialist candidate, however, captured a meager five percent (20,117) statewide. Of 5,654 votes cast for president in Goodhue County, just 178 went to the Socialist. Such voter rejection of Socialist candidates indicated NPL campaigners in Goodhue County might face stiff opposition.[54]

Minnesota's business and industrial leaders and their Republican Party allies, the natural enemies of the Nonpartisan League, looked for a way to counter the League's encroaching brand of socialism. The election of socialist Thomas Van Lear as Minneapolis mayor was dangerous enough, but as Minnesota historian and Goodhue County native Carl Chrislock pointed out, there was a another issue: "If anything, the situation in North Dakota, whose citizens had long regarded the Minneapolis-based grain trade as a colonialist oppressor, was even more alarming…the Nonpartisan League had won a sweeping victory on a platform that directly threatened the interests of the Twin Cities industrial complex."[55]

America's entry into the Great War in April 1917 provided Republicans a critical wedge issue for the upcoming 1918 elections. They would flaunt their complete and uncompromising support for the war effort and compare it to the NPL's more nuanced endorsement and second-guessing.

Then, a half-year after the war declaration, a new and alarming form of socialism materialized in Russia. Following that nation's October Revolution in 1917 and throughout 1918, insurgents fought to install a communist government. Bolsheviks—a faction of Social Democrats under Vladimir Lenin that morphed into the ruling Communist Party—led this prolonged and ultimately successful revolution. Bolsheviks planned to create a complete socialist state by destroying the existing Tsarist regime and establishing a dictatorship of the people. Bolshevik governmental plans were roughly similar in theory to those advanced by the NPL, even though, in practice, the Russian model would result in a dangerously oppressive totalitarian state.[56]

But to Nonpartisan Leaguers, a people's uprising in Russia, even one led by radical Bolsheviks against a centuries-old ruling aristocracy, sounded like progress. In the NPL's declaration of principles earlier that year, Joe Gilbert called for the American government and its European allies to support "the new democracy of Russia…." With statewide elections looming, Republican critics and the Commission of Public Safety would use such statements to depict NPL leaders as radicals of the socialist and communist ilk. They would find more such ammunition in the coming months, adding momentum to a campaign that branded the League as anti-war and pro-German.[57]

An aptly titled anti-Nonpartisan League screed, *Are You Ready to Hand Over Your Farm to a Bunch of Socialist Adventurers: That's What Townleyism Means, Mr. Farmer*, attempted to convince its targeted audience that, by joining the NPL, farmers were aligning themselves with dangerous socialist provocateurs. "There is no doubting the statement that Townley, Le Sueur, Gilbert…and all other leaders of the Nonpartisan League are radical socialists—not one has ever denied it."[58]

Nonpartisan Leaguers saw themselves as enemies of corporate interests. As the costs of the war increased, "profiteers" grew fat from the labor of others. In this political cartoon, a determined NPL bulldog is dealing with a profiteer.

Getting Rid of Parisites

NPL recruiters used a fleet of "Tin Henrys" (Model T Fords) to reach and enlist North Dakota farmers. Rodent-sized Model T's plague this farmer. In 1916 and 1917, Nonpartisan Leaguers also chose to use autos in Minnesota to spread their message of farmer unity. This anti-League cartoon shows a North Dakota farmer being attacked by NPLers.

This political attack on Arthur Townley, founder of the farmers group called the Nonpartisan League, shows the silk-hatted Townley beckoning carloads of "commission men." These League organizers—"salesmen" to critics—received a portion of NPL dues paid by farmer recruits.

☆   ☆   ☆

Norwegian and Swedish wheat farmers made up the majority in Minnesota's Nonpartisan League membership as recruiting began in 1916. But in less than a year, a surge into the League of wealthier German American corn and livestock producers greatly increased the NPL presence.[59] Critics of the Nonpartisan League noticed its gains in German membership. Citizens had not forgotten that during the nearly three years the United States remained a neutral power, the nation's German Americans offered steadfast support for their European fatherland. After the United States declared war on Germany in April 1917, the general public pondered: Were pro-German citizens lurking among the nation's 8.3 million German Americans? Those lingering suspicions would dissipate with the passage of time and ample proof of German American loyalty. In the short term, however, Germans in America and Minnesota, particularly those with Nonpartisan League connections, would come under suspicion.[60]

Membership in the Minnesota Farmers' Nonpartisan League neared 50,000 as 1917 ended. League officials expected to boost those numbers. Their strategy, however, contained flaws that threatened the organization's growth and even its ability to survive. League founder Arthur Townley shrugged aside advice and badly misjudged his Minnesota audience. Earlier, in January, Joe Gilbert issued Townley a warning about NPL plans for the state. He later recalled his admonition: "Now Townley you've got to have different tactics here [in Minnesota] from what you had in North Dakota."[61]

Gilbert declared Minnesota's mixed agricultural and industrial economy—like that found in Goodhue County—was significantly different than that of Townley's "purely agricultural" North Dakota home. Minnesota also included more urban communities populated by voters unfamiliar with League concerns. NPL attorney James Manahan agreed with Gilbert, writing, "The farmers in the more prosperous parts of the state are naturally more conservative by nature and were reluctant about joining."[62]

Unlike their North Dakota wheat-growing brethren who seethed over the Twin Cities grain monopoly, many Minnesota farms had evolved from traditional self-sustaining operations into profit making businesses. Minnesota growers employed crop diversification. Corn, oats, barley, flax, potatoes and more shared space in fields once dominated by wheat. Scientific advances in dairying created a new source of revenue. Those farmers still relying on wheat as their cash crop would prove most likely to take a sympathetic interest in NPL ideas.[63]

Nonpartisan League organizers discovered receptive recruits in Goodhue County's rural districts, but not in the same large percentages found in North Dakota. The predominantly German American townships of Hay Creek, Goodhue, Belvidere, Zumbrota and Pine Island emerged as sympathetic to the League. More ethnically diverse townships like Featherstone, with strong German, Swedish and Yankee districts, also supported the League. Henry and Esther Hinrichs farmed in Featherstone and recalled farmers there were "100% Nonpartisan Leaguers," with the exception of a small group living around the town hall. The NPL could count on farmer support throughout the county, but not in the numbers they hoped for.[64]

Joe Gilbert: The "Brains" of the Nonpartisan League

Not quite five-foot-six-inches tall, the bespectacled Joseph Gilbert, with his professorial demeanor and skilled debating style, did not have the look of a dangerous radical. Nonetheless, leading NPL orators, including Gilbert, the man whose Goodhue County conviction for sedition would become a national issue, often demonstrated the ability to convince their listeners to oppose a system that the League claimed was rigged against them.[65]

Gilbert grew up in England. Orphaned at nine, he fought his way through school. One of the smaller boys, he recalled in detail his ongoing battles with bullies as well as an encounter with a head-master whose hard rubber ruler left a permanent scar on his head. His angry instructor, questioning Gilbert's parentage, snarled at his insolent student, "Who owns you, anyhow?" Gilbert replied, "No one owns me." At 14 he was indentured into a trade, carpet designing, and learned to despise the English caste system. His Dickensian years ended in January 1884 when, at age 19, he used his meager savings to buy a passenger ship ticket (in steerage) to New York. He was an American citizen and attorney by age 31.[66]

Arthur Townley chose wisely in selecting Joseph Gilbert to help manage the Nonpartisan League's move into Minnesota. Gilbert immodestly but accurately claimed that during the formative period of the NPL in Minnesota, "… I had the reputation of being the 'brains' of the organization because, well, I had had an awful lot of experience." He quickly proved his worth to the League. In March 1917 the Wisconsin Society for Equity fought an NPL organizing move in that state until Gilbert ably brought the disparate forces together. Later that month, Townley, recognizing Gilbert's talents, made him the League's national organization manager.

When the Nonpartisan League came under fire in April 1917 following the United States declaration of war against Germany, Gilbert was chosen to craft a statement of its principles. Copies of his treatise quickly circulated through the Upper Midwest and received enthusiastic support from NPL members. Gilbert arose as a charismatic farm-country orator, speaking frequently at League-organized functions, particularly in northern Minnesota. As a fraternal NPL delegate,

Gilbert led in forging first-time League links with the state Federation of Labor during that group's raucous July 1917 state convention in Faribault. At that time, he also held talks with powerful railroad brotherhoods and other labor unions—early steps in shaping a future Farmer-Labor political coalition.[67]

In spring 1918 it became clear to Gilbert that he faced a coordinated effort to discredit his ideas and mark him as a disloyal seditionist, a traitor to the United States. Vigorous and obstinate, he defied threatening crowds, hostile prosecutors and juries—tactics that would ultimately fail him. Convicted of sedition in Goodhue County, he would eventually plead his case before the United States Supreme Court.

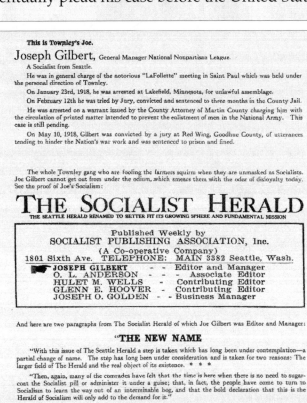

This full-page broadside is aimed specifically at Joseph Gilbert, the Nonpartisan League manager and influential strategist. It points to Gilbert's record running a socialist newspaper in Washington and has a sketch linking the NPL to the Russian revolution, then underway.

Benjamin Briggs Herbert brought national attention to his Red Wing newspaper and himself on February 19, 1885, when he met in New Orleans with some fifty newspaper men and women interested in his brainchild, the National Editorial Association (NEA)—later the National Newspaper Association. Herbert, publisher of Red Wing's *Advance-Republican*, a forerunner of Jens Grondahl's *Daily Republican*, believed the quality of America's small town newspapers could be improved through the education and professional development of their owner-operators.[68]

The future editor had moved to Red Wing in the late 1850s to attend Hamline University, then based in the city, and in 1873 became co-owner of a pro-National Grange weekly. It was as the NEA's president that B. B. Herbert organized its first formal convention in Cincinnati on February 23, 1886. Larger metropolitan dailies,

seeing the need Herbert identified, created their own professional organizations, but credit went to the NEA for beginning the newspaper-improvement movement.

Goodhue County newspaper publishers took pride in B. B. Herbert and his fame as an important leader in their industry. Herbert visited Red Wing shortly before his death in 1917 to be honored by the placement of a plaque near the entrance of the new Red Wing Printing Company building. As the direct heir to Herbert and his earlier version of Red Wing's *Republican*, Jens Grondahl had an impressive tradition to live up to.

American newspapers of the World War I era, including those in Goodhue County, did not require the objectivity their profession would later demand.

Benjamin Briggs Herbert, front middle, founder of the National Editorial Association, stands with Jens Grondahl, front left, and Grondahl's wife, Ottonie, outside the Red Wing Printing Company building in 1917.

Editors of small daily and weekly papers typically kept to the facts of a story, but allowed their personal views to occasionally appear in news columns. Most often, they owned at least a part of their publications.

As the United States joined the Great War, Goodhue County editors made little pretense of neutrality in their coverage. They stood wholeheartedly behind the national war effort. *Red Wing Daily Republican* editor Jens Grondahl's postwar comments praising his fellow county editors explained the situation: "During the great world war the Government depended…upon the newspapers of the country to stimulate patriotism and create a sentiment in favor of the various Liberty Loans and other war activities…. [The editors] never failed to respond to the calls of their country… [and] it may be said that the newspapers of this county were wholly in the service of the Government."[69]

Such unconditional support from local newspapers, the only reliable news source for most Americans and to which nearly every household subscribed, proved invaluable to the government's prosecution of the war. Newspapers run by intensely loyal editors brought about growing public support for the nation's wartime policies. Daily and weekly papers had carried news of the war in Europe to customers' doorsteps since fighting began in 1914. When America joined the struggle, editors described the need to build a modern military machine. A few Minnesota newspapers raised questions about the American involvement in the conflict. NPL's *Nonpartisan Leader* and the radical Norwegian-language weekly *Gaa Paa* [Walking On] were prominent among them. But such papers had little influence in Goodhue County where community newspapers dominated.[70]

Small town middle class residents—newspaper editors, business owners and professionals—typically developed mutually beneficial working arrangements. Nonpartisan League radicals and many of the NPL's farmer and working class supporters believed that system worked against them. Newspaper and business owners, dominantly Republican in Goodhue County, displayed a wary respect for the NPL's political potential, and were determined to fight it. Newspaper editors and their middle class supporters were no friends of the League and its brand of socialism.[71]

A trio of Goodhue County newspaper owners and editors with close political ties to the Republican Party—two had been elected to the state Legislature, one was in office, and another would soon serve there—stood ready to resist the Nonpartisan League and others they considered subversive. Jens Grondahl of the *Red Wing Daily Republican*, a regional newspaper power, had thrice been elected to the House. Future lawmaker Andrew Finstuen co-owned the *Kenyon Leader*, and incumbent state senator Anton J. Rockne shared ownership of the *Zumbrota News*.[72]

Grondahl of the *Red Wing Daily Republican*

At age 47 in 1917, Jens Grondahl neared the peak of his power and influence as the United States decided to intervene in the Great War raging in Europe. Grondahl's *Red Wing Daily Republican* afforded him ample access to residents of Goodhue County's largest city. Mail subscriptions, meanwhile, extended his reach across the county and into western Wisconsin. He also ran Red Wing Printing Company, parent of the *Republican*. Grondahl, a former state legislator, was also an important Republican Party leader—he frequently earned delegate status at state and national party conventions and had served as secretary of the Minnesota Republican Editorial Association. As a newspaper owner, Grondahl maintained comfortable ties to the city's business and industrial sector, serving as president of the Commercial Club and as a member of the city's Manufacturer's Association.[73]

Grondahl's family brought him to Red Wing in 1881 when he was 11. He attended local public schools and Red Wing Seminary, a young men's institution operated by Norwegian Lutherans. He joined the *Daily Republican* staff in 1892, soon becoming involved with the Republican Party. True to his roots, Grondahl edited *Nordstjernen* (*The North Star*), a Norwegian language weekly newspaper also printed in Red Wing. The *Daily Republican* and its direct predecessors had produced a line of pro-Republican Party newspapers that began with Abraham Lincoln.

Grondahl, however, was conflicted by a personal issue that called his performance into question. As a newspaper editor, he proclaimed himself an ardent opponent of alcohol use and advocated for its prohibition. In one celebrated 1908 escapade, Grondahl and the Pierce County, Wisconsin, sheriff led a score of deputies in an early morning cross-border raid onto Wisconsin's Trenton Island. "The Island," best known for "dens and dives" that featured illegal liquor operations, was across the Mississippi River from Red Wing, a short walk or ride over the 1895 High Wagon Bridge. Among the driest of Minnesota's anti-alcohol activists, Grondahl, nonetheless, was known in the city "to imbibe [alcohol] quite liberally on occasion." Whispers of hypocrisy regarding his alcohol abuse dogged Jens Grondahl and damaged his credibility as an editor and reporter.[74]

Attorney Andrew Finstuen, who combined with O. Clarke Cole in 1910 to run the *Kenyon Leader*, would enter the state House of Representatives in 1923. An avid supporter of America's 1917–18 war effort, Finstuen emerged as a determined opponent of anything less than "100-percent Americanism." As an editor, however, he presented balanced pre-war coverage of the Nonpartisan League, a group he opposed. The son of Norwegian immigrants, Finstuen grew up in Roscoe Township, attended Zumbrota High School and the University of Minnesota Law School, graduating in 1902 at age 27. The lifelong Republican made Kenyon, in the heart of the county's Norwegian American community, his new home, and served as village council president and secretary of the Kenyon Commercial Club (forerunner of present-day Chamber of Commerce). Both Finstuen and Grondahl would be called to testify in the Goodhue County trials of Nonpartisan League representatives.[75]

Andrew Finstuen

Anton J. Rockne earned a law degree from the University of Minnesota, and in 1894 moved to Zumbrota and launched a career as an attorney. The following decade

Edgar F. Davis

found him busily moving in other directions, buying the *Zumbrota News* in 1897 and three years later bringing in Edgar Davis as co-owner. Rockne, a stalwart Republican, earned election to the state House of Representatives in 1903 and became House Speaker in 1909. By 1915, the Zumbrotan was in the Senate. The senator became even more prominent in the 1930s when he fought the progressive reforms of Gov. Floyd B. Olson. But in 1917, the socialists confronting Rockne and Davis were Nonpartisan League activists.

Four other Goodhue County editors adhered to the Republican Party pro-war line. Silas S. Lewis, a staunch though open-minded party loyalist, ran the *Cannon Falls Beacon*. Ole G. Sandstad, owner of *Kenyon News*, a proud Spanish-American War veteran and Minnesota National Guard member, offered a fierce advocacy for the war and was a frequent critic of the NPL and radicals. Ralph W. Holmes, a strong anti-NPL pro-war editor, managed *Pine Island Record*, and another advocate for the war, O. W. Hennings, was in charge of the *Wanamingo Progress*. More politically moderate Dwight and Florence Pierce teamed up to print *Goodhue Enterprise*. N. P. Olson and his sons published the *Red Wing Daily Eagle*, a Democrat-leaning daily that proved to be the only county newspaper holding some sympathy for the NPL and organized labor.

Silas S. Lewis

Ole G. Sandstad

N. P. Olson

Ralph W. Holmes

Dwight & Florence Pierce

O. W. Hennings

America, Goodhue County, and the Onset of War

Goodhue County men enrolled at a rapid pace during the nation's first draft registration day, June 5, 1917. Federal military conscription law required males from the ages of 21 to 31 to sign up. Over 400 registered in Red Wing by three o'clock, with 669 mustered by day's end. It was the same across the county. In all, 2,567 men reported. How the American military would organize, train and then ship that force, expected to number more than a million, across an Atlantic Ocean infested with German submarines remained to be seen. Selection of the nation's first draftees would not begin until mid-July. American soldiers would not make a major impact in the fighting until summer 1918.[76]

Ironically, many Goodhue County men drafted into the armed forces would reach France before local National Guardsmen already in training. Shortly after arriving at Camp Cody, New Mexico, members of the Guard were transferred to other units for lengthy retraining. They would cease being infantry and be transformed into artillerymen. The county's first group of 224 draftees reported to Red Wing's Odd Fellows Hall for physical exams on Saturday, August 4, 1917. The spacious third floor hall was located in Bush Street's Lawther block. Physicians examined 75 men on that first day, 75 more the next day, and the final 74 on August 6. A monthly draft continued throughout the war.[77]

Red Wing's National Guard Company L marches past Christ Episcopal Church. Volunteers filled openings in the ranks following the U.S. April 6, 1917, declaration of war; some men do not yet have uniforms.

There was more irony in the Goodhue County draft. Some local political leaders, including Zumbrota state senator Anton Rockne, believed if the county filled its National Guard companies to capacity, the first local draft would be small. Rockne, who relied on information from Congress, reported, "I told people here…not over fifty to fifty-five men" would be conscripted during Goodhue County's first draft. "I urged all the boys to join the local militia companies at Red Wing and Zumbrota, arguing they would be better taken care of and could be reached better from home…." But federal officials later ruled that only those who enlisted in National Guard units *prior to June 30* would be credited against the county's draft allotment. Thus, the 80

Right: National Guard troops gather at the Goodhue train depot in a photo dated June 6, 1917.

Below: Soldiers of Zumbrota's Company D await the train that will bring them to an advanced training base at Camp Cody, New Mexico.

Goodhue County men who enrolled in the Zumbrota and Red Wing guard units after that date did not count toward the draft quota.[78]

Making matters worse for Rockne was the Regular Army's decision to reorganize National Guard units as they reported for training. "Since going to Camp Cody both [Goodhue County] companies have been disbanded and scattered more or less around," he noted [see pp. 136–37]. Dismemberment of county contingents discredited Rockne's contention that local Guard soldiers would be better cared for and easier to contact.

Rockne took damaging political flak over his failed draft theory. "I had…so much bad luck with my talks this spring [1917] that I hardly know what to say to the people now," he said. Complained the senator, "…now these Non Partisan [sic] League men are around telling the farmers that I knew this all the time and that I deliberately went out and misrepresented [military draft] matters to them, and many believe it." Rockne added, "It is things like these that we have to contend with in the country district…."[79]

Despite their training and willingness to fight, no one with knowledge of America's military readiness regarded its National Guard units as properly prepared for modern warfare. The standard training regimen for those soldiers included 24 drills per year, along with a summer encampment. Perhaps more shocking than the militia's semi-trained status was the diminutive size of the United States Regular Army: It totaled 80,804 officers and men. And when troops assigned to defending the nation's far-flung territories of the Philippines, Hawaii, Alaska, Puerto Rico, Panama Canal Zone and coastal defenses at home were subtracted, Regular Army soldiers available for war in 1917 fell to 24,602. When integrated into the army, the 180,000 guardsmen provided some help, but the United States would need about two million men to fight in the Great War.[80]

Goodhue County's Mobile National Guard

Orders to prepare for war duty led Goodhue County's National Guard units, Zumbrota's Company D and Red Wing's Company L, to mobilize on July 15. They began training locally in preparation for the call-up. These soldiers, along with Guard commands from other towns in the state, would comprise the Third Minnesota Infantry Regiment. Veterans of both Goodhue County companies understood the routine. Company D, Zumbrota's detachment and Minnesota's oldest militia company, had been home for just eight months, having taken part in the 1916 American expedition along the Mexican border. Now, the company, led by Captain Chris Nesseth, prepared for action once again. Even earlier, in 1898, Red Wing's guard unit, then known as Company G, and Zumbrota-area Company D mustered into service during the Spanish-American War. The Red Wing company, part of the Thirteenth Minnesota Infantry, was dispatched to the Philippines for 15 months where it engaged in combat with Spanish forces and, later, Filipino nationalists. [81]

Deployment of the Zumbrota and Red Wing companies to the Mexican border in 1916 progressed with remarkable speed. Following an alert from state officials in late March, the units were ordered to Fort Snelling on June 18. Physicians examined the men, and they were immediately sworn into federal service. Within 24 hours the guardsmen found themselves en route by train to Llano Grande Camp in Texas, six miles from the border with Mexico. The Goodhue County companies were assigned to the Third Minnesota Infantry. American forces soon launched a "Punitive Expedition" to retaliate against Mexican revolutionaries who had attacked a New Mexico town. The border war flared for several months, largely taking place north and west of the Minnesotans' positions. The local soldiers did not see combat and were ordered home on December 15, 1916.[82]

On July 15, 1917, the federal government recalled the two Goodhue County Guard companies, this time ordering the men to prepare for action in Europe's Great War. Other elements of the Third Minnesota Infantry joined in the mobilization. Soldiers received physicals and were fingerprinted and vaccinated against smallpox.

Patriotic citizens in Zumbrota and Red Wing prepared enthusiastic sendoffs for the soldiers. On August 26, the day before the Guard's departure, hundreds gathered in Red Wing's Colvill Park for an oversized Sunday afternoon community picnic. On that same day, a farewell banquet at the Zumbrota House honored Company D's guardsmen. Their meal was followed by a trip to the crowded armory for a meeting featuring "patriotism as the keynote." On Monday morning Company D, led by Zumbrota's town band and Civil War and Spanish-American War veterans, marched down Main Street to the Milwaukee Road Depot. Soldiers boarded their troop train, some leaning out windows for final good-byes, as the flag-waving crowd cheered lustily.[83]

Similar scenes were witnessed in Red Wing as its soldiers marched from the armory to Central Park for speeches and their official sendoff. They then trooped to Levee Park and the Milwaukee Road riverside depot. Their train departed the city at 2:45 that afternoon. The Zumbrota train, meanwhile, chugged west through Wanamingo and Kenyon toward a Third Regiment rendezvous. Carloads of friends, families and supporters drove on to Faribault to offer Company D a final farewell.

Not long after their trains pulled into Camp Cody, New Mexico, the Goodhue County infantrymen learned they would be reassigned. Considering the array of specialized assignment a modern army required, the men should not have been surprised. Most members of the Red Wing company were sent to the 125th Field Artillery, while Zumbrota soldiers were to be scattered among three artillery units, the 125th, 126th and 127th. About fifty Red Wing soldiers were reassigned to machine gun battalions. Extensive training awaited the rookie artillerymen: gun drills, mapping, gunnery, signaling, and also learning to break in and ride horses. It would take more than a year to get most of the Minnesotans combat ready. The massive reorganization of the men dissolved both Goodhue County-based National Guard units.[84]

Crowds assemble around Red Wing's Milwaukee Road train depot waiting for Company L to depart.

Cannon Falls Beacon editor S. S. Lewis had kept a watchful eye on rural Goodhue County residents since the April 6, 1917, United States entry into the Great War. Editorially, Lewis was a "100% American," favoring the war and printing his own patriotic poems, "The Call From Beyond," "A Song of Freedom," and "Goodbye," in the *Beacon*.[85] He blasted alleged pro-Germans, including Goodhue County Nonpartisan

League organizers and those who appeared to equivocate about America's involvement in the conflict. On June 1 Lewis wrote, "Every word now spoken in defense of Germany by a [U.S.] citizen…is treason and the man who utters it is a traitor and should be dealt with as traitors are dealt with." Three weeks later he called out the NPL, charging, "In politics the most partisan thing we ever heard is the so-called Nonpartisan League."[86]

In August, editor Lewis reported that George C. Breidal, a League man from North Dakota, had been canvassing Wanamingo Township and had enlisted "quite a number" of local farmers. The Cannon Falls newsman filled in readers about NPL organizer Louis W. Martin and his appearance in Minneola Township that month. In September the *Beacon* reported the NPL held meetings for farmers in Wastedo and Aspelund to elect delegates to the League's St. Paul convention. Members selected Lars J. Gjemse and L. E. Johnson from Wanamingo Township and Andrew Larson of Leon.[87]

A Nonpartisan League organizer attempts to enroll a farmer.

Louis Martin kicked off an NPL recruiting campaign with an August 15, 1917, speech at a "Farmer's Club Social" held at Olaf Haugen's Minneola Township farm. Martin rallied listeners to the NPL cause and its promise of farmer empowerment. He announced Kenyon as his next stop three days later. Martin had enlisted Joseph Gilbert, one of the League's leading orators, and another organizer, N. S. Randall, to speak. Randall also ranked among the Nonpartisan League's "top speakers." Gilbert and Randall, en route to a Sunday gathering in Plainview, Minnesota, had agreed to a Kenyon stopover.[88]

Kenyon Leader editor Andrew Finstuen, suspicious of League intentions, nonetheless agreed to chair the Main Street meeting and introduce the Nonpartisan League visitors. Standing on a portable bandwagon before a crowd of about 200, Martin made some brief comments and then called on Randall, who spoke for a half-hour. He restated one of the League's fundamental positions: America's wealthy were profiting from the war and not helping pay for it. Among Randall's assertions, "If the money of the rich was thrown into the war-chest, this war would end immediately."[89] Joe Gilbert, who spoke next, later remembered the Kenyon audience as a "typical small-town Saturday night crowd." NPL supporters encouraged Gilbert, but hecklers could be heard. Their numbers increased. Speaking for 20 minutes, Gilbert asserted that if men can be drafted into military service, the nation's industries should also be "conscripted"—taken over by the government. Catcalls of "Pro-German," "What's the matter with [U.S. President Woodrow] Wilson?" and "Let's roll the bandwagon into the river" were heard and deflected by Gilbert. The meeting ended, and the visiting

NPL men (Gilbert's wife, Julie, was also with him) walked to their hotel.[90]

No one in the crowd that day could foresee that the Kenyon NPL rally would become the focal point of several Federal District Court trials, a Minnesota Supreme Court decision and a ruling by the United States Supreme Court. And, another event in Kenyon involving Martin would also have far-reaching ramifications.

A month after the events of August 18, Louis Martin walked into a Kenyon barbershop and asked if someone could "give a pro-German a shave?" The flippant remark caught the attention of four local men inside the shop, barbering brothers Clarence and Martin Bakko, Joseph A. Gates, and George Brobeck, a local soldier in uniform getting a shave. Both Gates and Brobeck had attended the August NPL meeting in town. Brobeck challenged Martin: "Who's a pro-German?" Martin allegedly replied, "I am."[91]

An angry Gates, a prominent Kenyon physician, civic leader and former state legislator, confronted Martin, asking if he accepted the ideas advanced in the August Gilbert and Randall speeches. According to witnesses, Martin said he did. Brobeck and Martin verbally sparred over comments made at the meeting, and Gates joined in. Trial records note Gates "took strenuous exception" to Martin's comments—the doctor had grabbed Martin and tossed him bodily from the barbershop. E. F. Davis of the *Zumbrota News* asserted, approvingly, that the NPL organizer hurriedly left town after learning a "coat of tar and feathers" was being prepared for him.[92]

Martin brought suit against Gates, asking for $50,000 in damages. S. S. Lewis, editor of the *Cannon Falls Beacon*, reported, "…in Kenyon Doc Gates gave a 'Non-Partisan-pro-German' something more smoothing then [sic] chloride and lime and now the scab is going to sue Doc for $50,000. Gee whiz."[93]

Joseph Gates

Russell Gates

Elnathan Gates

A Patriotic Family

Dr. Joseph Gates publicly exhibited a deep commitment to America's involvement in the world war. The Kenyon physician served on the city's committee to recruit men into the military, was a board member of the Goodhue County Fuel Administration, headed the Kenyon America First Association, backed war bond drives and became a frequent speaker (a Four Minute Man) at pro-war rallies. In Gates's view, Nonpartisan League leaders and their pro-German allies were traitors.[94]

The Gates family also made personal pledges to the cause. Joseph and his wife, Jennie, saw their two sons off to war. While Jennie volunteered for the Red Cross, the Gates's oldest, Elnathan, joined the U.S. Medical Corps and later the marines before shipping out to France. Russell, the second son, left the University of Minnesota to sign up. Dr. Gates then followed their example, enrolling in the Medical Corps. All returned to Kenyon following the war.

In June 1922, with memories of the divisive World War home front fading, Joseph Gates was killed in a shocking auto-train accident. A crowd reportedly numbering 4,000 attended the Kenyon community leader's funeral. Joseph A. Gates American Legion Post was named in his honor and, at the time of this writing, is still active in Kenyon.[95]

In another August incident, nervous officials in Goodhue village concerned about the coming war and the large German American population in nearby townships took action. Just prior to the unrest during the Nonpartisan League rally in Kenyon, Goodhue village Mayor Charles L. Parkin wrote John S. Pardee, secretary of the Commission of Public Safety, requesting "secret service" help. Parkin contacted Pardee instead of the MCPS intelligence section, likely because he knew the secretary from his turn-of-the-century days as a Red Wing and Goodhue County newspaper editor. Pardee sent an August 7 memo to Thomas Winter, the commission's intelligence bureau chief, noting the village "is largely surrounded by German sections," and the mayor wanted "two good secret service men for a month or two, especially Saturday and Saturday nights." Pardee discounted Parkin's worries in a letter to Winter, "I am well acquainted with that part of Goodhue County, and it is not a most pressing case before us."[96]

October proved to be a challenging month for Nonpartisan League leaders and organizers around Goodhue County. On the fourth, the League's top attraction, its founder A. C. Townley, reserved Lake City Opera House for a proposed speech. Situated along the scenic shores of Lake Pepin, a widening of the Mississippi River, Lake City provided Townley a handsome venue. The town's location also gave him access to newspaper attention in two counties: The Goodhue-Wabasha county border sliced through Lake City. Members of the Lake City Commercial Club and City Council, however, wanted no part of Townley. Julius E. Boehlk, Wabasha's county sheriff, informed the NPLer by letter that civic leaders believed, "in the present temper of the people of the city of Lake City, and vicinity that such an [NPL] meeting is almost certain to result in disorder, disturbance and very possibly bloodshed…I have concluded that this meeting should not and must not be held." Boehlk cautioned, "I accordingly notify you not to allow the [meeting] to be held as advertised."[97]

Arthur Townley, right, poses with Henry Teigan, secretary of the Nonpartisan League (left) and Magnus Johnson, a Meeker County farmer, NPL supporter and future U.S. Senator (Farmer-Labor party) from Minnesota.

On October 19, two months after his Kenyon NPL rally talk, N. S. Randall found himself in Pine County and in danger. Prior to his scheduled speech, Randall encountered a citizen promising to exercise his civic rights by personally breaking up the League rally. In a sworn affidavit, Randall reported a group of five men confronted him as he arrived at the Rock Creek meeting place. They asked if he was the speaker; Randall replied that he was. A member of the quintet, later identified as the Pine City postmaster, said, "Then you are the son-of-bitch we are looking for." Randall was beaten during unsuccessful attempts to tar, feather and lynch him. While the county sheriff calmed the crowd, Randall was taken to safety out of the county. He would reappear in Goodhue County.[98]

Louis Martin, the NPL organizer who had been at the League's August rally in Kenyon, returned to Goodhue County for an October 22, 1917, speech. As featured speaker, he would address a gathering of the Goodhue County Farmers Association at a Belvidere Mills hall south of Red Wing. But Martin was late to the meeting, and Red Wing banker William Putnam, along with a group of supporters, seized control of the event. Putnam introduced four speakers: Goodhue County Attorney Thomas Mohn, Rev. William S. Middlemass, Rev. J. F. Powes and attorney Arthur E. Arntson, all of Red Wing. They gave "rousing" patriotic talks and touted Liberty Bond buying to the 100 or more farmers on hand. Martin finally appeared and halted the patriotic pep talks.[99]

Putnam had emerged as Goodhue County's most powerful public official at the war's onset, and was not shy about using that position. In May 1917, five weeks after the U.S. declaration of war on Germany, Governor Burnquist and the Minnesota

Commission of Public Safety (MCPS) appointed a banker-heavy group of men to serve as county public safety commission directors. William Putnam, a longtime Red Wing banker with a statewide reputation in banking circles, received the nod to chair the Goodhue County CPS board. Martin Halvorson, namesake of a pioneering Wanamingo merchant and co-founder of Farmers State Bank of Wanamingo, became its secretary. Other Goodhue County commission members included citizens from a broader sampling of occupations. It was in his capacity as chairman of the county MCPS that William Putnam assumed control of the October farmers meeting at Belvidere Mills.

William J. Bryan, president of the Farmers Association, along with board members W. Edwin Peterson, vice president, A. O. Naeseth, secretary, and Carl Degner, treasurer, vigorously protested the takeover of their meeting by the Putnam-led group. Bryan described the interlopers as "a few citizens of Red Wing who saw fit to appoint themselves guardians of the farmers…." Bryan asserted such interference would "stir up bitterness between the rural American citizens and the American citizens of Red Wing and any other city or village using the same methods." Writing to the *Zumbrota News*, William Bryan asserted he and the other association officers had heard Nonpartisan League organizer Louis Martin speak on several occasions, noting, "…we testify as loyal American citizens that he has not made one disloyal utterance." The farmer leader "demanded" Martin be "treated like as any other loyal American citizen." As for the NPL, Bryan declared, "The farmer is going to decide whether or not he wants to join the Nonpartisan League and if he does join, he should not become a subject for public abuse."[100]

A concerned William Putnam reported details of the meeting in a handwritten letter to Henry W. Libby, secretary of the Minnesota Commission of Public Safety and soon-to-be board member of that all-powerful body. The frustrated Putnam complained that after he and his group left the meeting, Louis Martin "secured a large number of members for his organization (the Nonpartisan League)." A specific comment made regarding the meeting's takeover by Putnam's group no doubt heightened the level of the banker's alarm. Wrote William Bryan in his letter to the *News*: "Such a proceeding can have but one result—to defeat the cause they represented (Liberty Loan sales)…." Putnam also chaired Goodhue County's bond drive.[101]

During a November 1917 meeting in Red Wing with William Putnam, a worried Anton Rockne, shown here, shared his concerns regarding the Nonpartisan League's growing power in Goodhue County.

Putnam's letter also informed Libby that State Senator Anton J. Rockne of Zumbrota came to Red Wing three days after the Belvidere Mills gathering to confer with the banker. Rockne, the influential Republican who chaired the Senate Finance Committee, argued, "Something should be done to stop the work [by the NPL] now being done among our farmers." He told Putnam, "It is almost impossible" to sell Liberty Bonds in Wanamingo, Cherry Grove,

Roscoe and other nearby townships." County Attorney Mohn, according to Putnam, believed a secret service man should be sent to follow Martin and "see if something can be done to get him out of this county."[102]

Rockne and Putnam had reason to be concerned. The Nonpartisan League familiarized farmers with socialistic theories that attacked exploitive big business. High on the League's list of farm-owner enemies were bankers and politicians who helped corporate interests perpetuate their power. Now, these wealthy insiders were demanding that farm folks and factory workers pay for the war by purchasing Liberty Bonds, the NPL said. Noted the League's newspaper, *Nonpartisan Leader*, in October 1917, "[T]hose men whose hands are white and whose skins are soft have more time to wave the flag. If we [farmers] spent as much time waving it as they do, the whole world would starve to death."[103]

In the wake of the Belvidere Mills meeting, Lars J. Gjemse, a Nonpartisan League defender from Hader, wrote an impassioned defense of free speech based on American tradition and law. *Zumbrota News* printed it. Gjemse's conclusion: "No people, reared in the atmosphere of freedom and raised in the love of liberty, with a government supposed to be by the people and of the people, will consent to have their rights and privileges taken away by a lot of petty politicians who are trying to blindfold and hoodwink the people by their cries of disloyalty and pro-German accusations. Let the people be their own judges, and they will see to it that pro-German speeches will not be tolerated or seditious actions go unpunished. The common laboring class in the United States are loyal and patriotic, and… [will] stand up for their rights at home, so that our liberty is intact when this world war is over."[104]

Goodhue County wasn't the only Minnesota locale in which Nonpartisan League organizers were being challenged. To combat this perceived injustice, the League's Joseph Gilbert secured an October 10 meeting with Governor Burnquist. The NPL manager planned to lodge complaints about what he labeled as outbreaks of "mob violence" across the state directed against League members. Gilbert and 40 NPL farmers marched from their Endicott Building headquarters in downtown St. Paul to the Capitol, where they crowded into the governor's waiting room. The protestors recounted stories of threats and intimidation. According to a *St. Paul Pioneer Press* report, the NPL group presented a petition "asking for permission to peaceably assemble and conduct our meetings…without interference from outsiders."[105]

Gilbert later told a biographer about a critical point in the meeting. The League manager asked Burnquist to instruct state peace officers and public officials "of their duty to protect these men and their property and see to it that meetings which they attend are protected from violence." Replied the governor, "Then you think they don't know their duty?" Gilbert snapped, "Well, by God, if they do, they are not performing it."[106]

On November 10 Louis Martin returned to Goodhue County for a short speech—a "monster farmers meeting"—at the Zumbrota Armory sponsored by Farmers Clubs of Minneola, Pine Island, Roscoe and Zumbrota townships. Other villages and townships sent large numbers to the gathering. Main speaker C. W. Barnes of St. Paul, author of two pamphlets critical of Governor Burnquist, commended Zumbrota for its "broad-mindedness in permitting the farmers of this county to use the best building in town."[107]

Stirred by continuing Nonpartisan League activity in the county, a group calling itself the Goodhue County Loyalty League met in Red Wing on November 15. They gathered at the St. James Hotel and then, led by the State Training School band, paraded to T. B. Sheldon Auditorium for a meeting. Delegates expected to create a permanent organization that pledged loyalty to the United States government. About 400 prospective members from around the county attended.[108]

Two weeks later, representatives from county farmers clubs with Nonpartisan League ties, including those from Zumbrota, Pine Island, Wanamingo and Minneola, met in Red Wing to protest a refusal to allow an NPL gathering there. Leaders proclaimed they would speak from the Goodhue County Courthouse steps if they couldn't get a hall. The farmer group met with success, securing the same venue used by the Loyalty League. On a bitterly cold December 14, about 300 farmers filed into the American-flag-bedecked Sheldon. Louis Martin, undeterred by his troubles with anti-League residents of Kenyon, chaired the meeting. John M. Baer, an NPL-elected U.S. Congressman from North Dakota, explained the League's aims.[109]

Red Wing's Company A, 5th Battalion, Minnesota Home Guard, was among units hastily formed to take the place of the state National

The advent of frigid Minnesota winter failed to cool tempers, and by December 1917, those on either side of the Great War's "Loyalty issue" had hardened their positions. The "100% Americans," Minnesota superpatriots unconditionally committed to America's war effort and led by the state's Commission of Public Safety, confronted organizations—the Nonpartisan League, socialists and trade unions in particular—that they believed held tepid or even traitorous views about the war. Jens Grondahl offered Goodhue County readers a personal definition of loyalty with an editorial titled "To Make Old Goodhue 100 Percent American."[110]

Labor unrest lingered on the Minnesota Iron Range and was growing in the Twin Cities as winter approached. State National Guard troops had departed for federal service and were now training in New Mexico as part of the Regular Army. The Commission of Public Safety and the Burnquist administration, concerned with an absence of emergency security forces, authorized formation of a "Home Guard," a military unit that would, for the time being, replace the absent National Guard.

In August, Minneapolis and St. Paul streetcar employees of the Twin City Rapid Transit Company (TCRTC) formed union locals—a measure management vigorously resisted. Union organizers called for an October 6 strike against the TCRTC, prompting some workers to stage a walkout. An uneasy, temporary truce followed. Peace prevailed until a December 2 union rally at St. Paul's Rice Park. Among that gathering's speakers was James Manahan, an attorney sympathetic to the union men and a leader of the farmer-based Nonpartisan League. The NPL visitor delivered a fiery assertion of support to the assembled workers—a precipitating factor in the violence that followed. Some angry pro–union men departing the meeting rioted and attacked nearby streetcars piloted by nonunion operators.[111]

When city police could not and the Ramsey County sheriff would not take situational control, Governor Burnquist ordered Minnesota Home Guard units, including

Guard. The MNG had been federalized into the U.S. Army.

Red Wing's 76-man Company A, 5th Battalion, to St. Paul and instructed them to restore order [see pp. 141–2].

With only four months of intermittent training behind them, members of Minnesota's Home Guard now faced their first major assignment. For the most part, the newly-minted citizen soldiers were in their thirties or forties, a mixture of businessmen, professionals and white-collar workers. But Red Wing's Home Guardsmen had taken training seriously and appeared prepared for duty. Those signing up for the unit faced careful scrutiny from a public wary that its enrollees were attempting to dodge the military draft. In May 1917, Congress had established the Selective Service System that compelled men to register for military service. A national registration day for all men between the ages of 21 and 30—the age range would widen to 18 to 45 in August 1918— had been held on June 5, with high compliance rates across the nation. Company A's post-war history made note of the caution taken in selecting its Home Guard members: "Only men whose exemption from the draft was beyond question were to be accepted."[112]

Captain Fred J. Seebach, a future Red Wing mayor, commanded that city's Home Guard unit, with Carl J. Heglund serving as first lieutenant. Company A was based at Red Wing's Plum Street armory. Orders to deploy to St. Paul, site of the streetcar strike, reached the company early on December 4. The soldiers, carrying full packs, assembled hurriedly and, joined by other companies, reached the capital city's armory that afternoon. Frigid temperatures greeted the Home Guard units. New sheepskin-lined overcoats offered protection.[113]

The enlistment papers of Charles J. Ahlers show the 40-year-old Red Wing electrical contractor joined the city's Home Guard Company A on June 27, 1917. Fred Seebach, company commander, signed the cover of Ahlers's enrollment form.

At 6 p.m., Home Guard soldiers began clearing demonstrators and the general public from St. Paul's downtown streets. They completed the job within two hours. Company A continued patrol duty until being recalled to Red Wing on December 13. Streetcar work stoppages had ended, and non-union workers replaced 800 strikers.

Minneapolis remained quiet during the St. Paul disturbances. With streetcar unionists on strike in the capital city, a worried Hennepin County sheriff rushed four companies of the well-armed paramilitary Civilian Auxiliary (CA) to the streets of Minneapolis. The anti-labor Minneapolis Civic and Commerce Association (CCA) had created this force, called an "illegal private army" by one expert on the organization. The CCA's Civilian Auxiliary, with approval from the Commission of Public Safety, kept the Minneapolis business district quiet.[114]

Introduction of Home Guard troops into the streetcar workers strike in St. Paul and the use of the Civilian Auxiliary in Minneapolis produced a simmering discontent in the ranks of organized labor. An estimated 15,000 unionists left their jobs and gathered on December 5 at the St. Paul Auditorium where they debated calling a general strike. Federal officials had been working to defuse the situation between the Rapid Transit Company and its workers, helping union members stay patient and await developments. After protracted negotiations, the federal mediators recommended concessions to the union—a request with which TCRTC officials abjectly refused to comply. The workers' defeat that followed proved a major triumph for Twin Cities industrialists and a galling setback for labor unions.[115]

Goodhue County labor groups and Nonpartisan League members warily watched developments in St. Paul. Might Red Wing's well-armed Company A be called out to confront them during future disputes with their organizations?

The Minnesota Commission of Public Safety found it had overreached during the streetcar strike. Unionists, Nonpartisan Leaguers and, to a lesser extent the general public, believed the MCPS had acted on behalf of powerful corporate interests. Then, a month after the St. Paul labor unrest, former Governor John Lind angrily stalked out of an MCPS commissioners' meeting following a vicious verbal attack by his colleague John McGee, the group's dominant figure. The loss of Lind, seen as a moderating influence on the MCPS, [see page 63 for more] was a major embarrassment to the commission.[116]

James Manahan's appearance at the December 2 rally of St. Paul union streetcar workers wasn't the first public Nonpartisan League overture directed at organized labor. Earlier in 1917, the socialist leadership of the Minnesota NPL had extended feelers. Upon joining the League in January, Joe Gilbert had advised leaders of the farmer group to cooperate with Minnesota labor organizations. Gilbert hoped to set up a loose farmer-labor alliance and, to that end, traveled to Faribault and the July Minnesota Federation of Labor (MFL) convention. That contentious gathering would become known as "one of the liveliest in the history of labor in Minnesota."[117]

MFL's conservative leadership, however, had little interest in cooperating with the farmers' League. During bitter convention debates, the more radical Minneapolis delegation tried to pass a resolution endorsing an earlier Nonpartisan League position. The assembly passed the Minneapolis proposal, but only after dropping the NPL reference. The time was not yet right for an MFL–NPL partnership. Nonetheless, with the crushing of the Twin Cities streetcar union strike at year's end, more labor leaders saw promise in allying with the NPL and its farmer base.

☆   ☆   ☆

Minnesota, Goodhue County included, maintained a large and secretive branch of the American Protective League (APL), a private organization headquartered in Washington D.C. with connections to the federal Department of Justice. Vigilant APL volunteers kept under surveillance individuals making or publishing comments critical of the American government and military. Red Wing businessman Fred E. Schornstein, new to the city as manager of Red Wing Power and Light Co., headed the Goodhue County branch of the APL. He had six volunteers from the community assisting him. Each county township had its own League chairman, backed by watchful deputies.[118]

According to *Goodhue County in the World War*, a 1919 history, the county's American Protective League operatives "...cooperated in apprehending pro-Germans and German spies," turning them over to the military. Red Wing newspaper editor Jens Grondahl ran Red Wing Printing Company, the publisher of that war history. The book's report on Goodhue County's APL effort proudly asserted, "Slackers were rounded up, draft evaders apprehended, people spreading false reports were given their choice of stopping the practice or going to jail." The author of the APL piece also explained, "Most people [in the county] were unaware of the existence of such an organization, and it was largely through this secrecy that the work of the league was so effectively performed."[119]

Considering Grondahl's outspoken support of the American war effort in the *Red Wing Daily Republican*—he was also chairman of the Goodhue County Recruiting Board and a member of the county Liberty Loan committee—it is certain that his views were reflected in *Goodhue County in the World War*. It appears likely that Grondahl authored the section praising the American Protective League's secret operations in Goodhue County.

Goodhue County had volunteer agents working for the secretive American Protective League in each of its townships; Red Wing had six. Fred E. Schornstein, manager of Red Wing Power and Light, headed the county APL.

America's war effort steadily gathered momentum and broad national support during the winter of 1917–18. Efforts to find and suppress groups or individuals questioning the nation's involvement in the war gained speed. "America First" clubs sprang up in Minnesota, holding "loyalty meetings" across the state. A *Minneapolis Tribune* report listed more than 30 such gatherings held on December 19 and 20 in Minnesota's southwestern counties. Those farm country prairie flatlands were thought to be fertile Nonpartisan League ground.

Goodhue County's America First Association spawned smaller groups in each township, village and town. Prominent 100–Percenters supporting the nation's entry into the European war assumed leadership in the association. Among them: William Putnam, Joseph Gates, Anton Rockne, Arthur Arntson, Thomas Mohn, and David Neill. America First organized a county-wide Loyalty Day program in November 1917, and nearly 100 county residents took part in Minnesota Loyalty Conventions.

Goodhue County America Firsters elected David Neill their chairperson. The Red Wing-area telephone company executive and Republican Party candidate for the state Legislature planned a lecture series through Goodhue, Zumbrota, Pine Island, Wanamingo and possibly other towns in early 1918.[120]

NPL organizers had tried to match the influence of America First and other loyalty groups by publicizing and holding their own functions. That January, League organizers preached the farmer group's philosophy wherever and whenever they could. But finding places to spread the NPL gospel was becoming a challenge.

Nonpartisan League headquarters in St. Paul learned of a last-minute January cancellation of a Goodhue County speaking engagement. Pine Island's Farmers Elevator Co. officials had invited Nonpartisan League organizer and lecturer J. Arthur Williams to address its annual stockholders meeting at noon on the 16th. Carl Degner of Pine Island, treasurer of Goodhue County Farmers Association and witness to the Belvidere Mills NPL meeting takeover, greeted Williams, Louis Martin and two other NPL men and informed them that city officials would not allow them to speak. According to Degner, described in an NPL report as a witness to the incident, Mayor Arthur Parkin was accompanied by a menacing, unnamed constable when they met with the visitors. Parkin informed Williams that, "should he attempt to speak the whole city would be alarmed." The mayor said that during a "mass meeting" held in Pine Island the night before, citizens demanded the Nonpartisan men be prevented from speaking "at all costs." Williams stated he would obey the law and not be part of the proposed gathering.[121]

Nonpartisans found many county officials and citizens hostile. Faribault County's Public Safety Committee threatened to burn an NPL-rented building; a mob, with the Scott County sheriff's backing, forced a League speaker into retreat; the Grant County sheriff struck a Nonpartisan League organizer after calling the group "a bunch of thieves." Redwood County's sheriff informed George Breidal and N. S. Randall, two NPL organizers well-known in Goodhue County, that no League meetings would be allowed because of the threat of disorder.[122]

Prosecutions of Nonpartisan League leaders, sometimes known as the Townley Trials, centered on NPL chief Arthur Townley and his top lieutenant Joe Gilbert. James Manahan, the League attorney who spoke for the group during the St. Paul streetcar strike and was a less than objective onlooker, later observed, "Men and institutions

```
                    MEMO:        Pine Island Interference,  League Meeting.  [January 19 1919]
            Nonpartisan League presented in persons of:                       Goodhue Co.
                                               L. W. Martin,
                                               J. Scott Martin,
                                               Howard R. Wood,
                                               J.Arthur Williams,-to speak
                  Witness,---Carl Degener, Pine Island, P.O., Farmer and League Booster,

                  Opposition headed by Arthur W. Parkins, Mayor of Pine Island,
                              Assisted by town Constable, President of Council, etc

                  ==================================================

            As near as we can recall incident occured as follows:

                          Arriving at Pine Island at Noon, January 16, 1918,
                  in answer to invitation from members of Farmers Elevator
                  Company, to have League speaker to appear before their
                  annual stockholders meeting that day, we were met by Carl
                  Degener with the information that the city officials
                  would not permit us to speak.

                          Upon going out on to the street we were met by the
                  Mayor and Constable, the former very vicious in manner,
                  and Mr. Degener was roughly asked if he intended to hold
                  a League meeting.  Upon answering that he was not a League
                  speaker he was left in peace and the Mayor turned upon Mr.
                  Williams.  Finding he was the one expected to speak the
                  Mayor immediately informed him that should he attempt to
                  speak the whole city would be alarmed and that in a few
                  minutes would be there to prevent Mr. Williams from saying
                  anything.

                          Upon Mr. Williams refusing to say one way or the
                  other until he could get better informed the Mayor took
                  that answer as an intention to speak and turned to the
                  Constable and ordered him to go ahead accordingly, which
                  orders the Constable turned away, apparently, to carry out.
                  The Mayor was very angry and said the sense of the Mass
                  meeting the night before was to prevent the meeting at all
                  costs and that he, in person, would lead the necessary action
                  to prevent a League Speaker talking.

                          Upon consultation with other League men Mr. Williams
                  informed Mayor he would not hold meeting.  That he was
                  there not only to obey the law, but to defer to the wishes
                  of the citizens of Pine Island.  That, therefore, the Mayor
                  could depent upon him not to attempt to speak on that day
                  in that city.  Later Mayor came to Mr. Williams and asked
                  further that he would not permit the soliciting of mem-
                  bers for the League that day which the latter agreed to.
                  At the time the Mayor complimented Mr. Williams on the
                  gentlemanly manner the League representatives had shown
                  in handling their side of the controversy.

            Signed,    January 17, 1918,  J arthur William

            Signed,    January   , 1918,_____

            Signed,    January   . 1918,
                                        _____
```

An incident report filed at Nonpartisan League headquarters in St. Paul provides detail on the Pine Island, November 16, 1917, confrontation between an NPL speaker and Mayor Arthur Parkin. The statement is signed by J. Arthur Williams, the NPL lecturer barred by Parkin.

who had been preying upon the farmers saw their opportunity to discredit their critics and become super-patriots over night." Their zeal, he continued, was based "as much on economic as patriotic impulses." The Nonpartisan League, asserted Manahan, had been "branded as disloyal and no one connected with it was safe. Treason was a common charge."[123]

☆   ☆   ☆

In late January 1918, Albert R. Allen and E. H. Nicholas, friends and attorneys representing Martin and Jackson counties, southwestern Minnesota neighbors located along the Iowa border, initiated the first in a protracted series of actions against Nonpartisan League leaders that would culminate in Goodhue County courtrooms. Nicholas opened the campaign by charging NPL leader Joseph Gilbert with discouraging military enlistments during a Lakefield (Jackson County) speech.[124]

A parrot played a compelling part in Gilbert's February 11, 1918, trial in Jackson County. That affair had dragged on until midnight when the judge, in a peculiar decision, approved an auction to benefit the local Red Cross. The bird, named Kaiser Bill—it was claimed he "talked German"—was produced and its owner shouted, "Bid on Kaiser Bill for benefit of the Red Cross." Chaos ensued.

Gilbert attorney James Manahan entered the bidding in the knowledge that buying a German parrot would make him appear pro-German, but refusing to bid might indicate he was anti-Red Cross. The canny lawyer made the winning bid of fifteen dollars. Then, playing the part of the big city attorney in a roomful of rubes, Manahan put the articulate bird back up for auction. He would rid himself of the parrot and raise more for the Red Cross. Manahan theatrically leaped onto a table and called upon the judge to open the auction, then taunted the opposing attorney Nicholas for not bidding. The feisty lawyer sneered at the audience, calling its members "lip patriots" and "tightwads."[125]

Fiery former U.S. Congressman James Manahan, NPL lawyer for Joseph Gilbert, caused chaos during a February 1918 Jackson County trial. The disturbance centered around a Red Cross fundraiser and an auction for a parrot named Kaiser Bill.

Arguments flared between Gilbert supporters and their rivals. Gilbert, whose running commentary on the courtroom action angered Sheriff O. C. Lee, was re-arrested. Infuriated by the new charge, Gilbert loudly protested the sheriff's actions. Soon, Joseph Gilbert found himself being marched to a judge's office, his allies and opponents trooping behind. Prior to the trial, wary Gilbert supporters suspected he might be jailed overnight—an incarceration that could result in dire consequences for their man. These local farmers had pre-signed appeal bonds ready for the use of the NPL leader. A watching crowd jeered as Gilbert, freed by the preemptive bail strategy, was driven away. Newspapers did not report on Kaiser Bill's fate.

Attorney Manahan, however, did not have Sheriff Lee's immediate protection. After the auction, he and a few Gilbert supporters slipped out a courthouse back door hoping to avoid hostile citizens gathering in front of the building. Manahan hurried down an alley, and at a boy's shout, "There he goes!" the panicked attorney ran. The fast-growing mob seized him, quickly hustling their prisoner toward the river. Years later the St. Paul attorney would admit, with shame, that he had lied to the assailants, pleading he was only a lawyer with "…no use for those damn socialists." He observed, "My cowardice and betrayal caught the sympathy of that cowardly mob." The *Minneapolis Tribune* reported Sheriff Lee appeared and intervened to save Manahan "…from a mob, which, yelling for a rope, chased [the lawyer] through an alley." Two days later Gilbert was found guilty and sentenced to three months in county jail. His attorneys appealed and he left town on bond.[126]

Pointing to the existing sedition charges lodged against Townley and Gilbert in Jackson County, Martin County Attorney Albert Allen ordered Sheriff Lee to halt Nonpartisan League meetings in his jurisdiction, using the threat of arrest. The outlawing of NPL meetings was a growing Minnesota phenomenon, with Goodhue County leaders among its earliest proponents. On February 15, meanwhile, a Faribault County deputy sheriff stopped Gilbert from addressing a group of 200. Earlier, orders had been issued banning League gatherings in that county.[127]

In late February, Allen issued new warrants of arrest for Gilbert and Townley, charging them with distributing seditious literature. Allen then overplayed his legal hand, ensnaring himself in a jurisdictional conflict with Ramsey County courts. He had directed Sheriff William S. Carver to track down and arrest Joe Gilbert in St. Paul and escort the NPL leader—Gilbert asserted he was "kidnapped"— to Fairmont, the Martin County seat. A St. Paul judge, responding to a plea from League attorneys, promptly issued a writ of habeas corpus ordering Sheriff Carver to produce Gilbert in the capital city. The chastened lawman complied. Gilbert commenced suing Martin County officials for false imprisonment, later settling out of court for $275. On March 11 Gilbert would journey back to Fairmont's Martin County District Court to face sedition charges. Constitutional issues regarding the indictment then prompted county officials to send the case to the Minnesota Supreme Court.[128]

Andrew Finstuen chaired the March 7, 1918, Kenyon town meeting that transformed into a 300-person search party on the hunt for suspected NPL organizer George Breidal, rumored to be in town. Finstuen is pictured in the state Legislature sometime during his ten-term service there (1923–1944).

While the Martin County courtroom drama played out, a Nonpartisan representative found trouble in Goodhue County. A businesslike community meeting held at Kenyon's city hall on March 7, 1918, devolved into a hunt for an NPL organizer rumored to be in town. Chaired by Andrew Finstuen, the mundane town meeting had produced a slate of officers being nominated for the coming year. Caucus goers then officially declared themselves "100 percent loyal Americans," ordering the incoming council to "put a stop to all disloyal gatherings and utterances and to drive all disloyal agitators from our community." At that point, a Kenyon resident burst into the room to report Nonpartisan League organizer George Breidal had been sighted in the village. According to a *Kenyon News* story headlined "Held Caucus and Drove Out Breidal," the caucus "voted to go in a body and invite Mr. Breidal to leave town never to return."[129]

Caucus members and other citizens, about 300 in all, marched toward the Commercial Hotel looking for Breidal. They detoured to the Lyric Theater after receiving a tip that the suspect was there. The NPL representative, answering a boisterous summons from the townspeople, soon appeared. An unnamed spokesman ordered the NPLer to get out of Kenyon, and then directed him to kneel and kiss an American flag. Breidal's escorts paraded their prisoner, now carrying the flag, to the hotel where he paid his bill.[130]

According to *News*

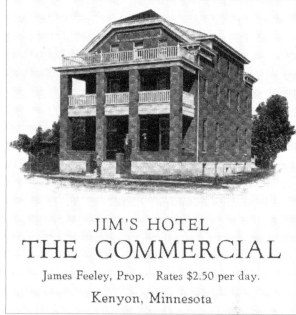

JIM'S HOTEL
THE COMMERCIAL
James Feeley, Prop.   Rates $2.50 per day.
Kenyon, Minnesota

The Kenyon crowd headed to the Commercial Hotel where their NPL quarry was reported to be staying. They eventually found Breidal at the Lyric Theater.

editor Ole Sandstad, Breidal "was not handled roughly," but seemed "humiliated by the bantering of the younger element...." He was taken to the train depot and put on a southbound train to Dodge Center. Breidal had asked to go north. The editor concluded, "The incident ought to be a warning to others of his kind to give Kenyon a wide berth." *Zumbrota News* editor E. F. Davis applauded the treatment of Breidal, pointing out, "It would be well for other towns in the county to follow their [Kenyon's] example." In its page one story, "Nonparty Agent is Deported by Village Caucus," the *St. Paul Pioneer Press* quoted a village official, "We want it understood that this community is undivided for America, and anybody who comes here must be 100 percent American."

Perhaps a letter from a Kenyon soldier sent the week before the Breidal incident inspired the actions of its townspeople. George Brobeck, in training at Camp Cody, New Mexico, had reminded village residents, "All the boys here are watching for the results of the [Nonpartisan League] trials...." Brobeck had written to *Kenyon News* editor Sandstad. The local soldier had been in the town's barbershop during the Louis

Kenyon News editor Ole G. Sandstad, he preferred "O. G.," was justifiably proud of his Spanish-American War service and his later leadership in veterans affairs. This ad from the county history of the World War shows him in his bemedaled 1898 uniform.

George Brobeck, an active participant in the Kenyon Bakko barbershop incident, kept track of developments in his hometown while training at Camp Cody, New Mexico.

Martin incident. Brobeck observed bitterly that he and his fellow recruits were "doing our best" while traitors back home were trying to "knife us in the back."[131]

The same March 7 edition of the *Kenyon News* that told of Breidal's fate carried a report from Cannon Falls regarding a Nonpartisan League request to rent the local opera house. Mayor A. R. "Tony" Mensing and the town's Civic Improvement Club, who handled booking of the building, denied the League's request. The popular Mensing had left his position at Minnesota Malting in Red Wing to open Commercial Grain and Malting in Cannon Falls. Village council members later joined in with their own anti-NPL resolution, forbidding that group from holding a meeting within the corporate limits of the community.[132]

An early March comment from the *Faribault Republican* applauded Kenyon's efforts against those suspected of failure to support the war effort. The praise was republished in the *News*: "Kenyon is developing a most unhealthy climate for disloyalists. There will soon be no place where a traitor can hang his hat." The village council had earned those plaudits by barring seditious or pro-German propagandists [meaning NPL organizers] from holding a meeting within Kenyon. C. J. Talle, council president, signed the unanimously approved resolution.[133]

Frontenac's Mrs. Fred Kingsley, vice chairman of the local Red Cross, looked with alarm at NPL organizational efforts in that Mississippi riverside community. Writing on March 1 to the state Commission of Public Safety, she reported, "The Non Partisan men are working in our township & we are in much need of some one to boost for loyalty."[134]

On March 14, 1918, a Goodhue County Grand Jury delivered a straightforward warning to those who would question the American commitment to the Great War. Meeting at the county courthouse in Red Wing, jurors issued nine indictments for sedition to men who, according to evidence, might have committed disloyal, treasonous actions. The charged included Joseph Gilbert, Louis Martin and N. S. Randall, all of the Nonpartisan League, along with county residents Herman Zemke, Goodhue, John C. Seebach and Carl Seebach, Red Wing, Henry J. Bang, Belvidere Mills, and Gust W. Kruger and William Ripetto, for whom no local addresses were provided.[135]

Prior to the arraignment, Red Wing's *Daily Republican* editor Jens Grondahl extended in print some stern advice to the grand jury: "The laws in America…are much too lenient in a crisis of this kind but they are sufficient to bring to their senses those ungrateful pro-Huns who have sucked the substance out of this country only to repay it with ingratitude and treason. It is hoped that the grand jury…will do its full patriot duty by helping to bring to justice the kaiser's admirers and spokesmen…."[136]

Indicted individuals learned the specifics of charges against them. John (Johannes) C. Seebach's indictment covered eight handwritten pages containing testimony and eight charges detailing his alleged efforts in "discouraging enlistment." Irony could

195

File # 895

The District Court for the County of Goodhue, and State of Minnesota, First Judicial District.

THE STATE OF MINNESOTA,

Against

N. S. Randall
N. S. Randall

} Indictment.

is accused by the Grand Jury of the County of Goodhue, State of Minnesota, by this indictment of the crime of *discouraging enlistment of men in the military and naval forces of the United States, and advocating that the citizens of said state should not aid and assist the United States in prosecuting and carrying on war with the public enemies of the United States,* committed as follows:

The said N. S. Randall

on the *18th* day of *August* A. D. 19*17*, at the *Village* of

Kenyon in the County of Goodhue, ~~in the~~ State of Minnesota, then and there being, did, then and there, at a public place where more than five persons were then and there assembled, unlawfully and wilfully teach and advocate by word of mouth and oral speech that men should not enlist in the military and naval forces of the United States and that the citizens of the state of Minnesota should not assist the United States in prosecuting and carrying on war with the public enemies of the United States, said United States being then and there at war with the Kingdom and Imperial Government of Germany; by then and there stating and expressing to and in the presence of Joseph A. Gates, Andrew Finstuen, Gilbert A. Flom, John A. Bradley, Thomas A. Toss, Charles Linderlow and Albert Hilstad, all being then and there citizens of the State of Minnesota, in substance and effect as follows, to-wit: The rot that is being pulled off nowadays by our government with reference to this war is something so disgraceful that you have no idea of it. If the money of the rich were thrown into the war-chest, this war would end immediately. We must save food for the Allies, they say; we must save food for them whether we get anything for ourselves. This is what makes high prices. The president of the United States has too much power in this country and he uses it to suit himself,

STATE OF MINNESOTA,

FIRST JUDICIAL DISTRICT,

DISTRICT COURT,

GOODHUE COUNTY.

THE STATE OF MINNESOTA,

AGAINST

N. S. Randall

INDICTMENT.

A TRUE BILL,

H. P. Hulebak
Foreman of ~~the~~ Grand Jury.

Thomas Mohn
County Attorney.

clerk of court
OFFICE ~~CLERK OF DISTRICT COURT,~~
GOODHUE COUNTY, MINNESOTA. }

Filed *March 14"* 19*18*

C. S. Dana.
Clerk.

Specific charges in N. S. Randall's indictment [shown here], as with those of the other defendants, are spelled out in Goodhue County Indictment Record 2, 1897–1922.

be found in Seebach's situation. He was an uncle to the two Red Wing military officers then most prominent in the war effort—Major Otto Seebach, who helped organize and lead the Minnesota Home Guard, and Capt. Fred Seebach, who commanded Red Wing's Home Guard Company A. Harry Olson, an employee at Red Wing's La Grange Mills where John Seebach, 59, worked as a manager and bookkeeper, stated his boss openly disagreed with the draft and didn't believe American servicemen should "protect the land of England and France." Olson testified Seebach demanded that he get out of the Red Wing Home Guard, said President Wilson "had no business getting the U.S. in a war," and claimed the people of the county would put the *Red Wing Daily Republican* "out of business" because of its support of the war.[137]

Martha Bergh testified that John Seebach suggested she write to her brother, Alex, when he got to France, telling him "to shoot high so as not to kill the relations of his." Alfred G. Nelson swore Seebach claimed a lot of men would refuse to cross the ocean because the government couldn't make them.

John Seebach also faced charges for preventing his sons, Carl and Walter, from fighting against the "mother country," allegedly contending he would rather see his sons shot than go to war with Germany. Carl, 24, was also indicted for discouraging enlistment, allegedly stating, within the hearing of Leonard E. Clayton and Herman Grosse, that U.S. involvement in the war was "absolutely wrong on principle," he would not fight, and would shoot anyone who "would come to get him."[138]

Others indicted faced single counts. Charles T. Parkin, John Stemmen and William H. Hennings stated that Herman Zemke said, in Goodhue village, "We had no business to go into this war with Germany," and "We will start a revolution here." Fred Tiedeman reported that Gust Kruger, while speaking to him in Red Wing, said that when the Kaiser and his German army came to the United States, they would show America "where to head off." Also, while in a conversation in Red Wing, William Ripetto reportedly alleged American soldiers were as evil as Germans and "murder innocent women and children," adding, "Germans are the only and most civilized people on earth." Belvidere storekeeper Henry J. Bang had complained about being coerced into buying a Liberty Bond, saying he did not expect to get his money back but believed rich men would get theirs.[139]

The three Nonpartisan League leaders, Joseph Gilbert, Louis W. Martin and N. S. Randall, were indicted for the August 18, 1917, statements they made before the public Nonpartisan League gathering in Kenyon. Eight men claiming to have been in the crowd, four of whom testified—Joseph A. Gates, Andrew Finstuen, John Wallaker and Albert Hilstad—alleged the three League orators discouraged their listeners from enlisting in the U.S. military. Martin's indictment also noted the September 22 incident at Kenyon's Bakko barbershop when he supposedly reaffirmed his support for the comments made by the NPL speakers on August 18. Clarence and Martin Bakko were called as witnesses against Louis Martin.[140]

Gilbert, the most prominent NPLer charged, was quoted directly and at length in the indictment, leading his defenders to publicly question how his accusers could recall and repeat exactly such extended oratory. Gilbert would deny that he spoke the words attributed to him. His statement, as shown in the indictment, read:

> "We [U.S. military] are going over to Europe to make the world safe for democracy, but I tell you we had better make America safe for democracy first. You say what is the matter with our democracy, I tell you what is the matter with it: Have you had anything to say as to who should be President? Have you had anything to say as to who should be Governor of this state? Have you had anything to say as to whether we should go into this war? You know you have not. If this is such a great democracy, for Heaven's sake why should we not vote on conscription of men. We were stampeded into this war by newspaper [sic] not to pull England's chestnuts out of the fire for her. I tell you if they conscripted wealth like they have conscripted men, this war would not last over forty-eight hours."[141]

The words attributed to Gilbert were similar to the rhetoric he typically employed as a Nonpartisan League representative. He also had put his thoughts on record in April 1917, authoring a statement of NPL principles regarding the war effort. Gilbert had asserted, "A declaration of war does not repeal the Constitution of the United States, and the unwarranted interference of military and other authorities [he referred to the Minnesota Commission of Public Safety (MCPS)] with rights of individuals must cease." That statement also criticized profiteering by "bloodstained wealth" and "private monopolies." League foes viewed that declaration as far less than a 100 percent commitment to the American cause.

The defendants pleaded not guilty, and Judge Albert Johnson set bail for each at $2,500. All paid and were released.[142] Jens Grondahl's *Red Wing Daily Republican* carried accounts of the grand jury indictments, leading the editor, furious over the defendant's reported actions, to direct a highly charged, menacing editorial, "The Mark of Cain," at Goodhue County's "pro-Germans." Excerpts are found below:[143]

> "Have the pro-Germans in this city [Red Wing] and other communities stopped to think of the future of their children and grandchildren who will continue to live in this country…. Have they given a moment's thought to the fact that when history is written and understood clearly as their children and grandchildren will understand it…they will hate their fathers and the memory of their fathers with that righteous hatred which a loyal citizen nourishes for a traitor—the same feeling with which the son or grandson of Benedict Arnold might think of that traitor?
> …these pro-Germans are hindering the government and prolonging

the war. That means the prolonged slaughter of American men by the 'mad dog of Europe.' The American blood sacrificed by the prolongation of the war through pro-Hun influences in America is upon the hands of the pro-Germans. They are murderers plain and simple, committing at the same time the crimes of treason and murder to which they will be called to account, as sure as there is a God in heaven."

☆   ☆   ☆

Along with the published March 14 indictments, presiding U.S. District Court Judge Albert Johnson and the Goodhue County Grand Jury issued inflammatory public commentary that placed their objectivity into question. As the proceedings closed, an impassioned Johnson cautioned jurors that they were "not discharged but merely excused…you may be called upon to go into secret session most any time because any person talking sedition or found in any way interfering with the prosecution of the war, should not have the comfort of waiting six months before he is brought to trial." Earlier, Judge Johnson not only joined the overtly pro-war American First Association, he chaired Red Wing's Second Ward committee.[144]

An ambitious Albert Johnson had been making a name for himself in Minnesota judicial circles in the four years prior to the 1918 trials. A longtime Red Wing resident, former attorney and clerk of court, Judge Johnson had served on the First Judicial District Court since 1909. He nurtured hopes of gaining a Minnesota Supreme Court seat, eventually making three strong attempts to win election. Johnson came closest to success in 1914, placing first among six candidates in the June primary. Nevertheless, incumbent George L. Bunn defeated him in the general election. Judge Johnson would fail to win election to the High Court again in 1920 and 1924.[145]

Following the indictments, all 23 grand jury members signed and then issued a resolution, "Upon the Loyalty of Goodhue County in Matters Pertaining to the War With Germany." Its text was later printed in the *Red Wing Daily Republican*. This remarkable document, an open and unveiled threat, warned war skeptics: "It is a well-known fact that in a good many communities in this county there have been some pro-Germans and some fifty-fifty [not 100%] Americans…. [T]hese people are going to be very carefully watched…it is their duty to…come out in the open and commit themselves to the successful prosecution of the war. It is not enough for them to subscribe and do things when they are asked…but they must voluntarily contribute their services and ask for the privilege of assisting in some way. In this way only can they remove from

Following the indictments for sedition in his Red Wing courtroom, District Court Judge Albert Johnson advised Goodhue County Grand Jury members to stay ready because "any person talking sedition should not have the comfort of waiting six months before he is brought to trial."

themselves the suspicions that have been raised in the last year. From now on we must all be boosters for the war and 100% American."[146]

Among "these people" to which the jury referred were those with familial ties to Germany or born overseas. Census data from 1910 showed more than 70 percent of Minnesotans were either foreign born or had parents who were, and 25 percent of those newcomers were ethnically German. And it was clear to those paying attention that ethnic Germans who had not been active in earlier Midwest farmer protest movements were now signing up for the Nonpartisan League. NPL membership in Minnesota had been primarily Norwegian and Swedish in 1916. Germans in significant numbers started enrolling in 1917, and that trend continued in 1918. This movement was, in the minds of its critics, apparently related to the NPL's less than 100 percent war support.[147]

After looking at the very public "loyalty" statements issued by judge and jury, the men indicted in Judge Johnson's courtroom were left to consider the likelihood of receiving a fair trial in Red Wing. Also pondering the court's warnings were county residents, particularly those carrying German surnames who had failed to "become boosters for the war." By this time, March 1918, such citizens might well have been under suspicion or were even being "very carefully watched."

In reality, the statements of intent issued by the judge and grand jury in the Red Wing courtroom aligned with the wartime philosophy of the Minnesota Commission of Public Safety. An excerpt from the commission's 1919 postwar report spelled out MCPS strategies for dealing with the perceived disloyal:

"The Minnesota men who were disloyal…formed a constituency of considerable size and there appeared leaders and spokesmen to organize them and give expression to their opinions. Misinterpreting the constitutional guaranty of freedom of speech and of the press, these leaders thought or pretended to think that even in war times, they could properly oppose the government's policies in speech and writings. These leaders were of three classes:

(1) Professional and theoretical pacifists who organized for a nation-wide anti-war campaign, the so-called People's Peace Council and similar bodies. (2) Men of pro-German traditions and sympathies, who were opposed to the war because Germany was one of the combatants….(3) Professional politicians of the socialist or Non-partisan league stamp, who sought to win votes at their country's cost by pandering to a treasonable sentiment. The Commission undertook to kindle the back fires [sic] of patriotism among the rank and file of this ilk by the devices already referred to. With the leaders it used the mailed fist."[148]

A Deepening Divide

"Farmers of Minnesota! The hour has come to strike." This strident call to action in the February 18, 1918, *Nonpartisan Leader* rallied readers to the League and its campaign to wrest the state from the grasp of what NPLers called "Big Biz"—Minnesota corporate interests. The Nonpartisan League wielded the same strategic club with which it so effectively battered North Dakota opponents. The League planned to infiltrate Republican and Democratic party primary elections with its members or allies and then place NPL-aligned candidates on the ballot. Charles Russell, a *Nonpartisan Leader* editor, later recalled that League creator Arthur Townley believed "mastery of the primaries was mastery of the state…."[149]

Always the socialist, Joe Gilbert had referred to the clique of capitalists dominating Minnesota two months earlier in St. Paul. Speaking before striking streetcar workers, Gilbert asserted that a functioning farmer-labor alliance could eventually put the working class in power. He proclaimed, "You have got to stand shoulder to shoulder and continue the fight, not simply for the sake of holding a job on the streetcars… And what should be your final goal?…[I]t must be the abolition of autocracy in industry."[150]

Just three weeks later, the Nonpartisan League leadership team stumbled badly as they formally opened their election campaign. League officials issued a surprising

THE SPIRIT OF MINNESOTA

A *Nonpartisan Leader* cartoon celebrates the budding alliance of Minnesota farmers and laborers in the aftermath of the NPL's March 1918 convention.

invitation to the organization's implacable political foe, Governor Joseph Burnquist. They suggested he address NPL members during their March 17 St. Paul Auditorium convention. League officials made the offer, apparently wanting to appear open and reasonable, expecting the anti-NPL governor to decline the invitation.[151]

Burnquist was having none of it. Instead, he issued a scathing RSVP—a written assault on the League asserting it had been "closely connected with the lawless I.W.W. and with Red Socialists." He accused NPL organizers of promoting conflict between social classes, and declared an individual who arrays class against class "…when our nation is in a life-and-death struggle is knowingly or unknowingly a traitor to his state and country…." The governor added, "For me there are during this war but two parties, one composed of loyalists [his Republican Party] and the other of disloyalists [Nonpartisan League and others in the pro-German element]." Newspapers around the state featured the gubernatorial message—unwanted publicity that immediately relegated the League to the defensive. With Minnesota primary elections just three months away, the NPL would be hard pressed to regain the initiative.[152]

NPL President Arthur Townley, temporarily sidetracked in Fairmont answering charges of discouraging enlistment in American military forces, managed a March 15 response to the Burnquist message. Townley accused the governor of insulting "over 100,000 organized farmers and their friends in Minnesota and 50,000 members of organized labor...."[153]

Just the day before Townley's riposte to the governor, a Goodhue County Grand Jury had indicted Gilbert, along with fellow NPLers Louis W. Martin and N. S. Randall, for sedition. The Nonpartisan League image had sustained another punishing blow.

Townley and the farmers he represented looked for encouragement from organized labor. Those living in the blue collar working class neighborhoods of larger cities, some with sizable immigrant numbers, appeared more likely to cast ballots for NPL candidates. Such citizens had demonstrated their power in November 1916 by electing a socialist labor leader, Thomas Van Lear, as Minneapolis mayor. Prior to that election, the city had suffered through a bitter machinist union strike, a crisis that helped Van Lear lock up the union vote and victory. The new mayor promised that city police officers would not be used as strike breakers, while laying plans to limit the power of those controlling Minneapolis street railways. Van Lear could count on the support of four Socialist Party members whom voters had placed on the city council.[154]

The NPL also relied on its Red River Valley strength, backing from reform-minded

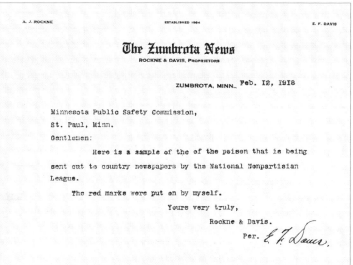

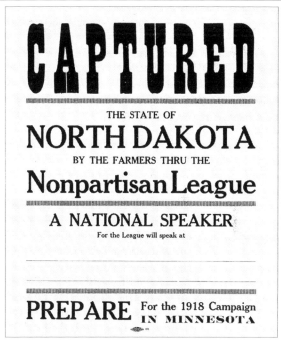

Zumbrota News editor E. F. Davis issued a February 11 warning to the Commission of Public Safety regarding NPL activity in Goodhue County. He included a flyer (above) advising League supporters to prepare for Minnesota's 1918 elections. `

farmers operating on Minnesota-North Dakota borderlands. Rural German American Minnesotans, as noted previously, looked more favorably upon the NPL and its nuanced support of the war against Germany. Minnesota representatives from the largely agricultural Third and Sixth Congressional districts, and a congressman from St. Paul, voted against the April 6 war resolution. That decision, strongly criticized by a majority of Minnesotans, did not hurt their political futures in congressional districts that included substantial numbers of German Americans. The three men would win reelection in 1918.[155]

The state's central and west central counties, a good part of which made up the Sixth Congressional District, gravitated toward the NPL. The district was home to Charles A. Lindbergh Sr., a well-known former Republican congressman. Townley and Gilbert would soon convince Lindbergh, who now found himself in agreement with Nonpartisan League policies, to be the NPL's choice during the upcoming Republican primary campaign for governor.[156]

With Lindbergh at the top of their ticket, Nonpartisan League officials expected endorsement from the state's Swedish American community to complement the anticipated support of a large segment of Minnesota's German American population. Sweden-born Lindbergh, along with the Swedish American press, had staked a claim for American neutrality when European powers went to war in 1914, holding to that position as America began its tilt toward involvement. In some quarters, including the state Commission of Public Safety, Minnesota Swedes were suspected of harboring pro-German and NPL sentiments.[157]

Early in 1917, Minnesota Congressman Charles Lindbergh Sr. spoke out against both the Federal Reserve Act of 1913 and the arming of merchant ships—radical positions to most, but attractive to the NPL leadership.

Charles Lindbergh carried unwanted political baggage into the campaign. In March 1917, just prior to the American declaration of war with Germany, he had been among the few U.S. House members to vote against arming merchant ships for their own protection. The vote was 403–13. St. Paul's Patriotic League claimed Lindbergh's vote was "un-American" and "cowardly."[158] Bigger problems lay with the July 1917 publication of his pocket-sized book *Why Your Country is at War and What Happens to You after the War and Related Subjects* in which he emphasized economic and political reasons for avoiding entanglement in the conflicts of other nations. Republican opponents and enemies in the press distorted Lindbergh's text in attempts to brand the author as disloyal—a practice made easier by the author's circuitous writing style.[159]

Even prior to the League's St. Paul convention and Lindbergh's NPL nomination, members of the League hierarchy and some of its foot soldiers had become familiar with the inside of jails and hostile courtrooms. Those arrests occurred while U.S. military strength in France was meager and losses small. Reinforcements would be arriving at a rate of 120,000 men per month in spring 1918. American public support for their soldiers in combat was bound to grow. Lindbergh, as the NPL standard bearer, faced a well-organized, ready-made opposition eager to take him on. To some, it appeared he was more likely to be arrested than elected.[160]

Lindbergh's Goodhue County Ally

Charles Lindbergh Sr. became familiar with Goodhue County, thanks, in large part, to his relationship with Frederick A. Scherf, an enthusiastic Nonpartisan Leaguer and NPL legislative candidate from Red Wing. Scherf, who had a farm in Wacouta and a house in Red Wing, was a former Goodhue County commissioner and treasurer. He was a key NPL man in the area. Lindbergh and his lanky teenaged son, Charles Jr., called on Scherf at the latter's Wacouta farm south of Red Wing. Scherf's daughter Mildred later recalled these visits. She paid particular attention to Charles Jr., a teenager who sometimes served as chauffeur during their visits. The young Lindbergh would go on to achieve international celebrity in 1927 when he thrilled a watching world with the first nonstop solo airplane flight across the Atlantic Ocean.

In 1918, Scherf, a native of Hay Creek, was running as a Nonpartisan League candidate for the Minnesota Legislature, with Lindbergh's support. Fred Scherf never backed away from a challenge during the election, standing up publicly for the League no matter how hostile the audiences. For his trouble, he faced a spurious contempt of court charge, was harassed and threatened at political meetings, was accused of being pro-German, and saw his Red Wing home splashed with yellow paint. Nevertheless, with rural support, Scherf would win election to the state Legislature in 1918. After the war in June 1919, Scherf, tired of the anti-farmer, anti-labor coverage he believed dominated Goodhue County newspapers, founded his own weekly, *The Organized Farmer*. Scherf's paper supported the viewpoints of NPL farmers and organized labor.[161]

Lindbergh ally Frederick A. Scherf was an unabashed, unapologetic NPL activist who proudly brandished his German heritage, even when such behavior in Minnesota and Goodhue County became suspect. Fred Scherf, a first generation German American, was 47 in 1918. His family settled in Hay Creek Township, one of Minnesota's most ethnically German enclaves. At the turn of twentieth century, students in Hay Creek's one-room schools received instruction in English, as Scherf did, but for just one hour a day. German was the classroom language for the remainder of the lessons. In 1916, before the U.S. entry into the Great War, Scherf wrote to Minnesota U.S. Senator Knute Nelson challenging Nelson's claim that Germany was Europe's chief offender of "Scandinavian neutrality." Scherf also lashed out at Nelson for his support of arms sales to warring nations, "Can it be possible that in your declining years (Nelson was 73) you will support a policy of bloodshed and the taking of human life?"[162]

During the 1918 Goodhue County campaign for governor, Lindbergh and Scherf employed a bold, straightforward approach to the issues, a stance that impressed followers and inflamed their Republican Party and superpatriot opponents. In League parlance, men like Scherf "would stick"—stay with the Nonpartisan League no matter how much coercive pressure they faced. Nonpartisan League-produced "We'll Stick" buttons were distributed to supporters. In accepting the Nonpartisan League nomination for governor, Charles Lindbergh Sr. reiterated the League charges against its enemies, declaring the loyalty issue to be a fraud and labeling the state's pro-war Republican Party and corporate interests "profiteers and politicians, pretended guardians of loyalty, who seek to perpetuate themselves in special privilege and in office."[163]

On April 19, within a month of Lindbergh's NPL nomination, John McGee, the Minnesota Commission of Public Safety point man and a loyal supporter of Governor Burnquist, made a clumsy political gaffe while in Washington D.C. In overexuberant testimony before the Senate Military Affairs Committee, McGee took an apparent swipe at Lindbergh when he questioned the loyalty of his state's Swedish residents. "The disloyal element in Minnesota," McGee contended, "is largely among the Swedish-German people." He claimed the nation

Burkhard's County Hotel in Hay Creek Township was owned and operated by Albert A. Burkhard Sr., a German immigrant.

had erred in not dealing with "these vipers" at the onset of the war. Minnesotans had become familiar with McGee and the MCPS and their questions about German American loyalty, but lumping Swedes and Germans together and calling them both "vipers" was a monumental blunder.[164]

Furious protests greeted John McGee's remarks and echoed across Minnesota. Calls for his dismissal were heard. Pressure from the Burnquist camp forced a reluctant McGee to explain himself. He made a mess of the attempt. The commissioner disavowed any intent of branding Swedish Americans as disloyal, but then lurched into another attack. He stated that in some Swedish and German areas of the state, local juries had been reluctant to convict the disloyal. He also blamed the press for creating the improper perception that, during his Washington comments, he had called Swedes

John F. McGee, the abrasive, self-assured power inside the state Commission of Public Safety, made a clumsy political blunder when, in testimony before a U.S. Senate committee, stated, "The disloyal element in Minnesota is largely among the Swedish-German people."

disloyal. Then McGee veered off course again and called for military courts to handle the seditious, contending "a prompt appearance of the guilty before the firing squad" would produce a "most restraining influence." Tactless, tone-deaf remarks such as those from McGee raised doubts about the MCPS and Burnquist's candidacy. Burnquist, of Swedish heritage, asserted his fundamental disagreement with McGee's hyperbole.[165]

Former Governor John Lind, a native of Sweden, and John McGee had been among the original MCPS commissioners appointed by Governor Burnquist. The two men clashed when Lind opposed McGee's plan to remove Thomas Van Lear, the socialist mayor of Minneapolis, from office. Van Lear antagonized Minneapolis traditional political interests when he organized a peace conference as Congress debated going to war. Lind told fellow commissioners that

John Lind, the former governor who grew up in Goodhue County, was a member of the Commission of Public Safety when John McGee attacked him during a CPS meeting. Said Lind, McGee called me "everything vile you can think of." Lind resigned.

Commission of Public Safety maneuvers to oust Van Lear would violate the law, and quashed the plan. An infuriated McGee bitterly denounced his colleague. Lind later told of McGee calling him "everything vile you can think of before the committee—with the governor [Burnquist] in the chair." Lind reported, "The governor begged me to come back [to the MCPS]. I told him I could not and would not with McGee on the board."[166]

Louis Martin, among those indicted for sedition by a Goodhue County Grand Jury on March 14, 1918, was back in Red Wing and Judge Albert Johnson's District Court on April 3, facing a different charge. The Nonpartisan League organizer stood accused of making disloyal statements in September 1917 during a Goodhue village NPL meeting.[167]

K. L. Anderson, Goodhue council president, justice of the peace and owner of the hall used for Martin's speech, testified first. In a statement supported by other prosecution witnesses, Anderson alleged the NPLer stated, along with other treasonous assertions, "I am a pro-German and am going to give a pro-German talk. The United States has no business in this war. The country is trying to rake England's chestnuts out of the fire…. This is a rich man's war and if the United States had kept out of it, the war would be over in 24 hours." Anderson was later recalled to the witness stand to back up his statement that the approximately 40 persons attending the meeting were "mostly Germans." Under close questioning by the defendant's counsel, Thomas

Davis, he could name only two.

The defense argued that Martin's alleged "pro-German" statement actually began with the words "The Twin City newspapers will say I'm pro-German"…and that his critics simply dropped off the first six words of the sentence. His attorney contended that Martin had urged his Goodhue audience to buy war bonds. On the witness stand, the NPL organizer recounted his speech, explaining how it had been mischaracterized. Six witnesses for the defense—B. E. Mann, Henry Buck, Ed Buck, William H. Hennings, Fred Vollmers and Conrad Meyers, "practically all league members," according to *Minneapolis Tribune*—had attended the Goodhue meeting in question and supported Martin's version of events [see p. 65].[168]

During the trial the prosecutor, Goodhue County Attorney Thomas Mohn, gave Louis Martin an opening. Mohn asked the defendant an open-ended question: What did you say to the Goodhue village audience? Martin jumped on the query, delivering a lengthy response while employing the colorful, well-practiced talking points he used as an NPL organizer. His words clearly had an effect. When they later deliberated, jury members leaned toward a "not guilty" decision, voting twice and each time producing an eight to four majority to acquit. On the third ballot, jurors returned a unanimous "not guilty" verdict. After the acquittal, some half-dozen farmers from the crowd witnessing the trial reportedly crowded around Martin, requesting NPL enrollment forms.[169]

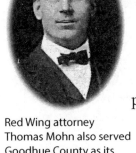

Red Wing attorney Thomas Mohn also served Goodhue County as its legal representative. With the Martin case, Mohn was just beginning prosecutions of NPL members that would continue into the 1920s.

Jubilant Nonpartisan Leaguers savored Martin's victory. After a prolonged series of bitter setbacks in Minnesota courts, the Martin acquittal in Red Wing gave NPL partisans hope that they might prevail in courtrooms and, perhaps, in the upcoming election. The League carpeted Goodhue County with circulars detailing Martin's acquittal. It claimed county farmers were "strongly in favor of the League," and that the trial had aroused "intense indignation against the anti-farmer gang which tried to 'frame-up' innocent men."[170]

Kenyon physician Joseph Gates drew special attention in the NPL flyer. "A certain Dr. J. S. (sic) Gates…was especially active against Martin and is said to have boasted he would drive him out of the county." The broadside reminded readers that the doctor had previously assaulted the League organizer. *Zumbrota News* editor E. F. Davis put his own spin on Gates's actions: "Sure he did [assault Martin], and if Martin said what he is alleged to have said, Gates ought to have broken his neck."[171]

In the *Cannon Falls Beacon*, S. S. Lewis offered a terse summary of the Martin trial: "Every pro-German in Goodhue County was delighted to hear L. W. Martin has been acquitted." An outraged Lewis offered a provocative prediction to his readers: "The fiend of disloyalty is stalking through this county and if the courts are powerless to check it, the people will eventually take it upon themselves to do it, and they will do it by the shortest route and most thorough manner." The editor then took a step back from what appeared to be an encouragement of mob violence, writing, he was not "advising breaking the law." Lewis finished with a threat: "…the country is fighting for its life and the people will not tolerate much longer sedition and treason."[172]

Days after the Martin acquittal, *Kenyon News* editor Ole Sandstad praised Warsaw Township residents for donating $150 to the Cannon Valley Red Cross, writing, "That's American 100 percent for sure." But then the editor tacked on his own characterization of the Warsaw effort: "[They] expressed their disgust, resentment and condemnation of all un-American pro-German draft evaders, disloyalists, seditionists, slackers and traitors." He predicted Warsaw citizens would rid themselves of such undesirables.[173]

> MARTIN CLEARED OF
> DISLOYALTY CHARGE
> --o--
> Nonpartisan League Organizer Is
> Acquitted By District Court
> Jury On First Ballot
> --o--
>
> L.W.Martin, Nonpartisan league organizer in Goodhue county, was acquitted last Friday of a charge of making disloyal remarks tending to obstruct the sale of Liberty bonds by a jury in the district court. The jury deliberated less than an hour and Martin was acquitted on the first ballot.
>
> Martin's arrest was the result of political persecution. He was unusually successful in organizing Goodhue county and soon aroused the opposition of a few professional politicians and bankers who feared the influence of the league. A certain Dr.J.S.Gates, defeated candidate for lieutenant-governor, was especially active against Martin and is said to have boasted that he would drive him out of the county.
>
> Politician Assaulted Organizer
>
> Dr. Gates assaulted Martin on one occasion and several times mob violence was incited against the plucky organizer. Hostile newspapers repeatedly published false rumors in the attempt to prejudice the people against Martin and to hamper his work. Last November Martin addressed a letter to the governor and the Public Safety commission asking for an investigation of the charges against him. He said that if he were guilty he should be in jail, but that if he were innocent that he was entitled to protection of the law. The governor ignored this letter and the Safety commission failed either to investigate or to protect Martin.
>
> Then Martin brought a suit against Dr. Gates for assault. His own arrest followed. It plainly was the result of a political conspiracy. All other methods had failed, and the gang fighting Martin evidently intended to put him behind the bars.
>
> Trial Vindicated Martin
>
> The trial, conducted before Judge Albert Johnson of the district court, was a complete vindication for Martin. It was shown that instead of being disloyal, he had advocated support of President Wilson. It was shown that instead of obstructing the sale of Liberty bonds, the parts of Goodhue county where he had spoken and organized were the sections where the sale of Liberty bonds was largest. The prosecution not only failed to make out a case against Martin, but the evidence showed beyond question that he was an industrious, hard-working young man of splendid character who was supporting his government by deeds as well as words.
>
> Joseph Gilbert, organization manager of the league, and N.S. Randall, league lecturer, also were indicted through the efforts of the anti-farmer gang which had Martin brought to trial. The cases against Gilbert and Randall have been postponed. The anti-farmer gang thought they had the strongest case against Martin and the failure of their plot has made them less ready to push the other cases.

Following Louis Martin's District Court victory in Red Wing, the Nonpartisan League celebrated with the flyer "Martin Cleared of Disloyalty Charge," widely circulating it in Goodhue County and throughout the region.
MCPS Main Files, Nonpartisan League Folders

Later that March, Sandstad found more good news for Goodhue County 100-Percenters. At a meeting in Kenyon's Nelson Hall, village residents joined with farmers from Kenyon, Holden and Cherry Grove townships to rally in support of the war effort. Dr. Joseph Gates drew enthusiastic applause with a " fervent patriotic address." Editor Sandstad observed with satisfaction, "those farmers and agitators who are stirring up class friction and hatred between farmers and others were conspicuous by their absence."[174]

Uncle Sam joined the Liberty Bond sales campaign to fund the war effort. Five national bond drives were launched.

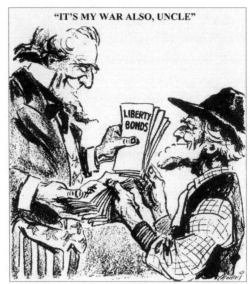

"With toil and money the American farmer is backing the nation in its hour of crisis. Men who already are wealthy may strive to gouge Uncle Sam in war contracts, and corporations may not contribute their share to the fighting fund, but the farmer is more than holding up his end of the load. And Liberty loan subscriptions have been beat in the district where the farmers are organized in the National Nonparetisan [sic] league."
Undated cartoon and caption from Nonpartisan Leader.

A cartoon touting the Third Liberty Bond drive shows an American pilot dropping a bomb on "Kaiserism." During the First World War, Germany was led by Kaiser [Emperor] Wilhelm II.

A bond-buying American uses wadded U.S. dollars to hammer nails into the head of German Field Marshal von Hindenburg.

☆　　☆　　☆

Although the human and economic cost of the coming conflict was impossible to predict, United States military and governmental leaders understood sending troops into Great War combat would be enormously costly. Three weeks after war was declared in April 1917, Congress authorized the Liberty Loan program to provide America's military with the financial backing needed to get the job done. Americans would be expected to support the war effort by purchasing U.S. Treasury-issued war bonds.

Red Wing banker William Putnam, president of the Goodhue County Bankers Association and head of the Commission of Public Safety, had announced the first Liberty Bond allotment at an April 1917 meeting with area bankers. Treasury officials established bond quotas for the nation that, in Goodhue County's case, amounted to $500,000. Liberty Bonds would earn 3.5% interest. A hurriedly assembled county bond sale campaign produced $372,750, a good showing but 25 percent short of the target amount. National bond sales also proved disappointing. Members of the county Liberty Loan Committee and its chairman, William Putnam, were determined to do better [see pp. 148–9].[175]

The Second Liberty Loan drive opened on October 1, 1917. Just over five months had passed since the first bond campaign. Despite Goodhue County's inability to meet the initial drive's goal, its quota had been more than doubled to a formidable $1.1 million. County directors stepped up efforts, boosted by a national publicity agency, the government-run Committee on Public Information (CPI) also known as the Creel Committee. The CPI labored to create support for the nation's participation in the Great War and its fund raising war bond campaign.

For those unable to pay for government bonds, the Treasury suggested individuals could "borrow and buy." In other words, citizens could take out a loan and buy bonds with its proceeds. The Federal Reserve supported this sales concept by funneling low interest loans to member banks. Such federal money, however, could only be used to purchase Liberty Bonds. Goodhue County residents more than doubled their First Loan effort, buying $841,600 in bonds, but once again, they failed to produce the quota set by the Treasury.

In the Zumbrota area, state Senator A. J. Rockne soon discovered a major flaw with the second loan effort. He explained the situation while writing to C. W. Henke of the Minnesota Speakers Bureau, an arm of the MCPS, just 11 days after the sale began. Rockne wrote, "...[T]here is considerable complaint here over the fact that the first bonds have not been delivered to them [bond buyers]. Have talked with several to-day asking them to subscribe for the new loan, and all…would like to have something to show for their first subscription before they subscribed to more." Rockne added, "We are going to make every effort to get the county to subscribe the amount allotted on the second loan."[176]

Zumbrota News reported that Liberty Loan offensives in Zumbrota and Pine Island townships where NPLer Louis Martin had been active had fallen far short of their goals. Zumbrota Township citizens faced a goal of $35,000 and bought only $4,200 worth of bonds, and rural Pine Islanders subscribed for just $2,500 of their $34,000 target. *News* editor E. F. Davis believed there was a direct link to the bond drive failure and subversive Nonpartisan League organizers.[177]

The first two Liberty Loan campaigns had proved controversial, especially to those living in rural districts. City businessmen, often bankers, as was the case in Goodhue County, headed such campaigns. Farmers resented bond sales committees prying into their personal financial affairs and then suggesting just how much they should buy. Studies done following the Second Liberty Loan campaign found roughly two-thirds of Minnesota's counties joined Goodhue in failing to meet their sales quota.[178]

"Our citizens didn't at that time realize the necessity of aiding the government by investing in these securities [Liberty Bonds]…." These words were written after the war and printed in the Red Wing Printing Company's *Goodhue County in the World War*. Jens Grondahl, who ran the publishing firm and edited the book, knew his topic.[179]

Goodhue County Liberty Loan chairman William Putnam seeks help from MCPS publicity director Charles W. Henke as the kickoff of the Third Liberty Loan drive nears.

Grondahl and Putnam would not tolerate such failure. The Red Wing men agreed to a much more aggressive sales approach as the Third Loan loomed in April 1918. A Liberty Loan Executive Committee led by prominent civic leaders from across Goodhue County was the result. And it would be chaired by Grondahl himself, the prominent 100% American. Members pledged not only to reach new quotas, but to "make up the amount we had fallen short" during earlier drives.

Each executive committee member assumed responsibility for one of the eight districts created for the Third Liberty Loan: Charles F. Sawyer, Belvidere, Goodhue, Belle Creek and Goodhue village; Tony Mensing, Cannon Falls (city and township), Leon and Stanton; J. C. E. Holmen, Kenyon, Holden and Kenyon Township; Henry M. Halverson, Wanamingo, Cherry Grove and Wanamingo Township; Leon L. Cornwell, Pine Island, townships of Roscoe and Pine Island; Carl Veek, Warsaw and village of Stanton; Leo Schafer, Zumbrota; Jens Grondahl, Red Wing.

Liberty Bond selling teams thoroughly canvassed the county, holding meetings and making calls. Some residents complained of high pressure from the sales force, but few spoke publicly. Belvidere storekeeper Henry Bang found himself indicted for sedition in March 1918 for reportedly grumbling, "I bought one $50 bond and was compelled to buy that."[180]

Nonpartisan Leaguers and German Americans in Goodhue County, especially those with family members living in Germany, were among those less likely to buy bonds at the expected rates. The 1905 Minnesota census reported 31,628 residents of Goodhue County. Of these, about 22% claimed German ancestry, with 1,757 German-born and 5,259 American born.* As the new century turned, German Americans took pride in the growing power of the "Old Country" carefully detailed in Minnesota's popular German-language press. These newspapers typically sided with Germany as the Great War in Europe took shape. German American newspapers came under close scrutiny after the United

Goodhue County Liberty Loan Committee.

1. W. H. Putnam, Chairman, Red Wing.
2. Jens K. Grondahl, Red Wing.
3. Henry M. Halvorson, Wanamingo.
4. J. C. E. Holmen, Kenyon.
5. L. L. Cornwell, Pine Island.
6. Carl Veek, Dennison.
7. Chas. F. Sawyer, Goodhue.
8. A. R. Mensing, Cannon Falls.
9. Leo. Schafer, Zumbrota.

Despite a respectable showing, Goodhue County was among the two-thirds of Minnesota counties that did not meet their quotas. Goodhue County's Liberty Loan Committee vowed to correct that problem with more aggressive sales tactics.

States joined the conflict in 1917, and their editorial stances, in most cases, were muted. With the war under way, their fellow Midwesterners took a closer look at German farmers in their midst. Particularly suspect were those who expressed agreement

---

* A specialist in political geography at Macalester College in St. Paul, Hildegard Binder Johnson was widely known as an expert on German immigration. Applying her vast experience in detailing the myriad complex cultural and geographic issues involved, Johnson wrote, "any attempt to summarize the origins of Germans by the geographical origins given in the census cannot be very meaningful." In this study the author relied upon Goodhue County census figures and the G. J. Kunau analysis of Goodhue County ethnic settlement in order to provide the reader with the number of residents who perceived themselves to be "German"—German born or of German ancestry.

with the NPL and that group's ongoing feud with business and industrial interests. Members of the German American community were being watched for indications of disloyalty. Refusal to produce the cash expected for Liberty Bonds was such a sign.[181]

The Third Liberty Loan drive opened on April 5, 1918, as the Goodhue County sedition trials of NPL officials and suspected local traitors were about to commence. *Zumbrota News* joined other newspapers in detailing how the new bond sales system would work. Prior to the campaign, local committee members would develop a card index showing the names of "every man, woman and child in the county," along with the person's income and property owned. Cards also carried "the minimum allotment of bonds each person is expected [to purchase]." Bond appeal officials were to create special blue cards to track those refusing to complete purchases.[182]

Not to be forgotten as the new war loan effort opened were the first two bond issues. Bulletins regarding the Third Liberty Loan program pointed out: "[T]he full amount that each person should subscribe for, for the first, the second, and the third [loans], *will be added together*" [emphasis added]. Thus, citizens who hadn't paid the suggested quota during the First and Second Liberty Bond efforts would see those missing amounts tacked onto their Third Liberty Loan commitment. "The government," the *News* story continued, would call for the balance of the three bond sales unless those "who refuse to take the allotment assigned them…can show to the committee that the allotment is not fair…." Cases where individual citizens still refused to purchase would be "submitted to the Federal authorities for final action." What the words "final action" might portend and why and how the federal government would be involved in county bond sales was left to the imagination of those deciding whether or not to pay.[183]

Grondahl and his *Daily Republican* adopted an effective, intimidating bond sales approach. He listed in his newspaper the names of city residents and the dollar amount of bonds they purchased. Having one's name on the bond register would be seen as proof of patriotism. Grondahl understood the public would comb through the lists of bond buyers, eager to learn who had bought them and how much they had paid. By their actions, those who were less than 100 percent behind the war bond effort might well earn the despised designation "slacker."

A Zumbrota Bond Buyer Guide
Zumbrota News explained to its readers the details of the Third Liberty Loan and its requirements. Failure by citizens to comply with these preconditions, noted the *News*, would result in their case being "submitted to the Federal authorities for final action."

CARD INDEX TO TRACK BOND GIVING
Zumbrota News, March 29, 1918
A card index system will be used in the next drive, and every

man, woman and child in the county will be card indexed before the drive begins. These cards will show what property each individual owns and what income he or she has and the minimum allotment of bonds each person is expected to subscribe for. These will be compiled within the next week by the committee men.

To make the matter still plainer, the full amount that each person should subscribe for, for the three issues of Liberty Bonds, the first, the second, and the third, will be added together. From this amount will be deducted the amounts subscribed for, for the two previous issues and the balance will be the amount which the government will now call for. Persons who refuse to take the allotment assigned them, unless they can show to the committee that the allotment is not fair, will be blue-carded as a last resort and his or her case submitted to the Federal authorities for final action.

It is the purpose to equalize the allotments so as to place an equal burden on the people of the community by basing amounts now to be subscribed to an extent on the amounts already subscribed to the two previous loans. That means, that the man who took less bonds than he should have done in the previous drives will be asked to buy more in proportion this time than the one who bought what he should, or more than he should in the previous drives, based on the financial ability of the individual. Those who shirked before will make up for the deficiency under the new plan.

The solicitors appointed for this village by Chairman J. D. Grover are A. S. Baken [sic], Ira D. Warren, Albert Severson, Aug. Perry and Anton Johnson. Other chairmen in neighboring townships have appointed their committees and the drive promises to be successful in every way.

At the drive's conclusion, a relieved Liberty Loan Committee announced $1,550,950 in subscriptions, $450,950 more than the Third Loan quota. The extra bond commitments made good Goodhue County shortages from the First and Second Liberty Loan campaigns. Cannon Falls (city) and Wanamingo (village) both doubled their quotas to lead, per capita, in purchases. Red Wing raised $435,000, over-subscribing by $150,000. Buoyed by their intimidating tactics, Grondahl and the bond committee had produced a bond bonanza.[184]

Five months later, questions about an expected Fourth Liberty Loan effort percolated through Goodhue County. What would be the new financial goal? How many more loan campaigns would follow? A partial answer came in early September 1918 when the new loan, this one to raise six billion dollars nationwide, was announced. Goodhue County's quota would be $1,980,000.[185]

Liberty Loan committee members and township chairmen, concerned with reaching this $2 million goal, gathered at the Red Wing Commercial Club to develop more innovative bond purchase procedures. The committee agreed to designate September 28, 1918, as Goodhue County's Liberty Loan Day. Advertisements printed in county newspapers explained what would happen on that Saturday. *Zumbrota News* announced, "The committee will not call on you as in the past. You are to call on the committee. Don't fail to report at the designated place for your city, village or township. Your committee will be on hand…to tell you what your allotment is and to receive your subscription." Advised the *Red Wing Daily Republican*, "YOU ARE REQUIRED to go to the place designated by your committee and take your allotment of Liberty Bonds. You must come to the committee, the committee will not come to you." Across Goodhue County the message from the loan committee was clear: We will tell you what you should pay and you will pay it. [186]

LIBERTY LOAN DAY

SATURDAY SEPT. 28

THIS MEANS YOU

Goodhue County Will Raise Its Allotment to the Fourth Liberty Loan in One Day, Saturday September 28

There will be no solicitation. The committee will not call on you as in the past. You are to call on the committee. Don't fail to report at the designated place for your city, village or township. Your committee will be on hand from 8 a. m. until 10 p. m. on Saturday, September 28, to tell you what your allotment is and to receive your subscription. You pay no money to the committee.

This advertisement prepared by Committee on War advertising and contributed by the Cannon Falls Beacon

A Liberty Loan advisory for the fourth war bond campaign, *Cannon Falls Beacon*, September 13, 1918

Hoping to kindle bond-buying cooperation among the reluctant, the Minnesota Commission of Public Safety issued Order 44, "Providing for Investigation in Connection With Sale of Liberty Bonds." Order 44 supplied a theoretical foundation for the prosecution of those who did not purchase their bond allotment. The *Red Wing Daily Republican* cautioned readers, "Slackers will discover there is no avenue to escape from doing their duty." Those alleged "slackers" would find such threats were earnestly authentic.[187]

For Liberty Loan committee members, the results once again proved gratifying. "Bond sales strong in the area," reported *Kenyon News*, "no problems in reaching the goal foreseen." "Cannon Falls Goes Way Over the Top," announced the *Cannon Falls Beacon*. At Red Wing's armory headquarters, some $300,000 in bond purchases had rolled in by early afternoon. Zumbrota experienced some shirking. According to the *News*, about 50 individuals failed to appear before their loan committee, and "two or three" refused to buy the amount they were allotted. Still, people in the Zumbrota area advanced toward their allotted goal.[188]

Grondahl offered readers accolades for doing their part in the Fourth Liberty Bond drive, although some self-congratulation was also in evidence: "No intelligent man or woman who reads a newspaper could have escaped complete knowledge with regard to the loan and what was expected of the people."[189]

Subscriptions to Third Liberty Loan

(Continued from yesterday.)

Red Wing Union Stone-
  ware Co. $15,000.00
Hoyt, E. S. 5,000.00
Hoyt, Hazel Fay.......... 1,000.00
Hoyt, Mrs. E. S. 1,000.00
Page, A. A. 500.00
Reichert, F. W. 200.00
Stickles, L. D. & famIly ... 500.00
Red Wing Shoe Co. 2,500.00
Shaw, M. T. 1,000.00
Herder, H. J. 1,000.00
Howe, Hiram 500.00
Putnam, F. D. 150.00
Red Wing Manufacturing Co. 500.00
Nelson, Harris G. 100.00
Red Wing Linseed Co. 1,500.00
Adler, H. F. 100.00
Stebbins, H. C. 2,500.00
Red Wing Milling Co. 10,000.00
Olson, Swan 800.00
Anderson, Chris. 300.00
Giles, Geo. W. 250.00
Pumplin, H. J. 5,000.00
Monson, John 200.00
O'Rourke, Jas. 500.00
Lee, Emil L. 500.00
Sargent, C. J. 1,000.00
Wilson, Emma 100.00
Olund, Ingeborg H. 50.00

Red Wing Printing Co., $1,000;
David B. Gustafson, $200; N.
Halvorson. $300; Bertha Kyl-
lingstad, $50; John L. Hempft-
ling, $100; Jens K. Grondahl,
$1,000; D. O. Merrell, $50; Rolf
Julsrud, $100; Harold V. D...
...erson, $100; Andrew ...
...ons, $100; Raymo...
$100; C. R. Joh...
...old Cochr...
Johnso...

SUBSCRIPTIONS TO LIBERTY LOAN

(Continued from page 1)

Olson, C. J. 100.00
Drew, Joseph H. 50.00
Howe, Roy N. 50.00
Swanson, Alfred 50.00
Swanson, E. 50.00
Lamberg, V. W. 100.00
Siefert, J. E. 50.00
Bender, Christine 300.00
Rehder, E. H. 300.00
Olson, Frances A. 50.00
Fritz, Mr. and Mrs. R. C. 50.00
Hempfling, A. R. 100.00
Prigge, Arthur E. ... 100.00
Morley, Mabel 200.00
Thygeson, Abel 50.00
Nesseth, N. P. ......
Sweney, W. M., Jr. ...
O'Roark, Anna ....
Graeber, Gertrude ....
Cambring Gust ......
Larson, D. ...
DeWitt, ...
Hoph...

McGrew, C. L. 100.00
Olson, Edward E. 50.00
Jablonski, William ... 50.00
Larson, Arthur 50.00
Thime, Carl 50.00
Jenkins, Charles 50.00
Belden, Lester N. ... 50.00
Tuggle, Thos. A. 50.00
Rethschlag, Wm. J. .. 50.00
Peterson, Peter 150.00
Bernard, Olaf 50.00
Johnson, Reuben .... 50...
Ommundson, B. J. ...
Hart, Charles ......
Anderson, Horace W. ..
Withers, Raymond ...
Johnson, Arthur ...
Engeldinger ...
Kuss, ...
Mel...

Gaugemeier, Dora C. 50.00
Howard, Mary C. 100.00
Howard, Rose L. ...... .00
Gilmore, Chas. M. ..... .00
Olson, Lenus R. .....
Olson, Arthur B.
Gardner, Chas
Holmes, ...
Wats...

...50.00
...50.00
...50.00
...200.00
...50.00
...50.00
...Mrs. F. A. 50.00
...F. 500.00
...antelman, H. W. .. 500.00
Holst, Henry 300.00
Enz, Geo. F. 500.00
Phillips, W. J. 150.00
Kruse, L. F. 100.00
Falke, Gust L. 50.00
Haustein, Geo. J. .. 50.00
Nibbe, Herman H. ... 50.00

Masthead: **Red Wing Daily Republican** — UNITED PRESS SERVICE — THURSDAY EVENING, APRIL 18, 1918 — VOL. XXXIII, NO. 198. — RED WING,

---

RED WING REACHES $400,000 MARK IN GREAT LOAN DRIVE

Over-subscribes Its Quota of $280,000 by Better Than 42 Per Cent.

TOWNSHIPS DOING SPLENDID WORK

Reports Coming in From Rural Districts Indicate County is Loyal.

This afternoon Wanamingo township reported Liberty Loan subscriptions of $52,000 up to last night. The township's quota was $44,000. Wanamingo village raised $12,000. Its quota was half that amount.

Over 1900 Subscribers to Third Liberty Loan in City

Figures compiled at Red Wing Liberty Loan headquarters this morning show that over 1,900 persons in this city subscribed to the Third Liberty Loan. Based on subscriptions of $435,000 already in, the average was $235 worth of bonds for each subscriber.

Reports from eighteen districts in the county, which are virtually complete show a total over-subscription of $317,450. When remaining townships file their returns, W. H. Putnam, county chairman, said Goodhue county will have over-subscribed its quota of $1,100,000 by $400,000.

The reports from cities, villages and township, showing quota for each district, amount raised and over-subscribed funds follow:

	Quota.	Raised.	Over-Subscription.
Red Wing	$280,000	$435,000	$150,000
Cannon Falls City	30,500	61,300	30,800
Dennison	6,500	10,000	3,500
Goodhue	12,000	17,000	5,000
Kenyon Village	33,000	55,800	22,850
Pine Island	20,000	36,000	16,000
Wanamingo Village	6,000	12,000	6,000
Zumbrota	25,000	38,750	13,750
Cannon Falls Town	25,000	26,550	1,550
Florence	23,000	30,050	7,050
Holden	48,000	60,850	12,850
*Kenyon Town	36,500	36,500	—
Leon	42,500	53,500	11,000
Pine Island	32,000	35,800	3,800
Stanton	22,500	28,000	5,500
Vasa	34,000	42,250	8,250
Warsaw	39,000	48,250	9,250
Welch	26,500	31,800	5,300
Total			$317,450

Two weeks after Goodhue County's Liberty Loan Day effort, bond crusade chairman William Putnam and his committee sat impatiently before loan shirkers who had been summoned to explain their failures. The *Republican* reported "a goodly number of men, several with wives and some with children" at the October 11 meeting in the Red Wing Commercial Club. The comfortable quarters atop the Goodhue County National Bank building served as a meeting place and clubhouse for Red Wing men involved in city business, industrial and civic operations. It was similar to Commercial Clubs then proliferating across the country. Those called to the bank building were "to show cause why they should not subscribe for the amount of the Fourth Liberty Bonds allotted them." Some recalcitrants stood up to the intimidation and refused to meet their assigned Liberty Bond target amount. Others pleaded their cases, providing reasons for their bond-buying shortcomings.[190]

The fourth floor of Red Wing's Goodhue County National Bank was home to the city's Commercial Club, a private group that included influential leaders in local business and industry. County residents who did not meet personal loan goals were summoned to the Commercial Club to explain their failure.

Red Wing's Influential Commercial Club

Red Wing businessmen and civic-minded residents joined a national movement in 1904 when they formally incorporated the city's existing Commercial Club. Its founders took special interest in promoting and expanding the city industrial and business foundations. The group's primary standing committees were: Manufacturers, Retail Interests, Roads and Highways, and Civic Beauty and Cleanliness. After obtaining written support of two members, any adult male in the city was eligible for election to the club.[191]

Pro-farmer, pro-labor groups, including the socialist-leaning Nonpartisan League, saw Commercial Clubs as a repugnant rival. Their antipathy was generally reciprocated by pro-business club members. When the United States entered the Great War in 1917, those espousing these opposing philosophies became bitter political enemies.[192]

In Goodhue County, members of the Red Wing Commercial Club

were outspoken and influential leaders in the political battle against the NPL and its allies. Three of the Red Wing Commercial Club's first four presidents, William Putnam, banker, David Neill, president of the local telephone company, and newspaper editor Jens Grondahl, were high ranking political and business chiefs. Newspaperman John Stone Pardee, a club incorporator, became the Minnesota Commission of Public Safety's first secretary. The club's John McLane served as chairman of the county's Four Minute Men, a pro-war Committee of Public Information-created speakers bureau. Also in the club was John Rich, Red Wing industrialist and investor, the first Federal Reserve Agent and chair of the Ninth District Bank's Board of Directors.[193]

Commercial Club associates held critically important courtroom positions in March 1918 when a Goodhue County Grand Jury indicted nine defendants for sedition. Thomas Mohn presented the prosecution's case, while U.S. District Judge Albert Johnson presided. County CPS chairman William Putnam's son, Robert, was a grand jury member. Mohn, Johnson and the Putnams were Red Wing Commercial Club colleagues.

Executive Committee members grilled individuals, ferreting out slackers. Grondahl, among the committeemen present, took his turn with the reluctant. He reported that suspects had "sharp questions hurled at them." Bond committee representatives Leo Schafer, Leon L. Cornwell, Tony Mensing, Carl Veek, Charles F. Sawyer and David M. Neill joined in the interrogations.[194]

One Zumbrota farmer resisted committee pressure, balking at his $400 prescribed loan subscription. Committee members promptly raised his quota to $1,000. The Zumbrotan re-thought his position, hustled to his bank and later returned with $400. Committee members accepted that amount. Six people, all with German origins according the *Daily Republican*, still refused to pay up. They received blue cards on which their bond buying failures were recorded. Holders of blue cards were subpoenaed to the First District courtroom for an inquiry led by William Putnam and representatives of the state Commission of Public Safety. Officers of the court were not present, but use of a courtroom for these interrogations gave the impression that government officials stood behind the inquiries. That implied threat added an extra measure of intimidation to the proceedings.[195]

Goodhue County contributors responded by surpassing the $1,980,000 quota, subscribing to $2,033,600. In just 17 months, the United States Treasury had issued four national Liberty Loan subscriptions totaling $17 billion. Goodhue County's contribution was $6,080,000.

A Fifth (and final) Liberty Loan drive, also known as the Victory Loan, opened in May 1919, five months after the war ended. In an announcement that came

Red Cross workers gather in front of Red Wing's City Hospital for a photograph.

far too late for those county residents who experienced heavy-handed coercion to meet assigned Liberty Loan goals, Arthur R. Rogers, chairman of the Liberty Loan Executive Committee of the Ninth Federal Reserve District, "advised" Liberty Loan committees that "it must be distinctly stated that all [loan] subscriptions must be voluntary and no compulsion used...." Goodhue County residents surpassed their $1.5 million quota by $6,200. Bullying tactics from the bond committee were not needed.[196]

Other Goodhue County fund-raising efforts proved far less coercive. The largest commitment in money and time came from supporters of the American Red Cross for its programs at home and in Europe. Volunteers organized the Goodhue County Chapter in the Northern Division of the American Red Cross. They raised $10,000 in their first wartime fund effort and another $44,500 during the second. Every township, village and city had an active Red Cross chapter. Kenyon village ranked first in per capita membership (2,846), and Vasa produced the most funds per capita ($3,508) from 145 members. Along with surgical dressings, books, clothing and other items, the Red Cross supplied county soldiers and sailors with well-filled comfort kits as they left for military training.[197]

More than 5,000 school children in the county enrolled in the Junior Red Cross when it was organized in February 1918. Led by Red Wing physician Grace Gardiner-Smith and Mollie Remshardt, county superintendent of schools, the Junior chapters adopted 17 French orphans, made hospital garments and sent boxes of clothing to war victims.

GOODHUE RED CROSS OFFICERS
Miss Minerva Backman   Miss Gertrude O'Reilly   Mrs. O. T. Parker
John McHugh   O. M. Haga

Goodhue County's Sedition Trials

A sensational kidnapping sidetracked the trial of N. S. Randall, the first of the NPL leaders to face charges of sedition in District Court. Judge Willard L. Converse had opened the proceeding in his Red Wing courtroom on Monday, April 30, 1918,

hearing testimony against Randall. At 9:30 that evening a group of men abducted Nonpartisan League organizer George Breidal from Red Wing's St. James Hotel. It was Breidal's second experience with Goodhue County street justice. Three weeks earlier, about 300 Kenyon townspeople captured the NPL organizer and ran him out of town.[198]

A group of court officers gather in the Goodhue County courtroom which was the site of the 1918 sedition trials. When this photo was taken in 1931, the original county courthouse was scheduled for demolition.

Earlier in the day Breidal had met with League officials regarding the Randall trial and was seen returning to the hotel. About a dozen men, said to be from Red Wing but unnamed in news accounts, entered the St. James lobby and asked to see Breidal. Considering his Kenyon experience, the NPL loyalist had to know a hostile reception awaited him. Nevertheless, he walked downstairs and was immediately seized and dragged to a waiting auto. As the car carrying Breidal sped west on Main Street, a dozen escort vehicles filled with men fell in line as an escort. According to a *Daily Republican* story, they "seemed to come from no where." Bystanders reported at least one of the abductors was armed.[199]

The convoy rolled out of town, turned left onto Vasa Road [Minnesota Highway 19] and drove for some eight miles before stopping. A gunshot rang out, but Breidal was not hit. Apparently the gunplay was an attempt to intimidate the persistent NPL organizer and convince him to leave Red Wing. The autos and their occupants dispersed. The captive was released with orders to get out of town and not return. A later *Zumbrota News* account reported that Breidal, "who had been making himself obnoxious," was escorted out of town by a "delegation of Red Wing citizens" and was told that the climate in that city "was not good for his health." County officials learned Breidal spent the night in Bernie Johnson's Vasa home, and Deputy Sheriff P. J. Lundquist returned him to Red Wing the next day.

Breidal's kidnapping occurred at the city's most prominent hotel and was perpetrated by a posse of unmasked assailants, identified in news accounts as Red Wing men. Considering those factors and the fact that the crime was committed in front of local witnesses, it seemed extraordinary that no bystanders could identify even one culprit. The ensuing Main Street motorcade accompanying the auto carrying the NPLer also produced no suspects. Red Wing buzzed with excitement and rumors.

Breidal's abduction, according to the *Minneapolis Tribune*, revved interest in the N. S. Randall trial to "fever heat." Judge Converse, aware of the emotions already heightened by the Randall case, announced he would sequester that jury and ordered the re-assembling of the existing grand jury on June 19 to investigate the Breidal incident.

WHERE THEY DIFFER WITH THE PRESIDENT

A *Nonpartisan Leader* June 24, 1918, cartoon depicts how NPLers and suspect German Americans viewed those opponents who resorted to violence.

Judge Albert Johnson stepped into the kidnapping case on June 18, questioning Converse's call for a grand jury investigation. Johnson stated that no evidence had been presented to the county attorney that would warrant such an inquiry, although he did not make it clear if any formal probe into the abduction had actually taken place. Also bothering the judge was the expense involved in calling a jury and the fact that harvest time was nigh. Breidal's capture by an anonymous posse of local citizens—at least one armed—was certainly one of the most brazen and widely witnessed felonies in Red Wing history. It went unsolved and apparently uninvestigated. And District Court Judge Johnson showed no interest in delving further into the crime.[200]

Judge Converse, meanwhile, allowed Goodhue County Attorney Thomas Mohn to move forward with the case against N. S. Randall. Mohn called key witnesses from Kenyon—Andrew Finstuen, Dr. Joseph Gates and Gilbert A. Flom—to testify. Albert Hillstad and Charles A. Lindholm later also took the stand. Mohn rested his case on Thursday, May 3.[201]

Randall's defense team called six eyewitnesses to the Kenyon incident, including the defendant's 16-year-old daughter, Fay. All refuted the testimony of Finstuen and the other Kenyon witnesses. John Aazie, a farmer and NPL member, emphatically supported Randall, asserting that the defendant said "nothing against the war." Aazie did remember Randall claiming "He would stand by [President] Wilson until hell froze over, even if he had to skate home on the ice."[202]

Judge Converse decided to limit the number of witnesses testifying in Randall's defense. The defense attorneys planned to call 27 individuals; Converse said only 12 could take the stand. The judge also ruled that Randall would not be allowed to repeat the entire speech he made in Kenyon, despite being questioned by County Attorney Mohn about its contents.[203]

Jurors deliberated for nine hours—their first ballot had eight for conviction and four for acquittal—before returning a guilty verdict. A visibly shaken Randall had hoped for a verdict matching that of Louis Martin, the NPLer who had been found not guilty of sedition in Goodhue County a month earlier. S. S. Lewis of the *Cannon Falls Beacon* approved the decision, "…a few more convictions will teach men like Randall and his ilk that they cannot with safety ignore the law and preach sedition."[204]

In another significant incident related to the Randall trial, Fred Scherf, Goodhue County's NPL leader, was ordered to appear before Judge Converse on contempt of court charges. Scherf allegedly attempted to influence Bert Rand, a member of the Randall jury, by asking Rand to be his campaign manager during the upcoming elections. Scherf, who was running for the state Legislature under the NPL banner, denied the charge and said he would be vindicated. His case was dismissed a week later.[205]

Four Minute Men

Goodhue County supplied its share of the 75,000 amateur speakers who helped assist with the national Four Minute Man support-the-war crusade. These volunteer orators presented brief talks, four minutes long or less. The announced goal of the speakers' bureau was to counter the "propaganda devices of the enemy" [material thought to be pro-German or NPL]. George Creel, who ran the national Committee on Public Information, came up with the Four Minute Man concept. Lecturers spoke wherever they could find an audience. Goodhue County speechmakers began their work in movie theaters before branching out to churches, public parks, auctions, fairs and street corners.[206]

Cannon Falls provided seven Four Minute men including T. R. Johnson, chairman, physician Owen Doely, Claire Tompkins and George Valentine. In Zumbrota, four men—Rev. Willis Beck, H. S. Froiland, Rev. J. L. Seager and Anton Rockne—made up the local speakers bureau. Goodhue's John McHugh, C. V. Varnum and George Johnson, and Bellechester's W. R. Sawyer "did much good work," according to the county's war history. Attorney and *Kenyon Leader* co-owner Andrew Finstuen chaired his village's eight-orator group that included Dr. Joseph Gates, J. C. E. Holmen and *Kenyon News* editor Oscar Strand. John M. McLane led Red Wing's ten-man speaking group that featured County Attorney Thomas Mohn and Robert Putnam.[207]

Four of Goodhue County's Four Minute Men—Mohn, Putnam, Gates and Finstuen—would become directly involved in the First District Court sedition indictments and trials of county residents and Nonpartisan League speakers. On March 11, 1918, Red Wing banker and Home Guard member Robert Putnam was chosen to be a member of the county grand jury. One week later, that jury indicted nine men who would soon be prosecuted by County Attorney Mohn. During the indictment stage, Mohn, who was also a member of the county selective service [draft] board, called upon Dr. Gates and Finstuen to testify for the prosecution. Gates had physically thrown one defendant out of a Kenyon barbershop.

Defense attorneys in upcoming Goodhue County sedition trials decided against formally challenging any of these Four Minute Men grand jurors, all well-known 100-Percenters, for possible bias.[208]

Four Minute Man Robert W. Putnam served in Red Wing's Home Guard Co. A. and as a grand juror in Goodhue County sedition trials. He and his father, William Putnam, chair of the county's Commission of Public Safety, were committed opponents of those they considered less than 100% American.

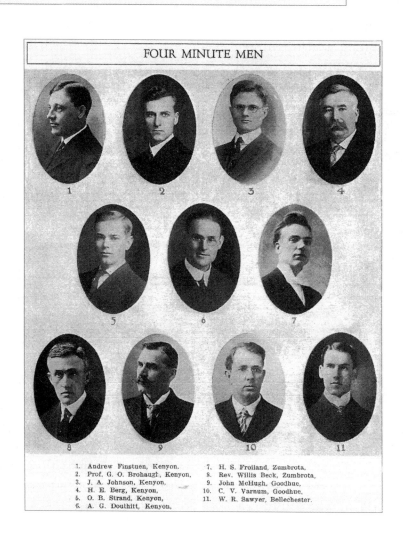

FOUR MINUTE MEN

1. Andrew Finstuen, Kenyon.
2. Prof. G. O. Brohaugh, Kenyon.
3. J. A. Johnson, Kenyon.
4. H. E. Berg, Kenyon.
5. O. B. Strand, Kenyon.
6. A. G. Douthitt, Kenyon.
7. H. S. Froiland, Zumbrota.
8. Rev. Willis Beck, Zumbrota.
9. John McHugh, Goodhue.
10. C. V. Varnum, Goodhue.
11. W. R. Sawyer, Bellechester.

On May 9, five days after the jury convicted Randall, Joseph Gilbert went on trial at the Goodhue County Courthouse on a charge of sedition. Four Nonpartisan League attorneys, led by George Nordlin, would handle his defense. State Attorney General Clifford L. Hilton assisted Goodhue County attorney Thomas Mohn for the prosecution. Hilton had just been appointed to his new post in March by Gov. Burnquist and was expected to add strength to the prosecution. As the trial opened, the Minnesota Commission of Public Safety considered Gilbert one of its prime Nonpartisan League targets. The governor would face the NPL-supported candidate, Charles Lindbergh Sr., in a Republican primary election in a month, and thus stood to benefit politically if Gilbert, a leading Lindbergh supporter, was found guilty.[209]

As the trial opened, District Court Judge Albert Johnson announced that Nonpartisan League members would not be allowed on the jury. NPL attorneys protested Johnson's decision, maintaining the banning of its members would result in League opponents only on the panel. The protest failed to sway the judge. Johnson also denied a defense attempt to show that some prosecution witnesses were biased against the League. Said Johnson, "The League is not on trial." A Gilbert biographer later put it, "In those days, you were either for the League or against it. Neutrals were rare."[210]

Andrew Finstuen, chairman at the Kenyon meeting in question, became the leading witness among the local residents called to testify against Gilbert. Finstuen relied upon extensive notes he claimed to have taken during the defendant's Kenyon speech. His testimony proved nearly identical to ten sentences found in Joseph Gilbert's indictment papers. Among Gilbert's statements, according to Finstuen: The American government is "the most damnable autocracy on earth," and, "If Congress would pass a law conscripting wealth the war would soon be over." All other prosecution witnesses—Gilbert A. Flom, Joseph Gates, John Wallaker, Albert Hilstad and Charles A. Lindholm—offered testimony that aligned perfectly with that of Finstuen—too perfectly for the defense to believe. Nine months had passed since Gilbert spoke in Kenyon, yet all the witnesses recalled his speech using the same sentences, reciting them in the same order.[211]

Andrew Finstuen's controversial handwritten notes detailing the 1917 NPL Kenyon speeches were the alleged informational source of the prosecution's "parrot chorus." Finstuen photo circa 1935

Gilbert's defense team asserted that the Kenyon witnesses had memorized the statements found in the indictment and simply repeated them on the witness stand. All those testifying denied having previously seen that document. Despite their perfect memory of the ten sentences, none of the men remembered any other comments made by Gilbert. They did recall that there were lapses of two or three minutes between the comments to which they testified. In Nonpartisan League circles, the prosecution witnesses became known as the "parrot chorus."[212]

Nonpartisan Leader, the NPL's national party organ, went after Finstuen and the parrot chorus with gusto. The *Leader* challenged Finstuen's ability to take accurate notes, considering they were made at night on a dark platform in a notebook perched on his knee. How, asked the *Leader*, could the notes used in court be so neatly written in pen and in normal handwriting? But the defense could not shake the witnesses or their testimony.[213]

Gilbert's lawyers called to the witness stand O. F. Henkel, C. C. Lawson, Peter P. Exeth, Lars H. Underdahl, C. P. Smith and H. Overholt. They supported Gilbert's contention that he had not spoken the words the Kenyon men attributed to him. Gilbert's defense took a hit with the Goodhue County jury when his supporting witnesses confirmed they were personally opposed to the war and had refused to take part in the Liberty Bond program. Lawson asserted Finstuen had not been taking notes at the meeting. When asked if he still opposed the war, Henkel, a Holden Township farmer, answered, "As a matter of choice, yes, as a necessity, no." Following the trial, Henkel claimed "a certain tribe of the [Joseph] Gates element" created "a very vicious feeling against me at Kenyon."[214]

Joseph Gilbert spoke on his own behalf, testifying about comments made during the Kenyon meeting. He told of defending the Nonpartisan League stand on the war— Gilbert had authored the paper giving the League's position in summer 1917—asserting his belief that if men could be drafted to

Cannon Falls Beacon

CANNON FALLS, MINNESOTA, FRIDAY, OCTOBER 18,

fight, material resources [industries] could also be conscripted. He had called for government ownership of industry to unite the war effort. Injecting some humor, the defendant stated he was English by birth and American by choice, "so it comes with pretty poor grace to call me a pro-German." Gilbert closed, "This organization [NPL] stands for mobilizing men and material for the winning of the war."[215]

Silas S. Lewis, editor of the *Cannon Falls Beacon*, wrote of Goodhue County NPL defendants, "In advocating the firing squad for traitors and seditionists, Judge McGee [of the MCPS] is right."

Gilbert's jury took only four minutes to find him guilty. "A good piece of work quickly done," wrote Jens Grondahl in the *Daily Republican*. S. S. Lewis, editorializing in the *Cannon Falls Beacon* during the trial, referred to the "enemy at home" and comments made by John McGee of the Commission of Public Safety two weeks earlier. McGee suggested an appropriate sentence for seditionists was "a prompt appearance of the guilty before the firing squad." Defendants on trial in Red Wing had been charged with sedition.[216]

Editor Lewis wrote: "Why shoot a deserter and let the man at home go scot free who was stirring up sedition and encouraging disloyalty and desertion? War means shoot to kill and the enemy at home has no more right to escape than the enemy abroad. In advocating the firing squad for traitors and seditionists, Judge McGee (MCPS) is right. If that be fire-eating make the most of it."[217]

"Goodhue county, Minn., finally has succeeded in getting two convictions against League organizers." With this lead to its story, "A Fleeting Victory for the Conspirators," the *Nonpartisan Leader* offered bitter congratulations to the prosecution. The writer quickly moved on to cite trial irregularities and conspiracies that produced a "frame-up" of Gilbert and Martin. Nonetheless, the *Leader* and NPLers expected the two Leaguers to prevail during the appeals process: "They [League members] know that the existing political and legal machinery of government is in the hands of their enemies in some localities, but they still have faith in American courts."[218]

Judge Johnson immediately imposed upon Gilbert a sentence of one year in jail and a $500 fine. Gilbert's attorney George Nordlin requested a stay of sentence, pending an appeal. Johnson agreed to the request with the condition that the Nonpartisan League halt all further activity in Goodhue County. Nordlin protested that he could not speak for the entire NPL. An angry Gilbert interrupted, "I'll tell you this: that never with my consent will the Nonpartisan League get out of Goodhue County." Johnson granted a stay of sentence on a $2,000 bond and Gilbert's promise to cease *his* activities in the county.[219]

Arthur B. Gilbert, associate editor of *Nonpartisan Review*, later presented the NPL view of the trial in a sensational, less than objective article subtitled "Frame-Up Case of Politicians Against Joseph Gilbert and L. W. Martin, Nonpartisan League Workers, Considered Only in Legal Aspects—Astounding Facts in First Trial Ignored." He claimed "desperate men" used "…the legal power of the state for framing up opposition leaders…. [P]revious to and during the trial, Goodhue County was terrorized by open and secret organizations opposing the League farmers." Arthur Gilbert cited the "parrot chorus" and said the judge "admitted the doped up book [Finstuen's journal] as evidence."[220]

☆   ☆   ☆

A cartoon strip shows three of the Nonpartisan League's stereotypical enemies—Big Biz, Kept Press and Old Gang.
Nonpartisan Leader, May 17, 1918

The attention of politically-minded Minnesotans now turned to the increasingly hostile Republican Party gubernatorial primary just a month away. Incumbent Joseph Burnquist faced former U.S. Congressman Charles Lindbergh Sr., the Nonpartisan League's choice. Nowhere was voter interest regarding the upcoming primary more evident than in Goodhue County. A jury in Red Wing had just found Joseph Gilbert and N. S. Randall guilty of sedition. In the eyes of many Minnesotans, the trial branded those men, their NPL colleagues and their supporters as traitors or, at best, dupes. NPL loyalists continued to rally around their candidates, but high profile trials of League members cost it assistance from the general public.

Tension in Goodhue County
A Sampling of Incidents, April–June 1918

•April 25, Kenyon: About 25 Kenyon men of draft age meet to protest the draft exemption of Adolph Zellner, who had been certified to go to Camp Dodge, Iowa, with 41 other men for basic training. Zellner had received an exemption to work on a farm, angering the protestors. The angry crowd "drafts" Zellner to ride a "binder pole" (long wooden poles four to six inches in diameter used to keep a wagon's load in place). He promises to join the military.[221]

•April 26, Goodhue village: The *News* reports a "big fellow who happens to be a nonpartisan leaguer" stopped in the village to have dinner when Tom, an ex-policeman [likely Tom Taylor, a former town marshal] confronted him. Tom told the League member "it was his move and he better beat it and get his eats elsewhere." The visitor hopped in his Model T Ford, which "was seen traveling south just as quickly as it could."[222]

•May 9, Goodhue village: *Goodhue Enterprise* editor Dwight Pierce criticizes the sentence of NPL's N. S. Randall, writing, "…the law ought to give him enough to cure him and to cure others who knew about it [Randall's alleged statements]. What does a little fine of $500… amount to?"[223]

Goodhue village, the county's youngest community, is pictured in 1909.

• May 10, Cannon Falls: Cannon Falls school superintendent E. A. Beito announces German language courses have been dropped from the curriculum. On June 12, Red Wing Public Schools announces the adoption of French language instruction for high school students in the coming year instead of the "dead" German language. The Commission of Public Safety reports that 59 Minnesota districts had dropped German instruction for the 1918–1919 school year.[224]

• May 23, Holden: About 25 men travel to the O. F. Henkel farm for a 1:30 a.m. "yellow paint party"—splashing paint around the farmstead. Kenyon police lead the raid, according to Henkel, who had testi-

fied for the defense in the Gilbert trial. He accuses allies of 100-Percenter Dr. Joseph A. Gates of turning up at his farm "with the evident intention of doing some bodily harm." Henkel and his three sons hold the intruders at bay while his wife walks through the dark to get help from neighbors.[225]

• May 24, Roscoe Township: Destruction of some NPL banners displayed in Zumbrota causes friction between

A pro-Nonpartisan Leaguer readies to battle Big Biz in what a sign says is to be a "Big Scrap to a Finish next November"—the 1918 elections.
Nonpartisan Leader, April 22, 1918.

"certain Zumbrotans and certain citizens and young men of Roscoe township." The *News* explained that Zumbrota had over 60 men in the military, thus, "to them the display of the Nonpartisan banners and anything that borders on it is evidence of disloyalty." Would it be asking too much of Roscoe young men, asks the *News*, "to cease displaying banners on Zumbrota streets?"[226]

• May 31, Cannon Falls: NPL Leader Arthur Townley speaks at the William Randall farm near Cannon Falls to a Nonpartisan League picnic that has more than 1,000 in attendance. Anton V. Anderson, a Goodhue County state representative (District 19), also addresses the audience.[227]

•Late May, Kenyon: In a story titled "About Our Yellow Neighbor," the *News* reminds readers that O. F. Henkel of Holden, whose home had just been attacked by members of a "yellow paint party," was deposed from the presidency of the Kenyon Farmers Mercantile and Elevator Company. His strong "pro-German" attitude is blamed.[228]

•June 6, Red Wing: Albert R. Allen and E. H. Nicholas, attorneys representing Martin and Jackson counties—which were among the first to prosecute NPL representatives, including Joseph Gilbert—address an audience at the Red Wing Armory. The two men, Minnesota leaders in prosecuting NPL speakers and organizers for sedition, warn that the NPL is "disloyal."[229]

•June 7, Cannon Falls: As the Republican primary nears, S. S. Lewis warns his *Beacon* readers, "Every vote cast for Lindbergh [the NPL candidate] is a direct slap at brave American boys who are bleeding and dying on the banks of the Marne [a French river]...."[230]

•June 8, Featherstone: Some 5,000 people attend a Nonpartisan League gathering at the H. V. Carlson farm in Featherstone. Fred Scherf presides. Anton V. Anderson and an NPL speaker from Oklahoma gave brief talks.

LOYALTY RALLY

ARMORY RED WING

THURSDAY EVENING JUNE 6

At 8 O'clock

SPEAKERS:

HON. A. R. ALLEN, of Fairmont
County Attorney of Martin County

HON. E. H. NICHOLAS, of Jackson
County Attorney of Jackson County

The Non-partisan League, Townleyism and Lindbergh plainly discussed

EVERYBODY WELCOME

Loyalty Committee of Red Wing and Goodhue County

Albert R. Allen and E. H. Nicholas, Martin and Jackson county attorneys, appeared in Red Wing to make anti-Nonpartisan League speeches. Historian Carl Chrislock pointed to a coalition of Minnesota groups, specifically the aggressive prosecution teams produced by Goodhue, Martin and Jackson counties, "as the most valuable component within the (MCPS) antisubversion network."

•June 10, Pine Island: Farmers from Pine Island, Minneola, Roscoe, and Zumbrota who support the Nonpartisan League hold a mass meeting in Pine Island. They call for unity in Goodhue County while decrying "mob action" and "lawlessness" from those opposing the NPL. They also protest against newspapers that censure farmers for disloyal behavior.[231]

•June 10, Red Wing: Citizens "swarm" city council chambers to object to that body's approval of a Nonpartisan League request for a rally in Central Park. James H. Doyle, C. S. Sultzer, George P. Pierce and William Cary speak for the dissidents, while Fred Scherf supports the NPL appeal. The chastened council, led by William J. Bach, unanimously approves alderman Harry G. Lillyblad's motion to deny the League use of any park in Red Wing. Jens Grondahl of the *Republican* declares, "It is the height of insolence…for such leaders [NPLers] who have been pronounced seditious…to intrude themselves on a patriotic community and…attempt to deceive right-thinking people."[232]

•June 13, Kenyon: A large group of men conduct a midnight harassment of prominent Kenyon-area farmer and NPL leader P. H. Volstead. He is bombarded with stale eggs and has his auto streaked with yellow paint. Volstead suffers a stroke during the incident and was reported in serious condition the following day.[233]

A Nonpartisan loyalist later offered his own version of the unrest that swept across the Midwest and beyond at the time. He singled out Minnesota for special attention in this 1920 piece:

"The charge of pro-German, disloyalists, seditionists and traitors were freely hurled at every man who belonged to, or represented, the [Nonpartisan] League. The more cunning and astute businessmen, politicians and newspapermen sat back safely in the shelter of their offices and incited the hair-brained and unreasoning into mobs of disorder and disturbance. For several months mob-law ruled in Minnesota, South Dakota, Nebraska, Montana and Idaho and there were minor outbreaks in other states. *But Minnesota probably held the center of the stage in this respect* [emphasis added]. Meetings were broken up, speakers and organizers were deported, tarred and feathered, threatened with hanging, beaten and assaulted. Farmer members of the League were rotten-egged, their automobiles damaged, tires punctured, curtains [car window shades] torn by jerking off banners; fences, houses, barns and places of business were painted yellow."[234]

With just six days left until the June 17 Republican Party primary showdown between party regulars and the Nonpartisan League, Goodhue County NPLers opted to pull off a bold campaign manuever. They organized a 100-vehicle motorcade to carry League members and their families on a meandering vote-seeking journey through Goodhue County. They would demonstrate support for Charles Lindbergh Sr., the Nonpartisan League choice in the primary race for governor. Those in the caravan sought support of like-minded residents in the county's ethnic German, Swedish and Norwegian rural districts—places where the NPL had shown strength. Along the way, NPLers planned to defy opposition from Republican anti-League forces that were entrenched, for the most part, in villages and towns.[235]

The Fiery Spirit of the Farmers' Parades
Long Motor Car Processions Drove Through Minnesota Towns Urging Votes for the League—Stories of the Campaign

Motorcades carrying NPLers for Charles Lindbergh Sr. generated voter enthusiasm and led to a mid-June auto procession through Goodhue County. This headline comes from *Nonpartisan Leader*, July 7, 1918.

Lindbergh's followers expected trouble. Auto parades were a staple of the Nonpartisans' 1918 campaign and had generated enthusiasm among League supporters, along with challenges from opponents. Disputes had occurred with an assortment of rivals, including Loyalty Clubs, business groups, county and village officials and traditional Republicans. Lindbergh banners and American flags typically bedecked the parade vehicles, political accessories that infuriated anti-League forces. Adversaries considered use of the nation's flag by persons they believed to be disloyal offensive.

Organizers planned for the convoy to form in Wanamingo and proceed to Kenyon, Dennison, Stanton, Randolph, Cannon Falls, Vasa and on to Red Wing. Some in the motorcade expected to continue traveling south through Hay Creek, Goodhue and Zumbrota. It was expected that other NPL backers would join in and some drop out along the way. The projected route would touch on at least 12 Goodhue County townships and nearly all of its villages and towns. Visits to Dennison, bordering Rice County, and Randolph in Dakota County promised helpful publicity in those counties as well.[236]

NPLers pulled out of Wanamingo at 10:20 a.m., driving west to Kenyon. Perhaps because of Kenyon's reputation as a pro-war community and the scene of clashes with the NPL, only scattered supporters of the League were to be found in surrounding rural districts. As the auto convoy approached the village a sentry rang the fire bell, businesses closed and residents deserted the streets. *Kenyon News* reported one person "paid his respects to the bunch by plastering about twenty cars with ripe hen fruit."[237]

With more than 100 autos now in the parade, the procession rolled on, reaching Dennison at 12:45 p.m. Town residents stayed inside, but left two dummies labeled "Lindbergh" and "Townley" propped up on a street. The elongated caravan snaked its way north.

An effigy dangling from a telephone pole outside the State Bank of Stanton now

A "Lindbergh for Governor" caravan travels to its next stop during the 1918 Minnesota gubernatorial primary race.

NO-PARTY LEAGUE BARRED FROM CITY

OFFICIALS HERE STOP NONPARTISAN LEAGUE PARADE

Demonstration Would Tend Only to Incite Riot Safety Commission Holds.

HOME GUARDS TO AID AUTHORITIES

Order Forbidding Flaunting of Non-Partiasn League Banners Is Issued.

The Nonpartisan league paraders, flying the Lindberg banners, reached the city limits at 4:30 o'clock this afternoon. Chief Jackson halted them and informed them of the order not to permit them to pass if the banners were displayed. They did not remove the banners and were discussing the matter with the chief at the time of going to press.

Police officers were stationed on the outskirts of the city to head off the Nonpartisan league members in case they attempted to parade the streets, flying their banners and the Home Guards were called out and in readiness at the Armory to preserve order, following the order forbidding a Nonpartisan league demonstration in this city this afternoon by the authorities.

Flying Nonpartisan league banners, one hundred and fifty automobiles, occupied by League leaders, members

ORDER FORBIDDING NONPARTISAN LEAGUE PARADE IN RED WING

TO WHOM IT MAY CONCERN:

Whereas, leaders and organizers of the National Non-partisan League have been indicted and convicted for making disloyal and treasonable utterances and statements against the United States and its just prosecution of the war; and

Whereas, it is believed by great many citizens that such leaders and organizers are disloyal and are by their teachings and activities giving aid and comfort to the public enemies of the United States; and

Whereas, it has been rumored and the undersigned have been informed that leaders and organizers of said League have planned and are about to cause a parade in the city of Red Wing, Minnesota, for the purpose of displaying certain banners or symbols of said League and otherwise promoting the desires and teachings of said League; and

Whereas, a great many loyal citizens, whose sons and relatives are fighting, bleeding and dying for the life of their Country and Democracy, and who by their acts and words are doing their utmost in supporting our Government in this hour of peril, consider and brand the banners and symbols of said League as badges of disloyalty and treason; and

Whereas, it is the firm belief and opinion of the undersigned that such parade and the flaunting of the banners and symbols of said League would incite and cause breaches of the peace and riots;

NOW THEREFORE, In order to prevent riots or other breaches of the peace and disturbances and solely in the interests of the public welfare, it is hereby ordered that the parading with, or the displaying of any banner or symbol of said League in the city of Red Wing, Minnesota, or the doing of any other act by any person or persons which may tend to a breach of the peace, is prohibited; and that all persons violating this order will be dealth with according to law and the Ordinances of said city. This order will be in full force and effect until further notice.

Given under our hands and dated at Red Wing, Minn., June 11, 1918.

W. H. PUTNAM,
County Director of the Minnesota Public Safety Commission.
THOMAS MOHN,
County Attorney of Goodhue County, Minnesota.

State of Minnesota, County of Goodhue—ss.

To the Sheriff of said County; the Constables and other Peace Officers of said County, and the Police Officers of the city of Red Wing in said County:

You, and each of you, are hereby directed to enforce the foregoing order and to preserve the peace and prevent riots.

Made and dated at Red Wing, Minnesota, June 11th, 1918.

W. H. PUTNAM,
County Director of the Minnesota Public Safety Commission.
THOMAS MOHN,
County Attorney of Goodhue County, Minnesota.

LOYAL MEN COMPEL COUNCIL TO DENY PARK TO LEAGUE

Nonpartisan League Leaders Will Not Be Permit- to Speak in City.

COUNCIL RESCINDS ORIGINAL PERMIT

James H. Doyle Protests Against Meeting—F. A. Scherf Makes Plea.

The Nonpartisan league was denied the right to use Central park for a political meeting next Saturday evening by the council last night following vigorous protest by a representative gathering of Red Wing citizens, who swarmed the council chambers after aldermen by unanimous vote, had consented to it. Jas. H. Doyle and C. S. Sultzer, chief spokesmen for the citizens declared that they were justified in demanding that the meeting be not held by reason of the fact that the Non-

(Continued from page 5).

Putnam-Mohn edict banning the Nonpartisan League auto parade from entering Red Wing

confronted the Nonpartisan Leaguers. The lifelike figure had detailed facial features, was well dressed with hat and shoes, and carried the label "Lindbergh NPL." The Lindbergh motorcade drove on to Randolph then turned east, stopping for lunch around one o'clock. Cannon Falls was the next stop.[238]

Goodhue County Sheriff John A. Anderson conferred with Cannon Falls mayor Tony Mensing as the NPL autos arrived. The two officials halted the motorcade and informed the group that William Putnam, county chairman of the Commission of Public Safety, had banned Nonpartisan League vehicles from Red Wing. Putnam's directive explicitly instructed "Constables and other Peace Officers of said [Goodhue]

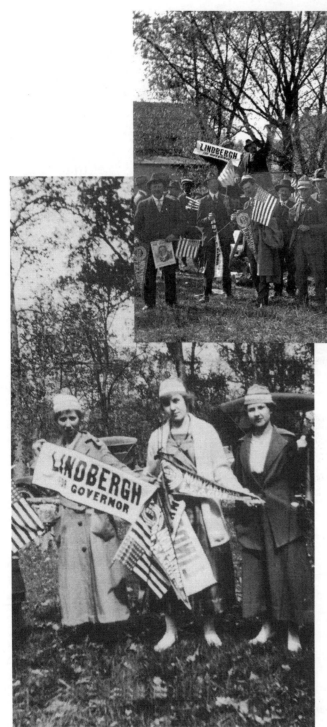

Lindbergh supporters pose with campaign materials during a Clarkfield Nonpartisan League picnic.

A group of supporters display Lindbergh campaign and NPL banners along with American flags. The Goodhue County MCPS chair declared "flaunting" of League regalia in Red Wing "would incite and cause breaches of the peace and riots."

County" to make certain the NPL campaign cavalcade did not reach the county seat. Sheriff Anderson apparently was uncertain if the directive meant the parade must now stop at Cannon Falls. He told the motorcade to avoid driving through the main streets of the city and also reminded the Lindbergh backers to refrain from entering Red Wing. The auto procession motored past a crowd of hecklers gathered at one Cannon Falls street corner and continued to Cannon Falls Township Hall, outside the city limits, to discuss their options. They agreed to press on to Red Wing.

Such was the Commission of Public Safety's power, as embodied in William Putnam, that leaders of the NPL farmer's parade did not question his right to wield such prior restraint. They did, nevertheless, choose to ignore it.

☆   ☆   ☆

Red Wing had been placed under martial law. With the assent of County Attorney Tom Mohn, Putnam ordered city police into action and mobilized the city's Company A of the Minnesota Home Guard. Invoking the name of the MCPS, Putnam assumed control of the city, preparing for what he believed to be a coming crisis. The Red Wing banker gave no indication that he had consulted elected public officials—the mayor or city council—before suspending civilian authority.[239]

Putnam issued his order banning the NPL political parade in the belief that "a great many citizens" would be so incensed by the disloyalty of NPL leaders that they might take the law into their own hands. Putnam pointed to rumors that Nonpartisan League members would display "certain banners or symbols of said League...." The "flaunting" of League regalia, Putnam wrote, "would incite and cause breaches of the peace and riots."[240]

"This is just about it," said a frustrated William Putnam earlier that day. He discussed the situation in Red Wing with a *Daily Republican* reporter after forbidding entry to the NPL motorcade. "Every peace officer in the city has been instructed to enforce the order and prevent the Nonpartisan League parade from taking place," he said. County Attorney Thomas Mohn explained the activation of Company A: "In cases where there is danger of riot and mob violence, the Home Guards can be called out. The peace of the community must be preserved."[241]

League members, families and supporters, meanwhile, had climbed back into their automobiles—70 now remained—and headed to the county seat by way of Vasa. Awaiting them at Red Wing's western border, at the time Bench Street/County Road 1 and Main, was Chief of Police Andrew G. Jackson and a detail of officers. In the downtown district, rifle-carrying Red Wing men of Company A patrolled the streets.

Shortly after 5:00 p.m., Chief Jackson stopped the Nonpartisan League autos at the city limits and, according to the anti-parade *Daily Republican*, told the motorcade drivers they could not pass as long as Lindbergh banners remained on their cars. A differing *Daily Eagle* pro-parade account claimed (after the *Republican* had gone to press) that Jackson asked the group to "stay outside the city limits." Parade leaders refused, "and immediately the line of automobiles began moving."[242]

Anton V. Anderson, a Goodhue County state legislator and one of the motorcade leaders—NPL's dauntless George Breidal rode with him—offered his version of the confrontation at the city limits. His group offered no concessions. Anderson said, "There were no banners or pennants removed before entering Red Wing. We told the Sheriff and Chief of Police that our banners and pennants would stay on even if we should never see Red Wing again."[243]

Driving east along Main Street, the autos moved steadily past the St. James Hotel, then two more blocks to Potter Street. They turned right [south] for one block before moving west on Third Street for three blocks. The motorcade made a

Red Wing Police Chief in 1918, Andrew Jackson, poses, billy club in hand, for a studio photo with an unidentified person.

left at Sheldon Auditorium onto East Avenue (then a two-way street) and drove south to link up with Zumbrota Road (State Highway 58). "There were no demonstrations of any kind," the *Eagle* observed, "no cheering or tooting of horns. Most cars bore Lindbergh and Nonpartisan banners." The emergency in Red Wing had ended.[244]

The following morning, County Attorney Mohn announced NPL autos had passed quietly and peaceably through Red Wing, and participants "didn't wave or flaunt the banners." Said Mohn, "There was no occasion to interfere with such a parade." It would seem, however, that the decision of Putnam and Mohn to place the city under martial law to avoid "riots" was the proper occasion to halt and arrest NPL lawbreakers.

Red Wing residents did not resort to mob violence as feared by Putnam, appearing to regard the NPL auto caravan as a curiosity. "Quite a crowd gathered to see the parade go through," wrote a *Daily Republican* observer. The same source claimed Lindbergh banners were snatched from autos, causing arguments. *Daily Eagle* reporters mentioned no such quarrels. Although his preemptive actions to halt the parade were heavy-handed, it would seem Putnam acted with good judgment in ignoring the fact that League supporters had pointedly disobeyed his order.[245]

Exiting the city, the NPL parade, still led by Anton Anderson, drove along Zumbrota Road toward Goodhue. Protestors intercepted and halted the motorcade outside

Two Goodhue County law enforcement officers—Red Wing Chief of Police Andrew G. Jackson, behind the wheel of a Model T "tourer," and County Sheriff John A. Anderson, standing to the rear—held critical positions during the NPL auto procession of June 11.

the village. Anderson reported in a letter to the *Daily Republican*, "The trouble at Goodhue started BEFORE any stop was made on the business streets and BEFORE any blockade of streets occurred (not after) and immediately after the paint was thrown on all of the members of my family who occupied my car." With yellow paint covering his windshield and an American flag, Anderson was compelled to stop his auto—a move that halted the line of cars behind him.[246]

Continuing, Anderson told of removing the "desecrated" flag and placing it in his auto. After nearly a two-hour stay in Goodhue, he prepared to drive to his nearby farm. Anderson swept away tacks placed in front of his car before leaving town. A number of the motorcade's auto owners later reported punctured tires.

S. S. Lewis of the *Cannon Falls Beacon* lampooned the yellow paint ambush of Anton Anderson with allusions to Bolsheviks (communists) who were then threatening Russia. NPL critics regularly used "Bolsheviki" in referring to League members. Lewis reported that League autos passed "quietly to Goodhue where the car in which the Duke of Goodhue [Anderson] rode had a bucket of yellow paint spilled on it by some careless downtrodden laboring man. A duma [a Russian governmental assembly] was held in Burnside on Wednesday and it is understood a ukase [Russian proclamation] was issued about the case."[247]

Lewis offered an editorial estimation of the NPL caravan: "Avowed pro-Germans were in evidence in the parade…they were there because they are for Germany and against America. The purpose of the parade was to create dissention and ill-feeling in the ranks of the people." Lewis failed to mention that the expedition's political nature had been clear; the Nonpartisans festooned their autos with Lindbergh banners and American flags for their cross-county drive. Protestors who harried the caravan along the way objected to the NPL's political beliefs and its candidate for governor. Adversaries of the Nonpartisan League had dealt yet another destructive blow to Lindbergh's Minnesota election campaign.[248]

Three Minnesota counties, including Goodhue, had taken the lead in prosecutions of the NPL and its leaders. Minnesota Commission of Public Safety historian Carl Chrislock wrote, "A coalition of groups on the local and county level *was the most valuable component* [emphasis added] within the safety commission's anti-subversion network. The Goodhue, Jackson and Martin county attorneys launched prosecutions against [Arthur] Townley and his associate Joseph Gilbert at the height of the 1918 gubernatorial campaign—prosecutions ultimately culminating in jail sentences." Governor Burnquist's advocates draped the shroud of traitor over Charles Lindbergh and his followers, and the Leaguers were unable to shrug it off.[249]

The Nonpartisan League's June 11 Goodhue County campaign cavalcade was designed to be a vote-getter for Lindbergh, not, as S. S. Lewis indicated, a rally for Germany. That fact, however, seemed lost amid a hail of rotten eggs, feigned lynchings, martial law and an American flag dishonored by the stain of yellow paint.

☆　☆　☆

If Governor Burnquist could prevail over the NPL's Lindbergh in the upcoming Republican primary, his return to office would be assured. A frail Democratic Party could provide only token resistance in the November general election. Courtroom trials of Nonpartisan League leaders and ensuing convictions for sedition had badly damaged, but not destroyed, the NPL image. Even without that disadvantage, Lindbergh's uneven, often clumsy campaign would have made incumbent Burnquist the odds-on favorite. A biographer of Lindbergh's famous son wrote of the elder's last campaign, "Worse than oblivion, he began sliding into political ignominy, becoming a crank."[250]

The primary campaign moved forward. Former Red Wing City Attorney Charles Hall scheduled a talk at Red Wing's Metro Theater on June 12 to support the war effort and Governor Burnquist's work in Minnesota. David Neill, chairman of Goodhue County's America First chapter, planned a June 13 Red Wing factory tour featuring speakers, including himself. Stops included Red Wing Shoe Co., Foot Tannery, Red Wing Furniture Co., and city stoneware and sewer pipe plants. They planned 15-minute "Loyalty Talks." A candidate for the Legislature in the 1918 elections, Neill

William Putnam (far left), chairman of the Goodhue County Commission of Public Safety, and Jens Grondahl (in profile), editor of *Red Wing Daily Republican*, proved strong backers of incumbent Minnesota Governor Joseph Burnquist (center). Putnam and Grondahl were pivotal players in Goodhue County's 100% American crusade. The men are pictured during the 1918 gubernatorial campaign.

also would have the opportunity to electioneer on his own behalf.[251]

Two days after the NPL's cross-county auto expedition, Jens Grondahl took a step back from his long-standing 100% American editorial policy. The Red Wing newspaper editor had encouraged, and even demanded, that Goodhue County citizens confront what he considered the area's abundant pro-Germans and Nonpartisan Leaguers. Now, perhaps embarrassed by the extralegal treatment of those in the League car caravan, the editor advised restraint in the June 13 *Daily Republican*, "…the people of Goodhue County no matter how patriotic [should] abstain from acts that are in any way unlawful." He worried such deeds would damage the "good name of Goodhue County."[252]

Dwight Pierce, writing in the June 13 *Goodhue Enterprise*, questioned NPL candidate Lindbergh's loyalty. He also encouraged readers to oppose Arthur Townley and primary election candidates supported by the Nonpartisan League, "most of whom are under indictment charged with making disloyal statements." The *Enterprise* editor concluded, "Are we ready to deliver the great state of Minnesota over to radical socialists?" *Kenyon News*, meanwhile, reported farmers living somewhere between Dennison and Wanamingo had hanged yet another crude effigy bearing the name "Lindbergh."[253]

Zumbrota News carried a list of candidates running in the upcoming primary election, but only included names of those on the "Loyalty Ticket" (Republicans). Editor Davis recommended a vote for those on a printed list it supplied to "keep good old Minnesota in the true blue loyalty column."[254]

Townspeople took to the streets of Red Wing on Saturday, June 15, for a final pre-election political rally and showdown between Burnquist and Lindbergh forces. Overnight, persons unknown had hoisted an effigy of Lindbergh in the middle of Main Street near Dakota Street. Signs attached to the figure read "Herr Von Lindbergh" and "The American German General." A spiked German helmet had been placed on the head. A pleased Jens Grondahl informed readers with the afternoon edition of the *Daily Republican* that those involved "performed a mighty good job." He wrote approvingly that scores of people flocked to the intersection and "left satisfied." Mayor Peter A. Nelson ordered the effigy removed.[255]

Also during the night, anti-NPL vandals splashed yellow paint on Fred Scherf's house at Bush and Sixth streets. The prominent German American had remained the highly visible local face of the Nonpartisan League and was running for the state Legislature. Rev. J. R. Bauman, pastor at St. John's German Lutheran Church, was among those to support Scherf. He said the guilty parties had "put on their own color."[256]

"Pre-election interest reached its climax in the city Saturday and candidates and party politics were subjects of heated discussions on every corner," observed *Red Wing Daily Eagle*. "Late in the evening several near fights were in evidence." On Bush Street, midway between Main and Third, a Lindbergh banner was torn from an auto and burned in the street. Police broke up the ensuing argument. The America First League organized talks from a speaker's stand erected in front of Goodhue County National Bank. Anton Rockne, James Doyle, Charles P. Hall and Thomas Mohn were among those addressing the audience.[257]

The largest Nonpartisan League gathering that night unfolded at the C. C. Sargent farm in Burnside Township adjoining Red Wing to the west. County and city folk attended. Crowd estimates ranged widely from 400 to 1,000. When the NPL speaker

During the evening hours of June 15–16, 1918, vandals splashed yellow paint on the Red Wing house of Frederick Scherf, a well-known leader in city and county German American communities.

did not appear, Charles P. Hall, a Four Minute Man who earlier gave an address in the city, filled the void with a rousing patriotic speech. Fred Scherf interrupted the speaker when his talk drifted toward politics. John McLane, chairman of the city's Four Minute Man group, asserted Hall was "speaking by government authority." Hall finished the address.[258]

For Charles Lindbergh Sr., the final weeks leading to the June 17 primary were a trial. A family friend wrote, "Violence followed Lindbergh everywhere. His opponents spied upon him continually; he was banned in Duluth and hanged in effigy in Red Wing. Several times unruly mobs dragged him from the speaker's platform. On one occasion Lindbergh came out of a meeting to find his driver badly beaten. He convinced the assembled mob to allow them to leave, only to be answered by a shower of bullets as his automobile drove away."[259]

Statewide, Governor Burnquist captured 57% of the Republican primary vote in recording a 199,325 to 150,626 victory over Lindbergh, securing the party nomination for the fall election. Lindbergh had demonstrated surprising strength, considering the two-front war—courtroom and campaign—he fought. Some 150,000 Minnesota voters, including Democrats who crossed party lines, spurned anti-League smears and sedition charges against Lindbergh. *St. Paul Daily News* pointed out that Burnquist backers could hardly boast of a victory for loyalty and patriotism when 40 percent of Minnesotans cast ballots against him.[260]

A *Nonpartisan Leader* editorial characterized the election this way: "If the charges [pro-German] against the League were true…Minnesota would be in a bad way. Out of every 34 votes cast in the entire state, 15 or 16, or practically half, would be sympathizers of the German Kaiser and interested only in knifing this nation in the back…and over 30 counties of the state would be populated by large majorities of German agents." The *Leader* blamed "the disreputable press of Minnesota, by its cry of disloyalty [for bringing] this stigma on the fair name of the state…."[261]

Red Wing Daily Eagle editor N. P. Olson had displayed sympathy for the Nonpartisan League in the past, and did so again following the June primary. He called Burnquist's recent success an "empty victory" for Republicans. Olson explained that

Red Wing Daily Republican

OFFICIAL RETURNS FOR GOODHUE COUNTY
Primary Election, June 17, 1918
As Returned by the Official Canvassing Board

CANDIDATES	1st Wd, 1st Pct	1st Wd, 2d Pct	2d Wd, 1st Pct	2d Wd, 2d Pct	3d Wd, 1st Pct	3d Wd, 2d Pct	4th Wd, 1st Pct	4th Wd, 2d Pct	Belvidere	Belle Creek	Burnside	Can. Falls Twp.	Can. Falls City	Central Point	Cherry Grove	Dennison	Featherstone	Florence	Goodhue Twp.	Goodhue Vill.	Hay Creek	Holden	Kenyon Twp.	Kenyon Vill.	Leon	Minneola	Pine Island Twp.	Pine Island Vill.	Roscoe	Stanton	Vasa	Wacouta	Wanamingo Vill.	Warsaw	Welch	Zumbrota Twp.	Zumbrota Vill.	Wanamingo Twp.	Total Vote	Plurality or Majority
REPUBLICAN																																								
Senator in Congress—																																								
Knute Nelson	128	110	187	192	118	146	150	222	88	100	65	97	245	13	124	57	62	88	116	77	66	124	108	233	130	134	73	119	132	85	163	9	81	151	95	76	241	150	4548	3277
Jas. A. Peterson	27	14	33	45	36	33	40	32	36	48	30	64	16	4	30	..	66	43	36	14	59	37	30	15	56	38	43	18	45	10	70	9	14	9	34	79	22	41	1271	
Governor—																																								
J. A. A. Burnquist	125	111	187	198	126	147	163	209	64	85	43	82	255	17	126	57	45	80	89	80	30	102	99	232	97	101	44	118	67	90	95	5	85	152	92	42	237	117	4084	1907
Chas. A. Lindbergh	32	21	42	48	34	40	32	49	97	79	55	97	15	6	36	..	111	71	96	14	134	68	48	23	106	83	95	30	128	10	141	19	8	12	51	123	33	85	2177	
Fred E. Wheaton	7	..	5	..	..	1	1	1	17	..	..	..	2	..	..	1	..	..	3	..	..	2	1	1	..	..	3	..	..	1	..	..	1	..	2	..	3	..	52	4
W. L. Comstock	4	..	3	..	..	1	3	8	1	..	4	..	..	..	..	..	..	1	..	5	..	..	2	2	3	..	1	..	..	1	..	4	..	2	..	4	..	48	
Lieutenant Governor—																																								
Ralph E. Crane	26	15	36	36	26	40	25	34	83	53	56	79	23	4	46	1	98	65	97	11	108	64	40	23	88	71	76	28	99	8	93	13	12	27	38	101	31	72	1851	
Thomas Frankson	92	80	133	149	86	100	124	146	40	65	30	54	179	10	90	43	34	54	70	66	29	74	81	132	73	13	39	75	55	75	98	9	56	101	66	44	199	87	3011	1160
A. D. Stephens	23	20	33	41	33	33	28	53	23	21	12	27	37	4	19	9	13	22	11	7	13	22	19	89	30	33	19	27	22	9	27	3	21	31	24	24	32	25	939	
Secretary of State—																																								
Carl G. Malmberg	32	22	44	63	51	59	47	78	35	58	39	56	52	4	35	6	56	41	53	8	43	65	43	41	79	55	43	21	66	11	122	8	29	30	48	61	35	63	1702	
Julius A. Schmahl	117	96	176	169	95	113	131	170	92	80	47	94	195	15	111	49	64	91	98	84	79	83	91	205	98	104	72	113	85	81	96	6	66	120	78	87	226	121	3901	2199
State Auditor—																																								
J. A. O. Preus	128	108	181	197	119	149	151	204	67	77	45	80	225	14	107	48	48	74	83	79	43	92	89	216	90	108	55	112	60	81	105	10	72	131	99	52	223	118	3940	2015
S. O. Tjosvold	19	10	31	40	29	30	29	38	73	68	52	78	27	4	44	5	96	84	89	12	101	67	49	28	97	70	78	19	118	12	115	14	23	24	48	113	37	74	1925	
State Treasurer—																																								
Albert H. Fasel	32	19	45	65	42	55	52	73	77	55	55	89	66	5	49	6	95	63	92	14	95	77	41	45	94	83	76	30	112	15	118	11	21	37	49	111	36	79	2169	
Henry Rines	103	93	159	158	92	109	117	161	61	81	38	65	178	13	96	47	45	77	72	75	46	78	87	192	87	90	51	91	57	80	100	10	72	108	73	50	225	109	3451	1282
Attorney General—																																								
Clifford L. Hilton	101	94	129	153	86	89	125	153	44	53	36	63	194	5	91	48	41	65	62	78	32	80	82	224	67	92	48	76	49	82	52	9	58	104	56	40	203	93	3186	705
Thomas V. Sullivan	44	22	78	70	52	74	49	83	93	86	59	91	42	10	61	6	100	77	100	13	112	76	54	22	111	82	83	46	119	12	130	13	32	46	70	121	52	90	2481	
Clerk of Supreme Court—																																								
Irving A. Caswell	70	59	106	87	46	66	88	101	40	39	32	35	137	7	48	39	80	48	45	47	24	43	47	121	44	67	30	69	36	69	40	5	35	84	39	41	172	52	2188	378
George G. Magnuson	46	32	57	82	57	61	46	90	15	49	25	49	64	4	51	7	17	25	33	29	22	52	42	86	57	34	23	27	26	11	38	4	46	42	59	15	49	63	1590	
Herman Mueller	24	14	39	49	33	36	35	81	56	38	67	32	6	46	7	92	66	84	12	101	52	44	31	80	66	76	29	98	10	86	15	10	24	28	109	35	65		1810	
R. R. & W. Commissioner—																																								
Fred W. Putnam	125	116	183	197	120	133	158	215	68	77	46	67	220	14	117	53	87	80	100	17	100	77	42	84	82	204	85	102	50	105	59	82	103	7	82	122	96	65	224	1895
Fred E. Tillquist	31	15	46	45	38	46	31	39	78	71	51	96	31	3	33	2	98	63	89	14	111	69	51	34	107	73	82	25	107	14	124	18	11	22	47	107	34	69	2025	
Rep. in Congress, 3rd Dist.—																																								
Charles R. Davis	65	53	100	121	91	94	118	121	71	87	65	107	98	13	83	6	70	78	104	28	81	104	75	105	118	110	71	73	102	28	155	12	50	42	97	102	136	132	3162	893
Charles R. Pye	79	52	106	108	55	79	64	124	45	37	26	47	138	4	66	49	42	43	34	49	45	47	60	139	49	44	34	56	41	58	61	6	41	113	29	42	104	49	2269	
County Treasurer—																																								
N. C. Lien	57	54	92	104	64	55	68	113	38	59	16	54	115	8	72	49	30	12	47	58	11	101	80	162	82	76	42	43	64	49	76	1	51	123	50	42	138	111	2388	1161
J. H. Seebach	78	49	100	111	57	76	79	97	110	76	68	78	52	6	43	6	120	102	107	24	141	39	20	39	65	61	68	74	78	16	125	16	22	11	70	121	69	66	2551	163
C. H. Tiedeman	33	34	52	33	31	56	48	52	12	31	16	36	81	3	41	1	5	33	30	16	10	23	36	49	37	41	18	25	38	21	27	7	25	24	25	26	104	42	1227	
Register of Deeds—																																								
Gust B. Freeman	110	79	147	176	105	127	129	164	90	97	68	132	212	12	137	49	85	112	123	79	106	114	110	234	144	141	69	100	143	66	193	17	89	138	119	113	229	161	4509	3438
W. C. Hawkins	9	16	15	21	26	10	19	18	7	13	22	16	10	5	6	1	16	7	9	6	18	3	11	9	6	18	3	6	10	11	10	6	7	7	13	12	13	10	443	
J. F. Wagner	48	39	77	50	27	50	50	73	50	58	10	18	19	3	11	3	37	22	36	11	42	24	14	14	18	23	46	22	17	10	16	4	5	17	14	37	24	24	1071	628
Sheriff—																																								
John A. Anderson	57	39	78	112	61	70	76	127	33	71	28	111	226	4	111	46	27	44	53	42	22	115	114	190	114	88	45	92	67	57	69	5	60	137	75	50	179	128	3053	1344
J. H. Bohmbach	23	10	32	32	18	23	25	37	78	33	38	19	4	3	10	2	92	48	80	8	112	12	10	13	20	15	25	4	28	3	58	12	4	2	13	36	26	20	1089	
E. Ellefsen	2	2	1	3	..	7	..	2	3	20	2	29	1	1	13	..	2	3	..	5	3	13	9	11	33	17	34	13	70	..	6	..	6	6	7	9	4	30	367	
Andrew G. Jackson	91	85	132	100	83	92	101	102	39	50	33	14	27	16	23	8	36	49	46	42	24	21	7	39	24	37	26	27	22	26	72	8	29	17	54	23	62	22	1709	614
Clerk of Court—																																								
Andrew Lindgren	23	25	33	49	21	31	38	60	4	9	9	17	27	2	3	3	10	6	7	1	3	10	4	7	3	..	3	12	16	7	3	..	12	16	7	5	5	152	
S. S. Lundquist	31	28	34	44	21	17	44	51	13	23	11	57	72	1	12	13	13	11	18	9	18	28	28	91	27	17	25	17	17	10	72	4	4	31	38	23	50	13	1036	
Harry N. Nordholm	64	52	92	74	91	82	64	79	40	12	7	7	31	4	4	..	27	28	30	10	51	5	5	13	7	16	10	8	15	23	36	6	..	13	26	32	30	1076	40

the governor's win over Lindbergh and the League would deprive the winners of "the sedition club which they have been swinging viciously in their effort to drive voters into the Burnquist fold." The question now was, to whom would the NPL voters and Democrats turn?[262]

Burnquist crushed Lindbergh in Goodhue County's cities and villages during the June 17 primary, garnering more than five times as many votes (2,273–421) as his opponent. The incumbent gathered 94 percent of the Cannon Falls vote (255–15), 91 percent in both Kenyon (232–23) and Wanamingo (85–8), 88 percent in Zumbrota (237–33), 85 percent in Goodhue (80–14), 80 percent in Pine Island (118–30) and nearly 80 percent in Red Wing (1,266–298). All 57 Dennison primary votes went to Burnquist.[263]

Ole Sandstad, the 100-Percenter *Kenyon News* editor, expressed frustration with the "23 yellow votes" [for Lindbergh] cast in the village. He was willing to wager none of those backing the League candidate would step up and admit to their deed. Sandstad added a threat to those who voted for the Leaguer, "…it may be interesting to these people to know the rest of the people have them pretty well spotted."[264]

Rural voters in the townships of Zumbrota, Pine Island, Cannon Falls and Goodhue opted for Lindbergh. Seventy-five percent of Zumbrota Township's ballots went to Lindbergh (129–42), along with 68 percent of those in Pine Island (95–44). Heavily German American Hay Creek Township chose the Nonpartisan League candidate 134–30, as did other townships with significant German populations, Belvidere, Featherstone, Burnside and Roscoe. Voters in predominantly Swedish American Vasa backed Lindbergh 141–91. Ethnic Germans, farmers and NPL voters had honored the "I'll Stick" promise bedecking League campaign buttons.[265]

The general election campaigns that followed provided a peaceful anti-climax to the raucous primary battle and its months of tumult. With scars of the divisive struggle far from healed, the Goodhue County electorate appeared eager to vote and put the past behind them.

On June 25, eight days after the 1918 primary, sedition trials resumed in district court in Red Wing. John C. Seebach, the La Grange Mills treasurer, was the first defendant. All members of Seebach's panel came from other counties since those in the local jury pool could not vow they were free of prejudice. A series of witnesses in the Seebach case, already known to the defense from appearances at the indictment hearing, testified that Seebach uttered disloyal statements regarding American participation in the war and discouraged employees and others from joining the military.

Seebach took the stand to deny all allegations made against him. The defendant contended his comments were misconstrued and misrepresented; one former employee supposedly testified to "get even" with him. The defendant denied saying he would not let his sons join the military, explaining sons Carl and Walter had been deferred from the draft because they operated a 240-acre farm that couldn't be run without them.[266]

During his charge to the jury, Judge Wilbur F. Booth echoed the Minnesota Sedition Act with its prohibitions on any activities that hampered the war effort. Booth declared that although there was no doubt about the constitutional right of an American's freedom of speech, "at a time like this it is proper and right that no one should be permitted to imperil the country's safety by abuse of this right."[267]

Jurors found Seebach guilty on three counts of violating the Sedition Act but recommended leniency in sentencing. Judge Booth chose not to go easy, ordering the Red Wing businessman to serve 18 months in federal prison and pay a $3,000 fine. Booth later denied a defense motion for a new trial, and Seebach's attorneys began preparing an appeal. Jens Grondahl's *Daily Republican* reprinted a *Minneapolis Daily News*

The Farmers' National Magazine—Read by Nearly a Million People

Efforts by *Nonpartisan Leader* and other pro-NPL publications to portray League farmers as patriotic citizens during the 1918 election put some Minnesota Leaguers in office, but not the governor's chair. Note the "We'll Stick" button on this NPLer's suspenders.

taunt directed at Seebach: "Seebach is a German name. You or your father brought it to America for just one reason—to find BETTER CONDITIONS. You have cashed in on American opportunity, John Seebach; you are known as a wealthy miller of Red Wing."[268]

On June 28, Louis Martin was tried in District Court for his part in the now well-known Nonpartisan League event held in Kenyon ten months earlier. Goodhue County juries had already convicted Joseph Gilbert and N. S. Randall, main speakers at the Kenyon gathering, for making treasonous statements. Martin had introduced Gilbert and Randall to the Kenyon League rally audience and later endorsed the content of their speeches. Considering the prior decisions against Gilbert and Randall, Martin appeared to have little chance in the Red Wing courtroom.[269]

Andrew Finstuen and Gilbert Flom were first to testify for the prosecution, describing comments made by Randall and Gilbert at Kenyon. Dr. Joseph Gates and defendant Louis Martin both took the witness stand to discuss their September 1917 dustup in the Bakko barbershop. They revisited the content of the NPL speeches. Martin's support of the League orators angered Gates, who grabbed and then shoved him out of the shop. Jurors found Martin guilty of "discouraging enlistment," and the defense team responded with a request for a new trial. That application was denied. Preparations began for a further appeal.[270]

As the summer of 1918 wore on, a welcome increase in social civility appeared to take hold around the state, Goodhue County included. Lindbergh's loss in the primary diminished the Republican grip on the loyalty issue. Ethnic and political strife appeared to be on the wane. German Americans, although still suspect in many quarters, experienced a lessening in overt nationalism. Nonpartisan Leaguers remained under suspicion, but the credibility lost during the elections and sedition trials had diminished the NPL as a political threat. A notable exception on the tolerance front was the state Commission of Public Safety. That organization persisted in issuing public warnings about radical socialists, German spies and sympathizers still supposedly on the loose.

Mobs in two Minnesota cities provided jarring exceptions to the hope for political decorum. In the southwest, the Luverne Loyalty Club tarred and feathered an elderly NPL farmer, then deported him across the state line. In Duluth, the Knights of Liberty assaulted a Finnish immigrant, and their victim was later found hanging from a tree. Authorities could not determine if the suspicious death was murder or suicide.[271]

Two volunteers with Red Wing's Company L, Minnesota National Guard were among the first Goodhue County soldiers to die in combat. A bomb from a German airplane killed Elof A. Ericson, left, on October 9, 1918, and Leo C. Peterson was killed in action six days later.

The Duluth incident and other lawlessness was shaking the belief, held even among their supporters, that Governor Burnquist and the Commission of Public Safety could control violent mobs. Burnquist issued a proclamation declaring "persons suspected of disloyalty [will] be given a fair trial and, if guilty, punished by lawfully constituted authorities, and mob violence shall not be tolerated."

Gunnar Bjornson, a former Minnesota legislator and state chairman of the Republican Party, expressed caustic criticism of the governor and MCPS in his *Minnesota*

Mascot newspaper: "The governor has made the discovery that there is a law against dragging a man out of his home and beating him up…. Mobs have been doing—free and unmolested—so many Hun stunts in this state that we had almost come to believe the mob was a new form of law and order enforcement." Coming from a respected party leader, the stinging allegations damaged Governor Burnquist.[272]

Lynn and Dora Haines, friends and biographers of Charles Lindbergh, later commented about the divisive political struggle, writing bitterly, "That 1918 campaign… will go down in the history of the state as one period in which Minnesota forgot the meaning of Democracy and turned loose the Cossack-minded to 'ride' down all those who had a different point of view. The things that happened in 1918, as one looks back upon them now, seem like a bad dream and in no way belong to the life of a sane, law-abiding people."[273]

County Soldiers in France

On June 25, 1918, the day troop trains carrying Goodhue County's monthly quota of draftees headed south for training, a U.S. Marine brigade deployed in France opened a determined assault on heavily defended Belleau Wood. It took the marines nearly two weeks of deadly fighting to capture this one square mile of heavily forested French soil. American units sustained 9,500 casualties; more than half of the men committed to the battle were killed or wounded in the assault. Among the dead was Clarence Elstad, a Red Wing man, the first county soldier killed in combat.[274]

Veterans of the county's two National Guard units were the first to leave for war duty, but they instead underwent retraining in New Mexico. Now part of 34th "Sandstorm" Division, the soldiers had impatiently and sometimes angrily endured the heat, sun and sand of Camp Cody for ten months learning to be artillerists while waiting to ship out for combat. Harvey Johnson's "Company L," a history of that unit, reported that when a June call went out for 700 volunteers to serve as replacements for units in France, "every one of the men wanted to go." About 50 men from the original unit were transferred. Three of them, Alfred B. Salmonson, Leo Peterson and Elof Erickson, were killed in action during the October Meuse–Argonne Offensive.[275]

In early August, Dr. Joseph Gates of Kenyon, a figure in the sedition trials, enlisted and became a captain in the U.S. Medical Corps. He joined two sons already in the military: Elnathan Gates, a marine serving in France, and Russell, a University of Minnesota student who left school in June and enlisted. Russell was in Officer's Training School. Kenyon's Commercial Club held a farewell reception for Dr. Gates.[276]

Elnathan Gates was wounded during the Second Battle of the Marne, part of the "Hundred Days Offensive" (September 26 through early November of 1918). Nearly 400,000 American troops and 135,00 French allies advanced against German-held trenches. The combat was typical of nearly all conflict on the Western Front—prolonged, brutal and deadly. In terms of soldiers killed and wounded, it was dreadful. More than 26,000 Americans died, and nearly 100,000 were wounded. Fourteen Goodhue County soldiers were killed, including men from Kenyon, Goodhue, Dennison, Zumbrota, Featherstone, Welch and Red Wing.[277]

Two weeks after the Nonpartisan League's campaign motorcade rolled through Goodhue County, auto drivers formed a column of more than 100 vehicles and commenced a different type of cross-county trip. Residents from Kenyon, Skyberg, Dennison and southwest districts had decided to escort area men newly drafted into the military to their Red Wing reporting point. Drivers steered vehicles through Zumbrota to Goodhue where cars from Wanamingo joined the procession, now two miles long. Autos from other townships also arrived, carrying their share of the 152-man June county quota. Upon reaching Red Wing, drivers sounded their car horns and kept them honking as they drove along flag-bedecked downtown streets.[278]

After registering at the courthouse, the men headed to the Red Wing Armory in mid-afternoon to await the rest of their comrades. Onlookers cheered in exuberant support as the parade of draftees, escorted by Home Guard Company A and the Elks Drum Corps, "wended its way through downtown streets between solid walls of humanity" en route to the Main Street YMCA and a 6 p.m. banquet. Along the way, some of the men broke ranks to hug family and friends in the crowd. Most of the spectators decided to wait for the troop sendoff and remained in the area or returned for the 9:45 train departure. The men were headed to military training at Camp Grant, Illinois. As their train rolled slowly into the station, Red Wing's Concert Band began playing "The Star-Spangled Banner." Those gathered stood in "reverent silence."[279]

The Great War still raged in Europe, and men entering the service on June 24 expected to soon be manning trenches in France. These prospective soldiers came from Goodhue County farms, villages and towns. Each township was represented in their ranks. As draftees boarded the train, the prolonged and bitter ethnic strife that had divided the people of Goodhue County since the United States' entry into the war was forgotten, for the moment at least. The crowd, a diverse collection of individuals possessing differing ethnic, cultural, political and class backgrounds, held just one quality in common: They were all Americans.

War Ends, Trials Continue

With its slate of sedition trials completed in June 1918, the First District Court in Goodhue County returned to more pedestrian legal matters. Citizens, meanwhile, showed support for county soldiers now in combat by taking part in Red Cross and Junior Red Cross activities and the continued purchase of Liberty Bonds. They conserved resources for the war effort: wheatless Mondays and Wednesdays, meatless Tuesdays, and porkless Thursdays and Saturdays came into being. Children joined the "fighting with food" effort, tending victory gardens at school and at home.[280]

In Cannon Falls, *Beacon* editor S. S. Lewis moderated the unyielding nationalistic tone of his political commentary adopted after the April 1917 declaration of war. At the onset, Lewis had been zealous in his support of attacks on citizens suspected of being less than 100% American—in particular, those defined as pro-German Nonpartisan League members. He had asserted, "Every word now spoken in defense of Germany by a [U.S.] citizen…is treason and the man who utters it is a traitor and should be dealt with as traitors are dealt with."[281]

Yet by late July 1918 Lewis was writing, "Patriots can find a better way to punish disloyalty" and "Innocent people may suffer." Lewis went further on August 2, affirming a concept that previously had been unthinkable to him: "…the vast majority of men" who had not backed U.S. entry into the Great War "were not and are not disloyal at heart." In doing so, Lewis echoed the sentiments of Red Wing's 100-Percenter, Jens Grondahl of the *Daily Republican*, who in June gently reminded readers to abstain from unlawful acts.[282]

During the summer of 1918, the Minnesota Commission of Public Safety bolstered its Minnesota Home Guard by adding a Motor Corps Division, a uniformed and armed unit made up of auto owners. It would be the first of its kind in the nation. In all, 2,583 "motor men" enlisted, with Goodhue County units at Zumbrota and Red Wing assigned to the Third Battalion. Red Wing police chief Andrew G. Jackson captained

More than 600 Motor Corps drivers gathered at Lake City's Camp Lakeview to practice for possible emergency deployment.

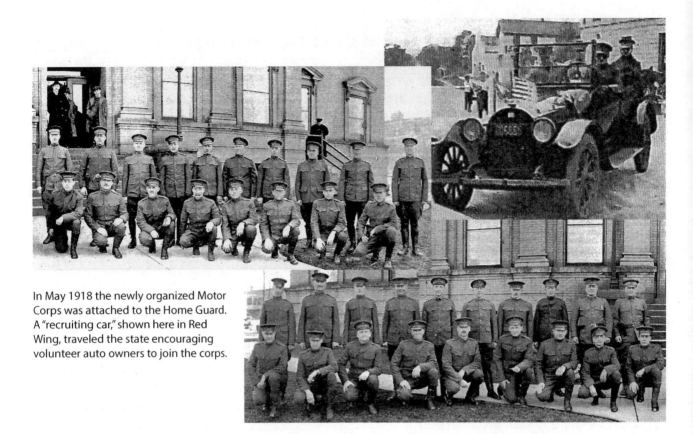

In May 1918 the newly organized Motor Corps was attached to the Home Guard. A "recruiting car," shown here in Red Wing, traveled the state encouraging volunteer auto owners to join the corps.

that city's unit, and Captain Frank C. Marvin headed the Zumbrotans. Minnesota Adjutant General Walter F. Rhinow praised the Motor Corps as "a military body of business and professional men who have offered their motor cars for duty…." Each enlistee pledged to provide a five-passenger motor car to be used in transporting troops. Summer drills brought more than 600 autos to Lake City and nearby Camp Lakeview on September 23.[283]

Explosive forest fires erupted in northeast Minnesota on October 12, necessitating a call-up of the Motor Corps, including 20 Red Wing autos and 16 from Zumbrota, manned by owners and co-drivers. The Motor Corps transported firefighters and troops between hot spots, transferred Red Cross supplies and personnel, and brought victims of the fires to safety. The Cloquet–Duluth fire and the inferno at Moose Lake killed 453 people and destroyed 30 communities. After working more than a week in the devastated areas, the county Motor Corps volunteers drove their battered vehicles home.[284]

Minnesota's deadly northern fires drew attention away from the war and France, but as the forests south and west of Duluth continued to burn, the state felt the effects of a far greater disaster: the influenza pandemic of 1918. The flu affected about one-quarter of the United States and a fifth of the world, killing 50 million people—more than the Great War itself.[285]

In Minnesota, a dangerous outbreak of influenza flared in October and eventually claimed about 12,000 lives. Kenyon, Cannon Falls, Red Wing and Zumbrota all suffered major outbreaks, with schools, churches and theaters closed. Public funerals for flu victims were banned; Cannon Falls officials ordered the wearing of face masks on the street and in public places; Red Wing police were ordered to escort any children seen on the street back home. The scourge of influenza was decreasing by mid-November, and citizens gradually returned to normal routines.

On November 5 politics again generated headlines as Governor Joseph Burnquist succeeded in winning the general election, but conspicuously without a majority of the votes cast. A varied slate of contenders drew support for the governorship, including candidates from the Democratic, Socialist, Farmer-Labor and National (Prohibition) parties.[286]

A Nonpartisan Leaguer convicted of sedition in Goodhue County took special interest in the Minnesota election. Writing from the safety of Jamestown, in NPL-friendly North Dakota, an unrepentant N. S. Randall sought information from Henry G. Teigan, the St. Paul-based NPL secretary. Randall asked about his post-election chances to overturn his conviction for treason. He claimed to have no regrets about the heavy personal cost of his NPL work in Minnesota, but also understood the legal threat still confronting him: "I will be glad when my period of exile shall have passed…. I'm chafing to be free of the restraint that is upon me…. I am glad, however, that we have gone through it, much as it has cost. Nothing could have stirred up the old moss-covered foundation of the capitalist system like this war. Goodhue County still looms in the distance and I can conceive of a situation where no quarter will be given should

The disastrous influenza pandemic of 1918 reached the Midwest in October, causing deaths in Goodhue County. Mourners gathered at St. John's Church in Goodhue for the funeral of Pvt. Adolf Jonas, a flu victim. He died while at Camp Grant in Illinois.

Spanish Influenza!
IS SPREAD BY THE SECRETIONS OF THE NOSE AND THROAT.

HOW TO PROTECT YOURSELF
Keep in good physical trim by regular habits.
Get plenty of sleep in a well-ventilated room.
Take a moderate amount of out-door exercise.
Avoid those who cough and sneeze.
Avoid common towels, common drinking cups, etc.
Avoid shaking hands.
Avoid crowds and public meetings.

HOW TO PROTECT OTHERS
Isolate all those in the household with the disease or having symptoms of it until they no longer cough or sneeze.
Sterilize their handkerchiefs, towels, and dishes by boiling.
Cough and sneeze into a handkerchief. Coughing and sneezing sprays the air with germs.
If you have influenza, don't pass it along.
MINNEAPOLIS CHAPTER OF THE AMERICAN RED CROSS.

Evans [David H. Evans, the Farmer-Labor candidate] fail of election."[287]

Nonpartisan Leaguers had stubbornly carried on the fight against Burnquist following Lindbergh's defeat by supporting organized labor's choice for governor, David Evans, a Tracy farmer and merchant. Their choice for lieutenant governor was Tom Davis, an attorney who had once been on Joe Gilbert's defense team. Evans and Davis called themselves the "Farmer-Labor" candidates. This was five years *prior* to the formation of the state Farmer Labor Party that would eventually combine with Minnesota Democrats as the DFL. The Evans candidacy generated enthusiasm and an impressive 111,966 votes.[288]

National Party's Olaf O. Stageberg, a professor at Red Wing Seminary, represented the Prohibition movement in the gubernatorial race. Stageberg also attracted scattered votes from reform minded pro-war Socialists and former Teddy Roosevelt backers. The professor collected the fewest votes (6,649) of the five candidates, with just 165 (under three percent) coming from the 5,737 ballots cast in Goodhue County.

Governor Burnquist polled 166,618 votes, while his opponents combined for 203,248. Fewer than half of Minnesotans voting chose the incumbent, the favorite of 100-Percenters. Election results presented a simple truth to state newspaper editors, the Commission of Public Safety, superpatriot groups and Burnquist backers: Minnesota voters rejected the contention that a vote against Burnquist was a vote for traitorous anti-war radicals. Many of those voting for someone other than the incumbent were not against the war; they were against Joseph Burnquist and the forces he represented.

Charles Lindbergh, meanwhile, had rallied after his primary election defeat, receiving an appointment to the War Industries Board in September 1918. Controversy ensued. Lindbergh's new assignment insulted and angered the many Minnesotans who still believed him to be pro-German. The ensuing firestorm of protest led Lindbergh to turn down the post. In a letter to his daughter, he contended the Federal Reserve Bank leadership in Minneapolis was influential in torpedoing him. John Rich, president of Goodhue County National Bank in Red Wing, had been the key figure in incorporating the Minneapolis Federal Reserve Bank in October 1914. He still held the position of Federal Reserve Agent in 1918. As a congressman, Lindbergh had been a leading critic of the 1913 Federal Reserve Act. He did not accuse Rich or any other member of the Reserve Board of blocking his appointment, but Lindbergh certainly knew of the influential Red Wing banker and industrialist. The determined attacks by his relentless critics in Goodhue County and Red Wing were still fresh in Lindbergh's mind.[289]

Fred Scherf, the Nonpartisan League candidate for Goodhue County's District 19 seat in the state Legislature, dealt his Republican opponent a humbling blow in the November elections. During the 1918 campaign Scherf had been arrested, assaulted, threatened at public meetings, publicly censured by city and village leaders and labeled pro-German, and had his house splashed with yellow paint. But Scherf never took a backward step in professing his beliefs. His opponent in District 19 was David

Neill, a prominent Red Wing executive and former president of the Federation of Minnesota Commercial Clubs—note-perfect credentials for the business community and those opposed to the Nonpartisan League.[290]

As expected, Neill polled well with Red Wing voters, but Scherf dominated in heavily pro-Nonpartisan League and German American districts such as Hay Creek, Vasa, Florence and Featherstone, with a vote advantage of 472–145. Scherf also found solid support in the county's other German American and Swedish American enclaves and narrowly prevailed, 1,459–1,310. Despite the long, bitter months of recrimination and repression since the onset of war, German Americans did not shrink from exercising their right to vote.

Results of the election battle between Frederick Scherf, left, and David Neill, Goodhue County candidates for the state Legislature in 1918, showed a polarized electorate. German American NPLer Scherf defeated the Red Wing businessman and former president of Minnesota Federation of Commercial Clubs by just 149 votes.

War news had brightened during early November as the Minnesota election neared. Allied assaults along the entire Western Front gradually rolled back German forces, compelling them to appeal for a truce. An armistice signing on November 11, 1918, closed the calamitous Great War. Raucous celebrations rocked Goodhue County for a full day. The "lid flew off in Cannon Falls," while in Zumbrota a parade of citizens heading for Pine Island encountered celebrants from that village. Both groups then veered off toward Mazeppa. A giant Barn Bluff bonfire culminated Red Wing celebrations. Some residents of Goodhue, however, still hadn't forgiven wartime grievances. Reported the *Enterprise*, "People paraded and sang into the night and splashed some yellow paint where it was needed."[291]

In less than a week's time, Minnesotans experienced an end to the most destructive

Welch Township men who served in the military during the Great War gather for a photograph.

war in world history and a jarring election defined by the state's toxic political and cultural divide. Tens of thousands of Minnesota war veterans awaited transfer to the United States and a return to civilian life, while at home the passions engendered by the 100% Americans and their loyalty crusade cooled. German Americans, Nonpartisan Leaguers and labor union members were finding that fellow citizens, newspaper editors and even political enemies moderated their views.

But what of the alleged pro-Germans and Nonpartisan Leaguers still appealing their wartime Goodhue County convictions? Election results sobered N. S. Randall, still self-exiled in North Dakota awaiting court rulings. On November 21, he wrote to Henry Teigan in St. Paul: "I have heard nothing from my case at all tho [sic] I have been expecting a summons to appear for a new trial in Red Wing." And again, December 15 to Teigan: "What do you know if anything about my case.... I am anxious to have it disposed of and if it is to go to jail." Teigan had been in touch with NPL attorney George Nordlin and replied reassuringly nine days later, "It isn't likely that you will have to spend any time in jail, in fact, it is almost a certainty that you will not."[292]

Ten days after the Great War's end, Red Wing *Daily Eagle* editor N. P. Olson lost patience with the Minnesota Commission of Public Safety. Fed up with the oppressive MCPS rule in the state, Olson penned an angry editorial, "Autocracy in Minnesota," asserting there was "no likelihood of the Safety Commission going out of business until forced out by the people...." He wrote that Minnesotans hoping to see despotic leadership suppressed in foreign countries "are not likely to tolerate autocracy [the MCPS] in their own state." Olson would have his wish, but it would take time. On January 14, 1919, the MCPS announced that as of February 5 its existing orders would no longer be in force, unless the Legislature decided otherwise.[293]

Gov. Burnquist opened his 1919 inaugural speech to the state Legislature with a supportive review of the Commission of Public Safety and its wartime activities and commended MCPS county directors for their effective service. The governor foresaw no immediate need to shut down the safety commission. Burnquist offered support for the Motor Corps and its possible continuation—"the war had not developed in Minnesota a more useful body of men...."[294]

Then, on February 4, the MCPS changed course, declaring its January statement was not meant to alter the status of the Home Guard, Motor Corps and, so it seemed, the commission itself. Commissioners pointed to legislation from Burnquist-backers designed to retain the Motor Corps as part of the National Guard. New laws would also be offered to fortify the legal underpinnings for the Home Guard's continuation.

Legislators with ties to organized labor and the Nonpartisan League, along with the union workers and farmers they represented, wanted no part of enhancing the state's existing military strength. NPLer Fred Scherf, the newly elected lawmaker for Goodhue County, hadn't forgotten how, in his view, members of the Red Wing

Red Wing's citizens celebrate the victorious end to the Great War with demonstrations continuing into the night. A huge bonfire at the foot of Barn Bluff capped the happy day.

Home Guard were employed as strikebreakers. They were deployed during the St. Paul streetcar labor dispute and later as enforcers of martial law in Red Wing. Other legislators with close links to labor unions and NPL farmer activists recalled heavy-handed interventions against their organizations. Moreover, the Minnesota National Guard showed no enthusiasm to share its mission with other military units. The Home Guard and Motor Corps would not survive.

A bill came before the Minnesota House on April 14 to dissolve the Commission of Public Safety. It passed overwhelmingly, 107–12. That law advanced to the Senate, where some legislators called on colleagues to remember the good works performed by the commission. To shut the MCPS down at this point, they argued, might well encourage disloyalty among the populace. The senators voted 48–13 to preserve the commission; an alliance of labor and NPL lawmakers made up the minority. While the Legislature debated the organization's existence, the Commission of Public Safety was losing relevance and public support. As historian Carl Chrislock observed, "Following its close brush with death at the hands of the Legislature in April 1919, [the MCPS] assembled twice: on May 13, 1919, and on December 15, 1920, when the commissioners finally closed up shop."[295]

The alliance between NPL farmers and union members, haltingly underway in 1916, was growing more powerful in spring 1919. In 1922, Susie Stageberg, a Red Wing NPL activist, urged creation of a Minnesota Farmer-Labor Party [F-L]. This political marriage came to pass. By the end of 1923, the Farmer-Labor party had claimed both of Minnesota's U.S. Senate seats and was advancing toward equality in the state's U.S. House delegation. By 1930, the F-L had elected its first governor. For her role in creating this potent political coalition, Stageberg would become known as the "Mother of the Farmer Labor Party."[296]

Representative Fred Scherf had viewed Stageberg as the perfect person to run a radical weekly newspaper that he was starting in Red Wing. Scherf wanted his weekly to counter the influential Goodhue County dailies and weeklies that opposed his views on farm and labor issues. He called his paper, *The Organized Farmer*, "the official organ of the Minnesota branch of the Farmer-Labor Party of America." Stageberg served as editor when its June 12, 1919, debut issue hit the street.[297]

With the war won and the national focus shifting to peacetime endeavors in most places, public interest in those citizens convicted of sedition in 1918 waned. Not so in Goodhue County. During the war, County Attorney Thomas Mohn, with assistance from the state attorney general, had gained nine indictments and four convictions under the Minnesota Sedition Law. Mohn still had business to conduct as he dealt with the ongoing appeals of those judged guilty—the Nonpartisan League trio of Joseph Gilbert, Louis Martin and N. S. Randall, and Red Wing businessman John Seebach. Gilbert, Martin and Randall had been found guilty of discouraging enlistments.

Seebach had been sentenced to prison on sedition charges. Those indicted for making less forceful anti-war statements in personal conversation—Herman Zemke, Carl Seebach, Henry J. Bang, Gust W. Kruger and William Ripetto—did not face trial.

Minnesota's Supreme Court surprised many observers in July 1919 when they reversed the order of a Goodhue County District Court that had denied N. S. Randall a new trial. The justices determined that Willard L. Converse, Randall's original judge, had made a prejudicial error. Although the High Court believed Randall's disloyal speech in Kenyon inferred his guilt, Converse had limited the number of his defense witnesses to 12. The defendant had asked to call 27. Further, justices said the trial court should have allowed Randall to repeat, if he could, what he told the audience in August of 1917 during his Kenyon talk.[298]

The High Court commented, "The main purpose of the speakers was no doubt to advance the cause of their own political organization…. In aid of that purpose it might be [proper] to decry rival political parties, including the one in power…. But we think it was for the jury to say whether in so doing they…went too far and taught what Chapter 463 [Minnesota Sedition Act] forbids."[299]

Randall was awarded a new trial. It was left to Goodhue County officials to decide whether to continue the prosecution. County Attorney Thomas Mohn weighed that possibility but did not announce an immediate decision. N. S. Randall would not be retried.

Meanwhile, the indictments against Joseph Gilbert and Arthur Townley had remained active and wound their way back to Jackson County Court in midsummer of 1919. In May 1918 County Attorney E. H. Nicholas had indicted the two Nonpartisan League officials, charging them with criminal conspiracy. The prosecution contended that Gilbert's January speech in Lakefield discouraged enlistment in the military. Nicholas also claimed Townley's speeches at other venues were so similar to Gilbert's—Nicholas introduced content from four such talks—it appeared that they had conspired to create them. A sensational, controversy-filled trial ensued.[300]

Throughout the war years 1917–1918, Nicholas and Albert Allen, his friend and fellow county attorney from neighboring Martin County, earned a well-deserved reputation as crusading prosecutors on the trail of "traitorous" Nonpartisan leaders. Allen took on Townley and Gilbert in February 1918 with a charge of discouraging enlistments, but ultimately failed at the Minnesota Supreme Court level. Nicholas stepped in again, indicting the two NPL leaders for conspiracy to discourage enlistment.[301]

In addition to their courtroom prosecutorial activities, ardent 100-Percenters Nicholas and Allen became popular anti-NPL speakers. As seen, in early summer 1918, just prior to the state primary, the two men conducted a well-publicized Minnesota tour dispensing pro-Gov. Burnquist and anti-NPL rhetoric. Considering Goodhue County's disturbing election-related tensions, it was no surprise that the Loyalty Committees

Political enemies of the NPL and its leader A. C. Townley feared the allure of Townleyism, the League's brand of socialism.

of Red Wing and Goodhue County invited them to make Red Wing a stop. Allen and Nicholas made a June 6 appearance at the city's armory. Allen led off with some strong jabs against NPL candidate Charles Lindbergh, and Nicholas followed with bigger swings at the League, charging its members with being "disloyal Red Guard Bolsheviki" and "dangerous to life and property and a menace to everything American."[302]

Later, evidence would show that Nicholas held a number of advantages as he pressed his Jackson County conspiracy case against Townley and Gilbert. Trial Judge Ezra C. Dean appeared to be far from impartial. Dean had previously criticized and opposed the Nonpartisan League publicly and, in an interview, had expressed his belief that German money was behind the League. Ferdinand Teigen, the county attorney's star witness, was an erratic former League employee who had been fired for dishonesty and recently jailed for forgery. There appeared to have been pre-trial collusion between Nicholas and Teigen. And although, according to the League, a third of Jackson County's farmers were NPLers, not one of the 144 men called for possible jury duty was a League member.[303]

Trial Judge Ezra C. Dean

In court, Nicholas asserted that Gilbert and Townley were part of a conspiracy to distribute two NPL pamphlets that discouraged young men from enlisting. The defendants allegedly dispatched a League operative to Jackson County to circulate the material. Teigen testified to having heard Townley make strong anti-war comments.

George Nordlin, the NPL attorney, had produced a March 27 letter from Nicholas to witness Teigen. It told of the

prosecuting attorney's planned campaign to expose NPL propaganda by distributing Teigen-created anti-League literature. The defense also obtained a copy of a May 25 telegram sent to Teigen from Nicholas' ally Albert Allen and stamped with "MONEY TELEGRAPHED." On June 13 Nicholas received a shipment of books from Teigen and confirmed by letter that he intended to sell them on behalf of the former NPLer [see pp. 146–7 for copies of NPL documents]. It would appear from the text of Nicholas's June 13

letter that the books in question were copies of Teigen's recently released anti-League tell-all, *The Nonpartisan League: Its Origin, Development and Secret Purposes*. That letter was addressed to Teigen at "Economical Research Publishing Co.," the St. Paul publisher of his book.[304]

Teigen had also received a suspiciously generous $50 stipend [more than $700, adjusted for inflation] from Nicholas for travel costs. The defense located potential defense witnesses willing to testify that Teigen told them about the $50 payment. Judge Dean ruled that information inadmissible. Further, Dean

E. H. NICHOLAS
COUNTY ATTORNEY OF JACKSON COUNTY
SECOND FLOOR, COURT HOUSE
JACKSON, : MINNESOTA

June 13th, 1918.

Mr. F. A. Teigen,

    Economical Research Publishing Co.,

       St. Paul, Minn.

Dear Mr. Teigen:

    I return to the office today for a few hours and find your letter and also the books which you sent. My understanding is that I can sell them for twenty-five cents (25¢) a copy. Am I right in that?

    I am sending some of them today to Adrian, Minnesota, and I believe that I can dispose of them. At any rate, I will do the best I can and account to you when we get through.

    I believe the book as it now stands, with your signature, is in good shape and makes a much stronger argument.

Sincerely yours,

E. H. Nichalas.

County Attorney.

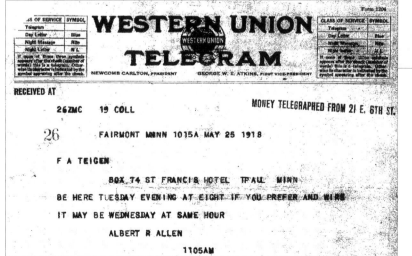

WESTERN UNION TELEGRAM

NEWCOMB CARLTON, PRESIDENT   GEORGE W. E. ATKINS, FIRST VICE-PRESIDENT

RECEIVED AT

26ZMC   19 COLL   MONEY TELEGRAPHED FROM 21 E. 6TH ST.

26   FAIRMONT MINN 1015A MAY 25 1918

F A TEIGEN

    BOX 74 ST FRANCIS HOTEL TPAUL MINN

BE HERE TUESDAY EVENING AT EIGHT IF YOU PREFER AND WIRE

IT MAY BE WEDNESDAY AT SAME HOUR

    ALBERT R ALLEN

       1105AM

Townley and Gilbert's defense team believed county attorneys Nicholas and Allen were conspiring with NPL turncoat F. A. Teigen to convict League officials. Two of the documents from the NPL files, microfilmed and located in Minnesota Historical Society's NPL papers, are shown here.

did not permit a trove of substantiating documents in support of Townley's patriotism to be admitted as evidence. These included transcripts of nearly 200 Townley speeches, letters, editorials, and a President Wilson thank-you letter praising Townley for his patriotism.

Arthur Townley in a December 1917 *Nonpartisan Leader* sketch

Serious questions regarding the legitimacy of the Townley-Gilbert trial made at the time and revisited over the following years would emerge. A 1957 study decided the prosecution "…was quite obviously part of the move by anti-League forces in Minnesota to destroy the organization before it gained much political power."[305] The *Nonpartisan Leader* printed a front page attack on the trial—"The History of the Jackson 'Frame Up'—" in which reporter W[alter] W. Liggett, head of the League publicity office, blamed the "vicious animus of the prosecuting attorneys [and] the bias of the judge" as factors in the conviction. Liggett used an NPL claim familiar to his readers when he wrote that Nicholas "was egged on by…Twin Cities special interests heads who were pouring out money like water…to defeat the farmers' movement which threatened to put a stop to their profiteering."[306]

Robert Morlan's highly regarded study *Political Prairie Fire: The Nonpartisan League, 1915–1922*, carefully detailed the Townley-Gilbert conspiracy trial. Indeed, a strong case could be made from the evidence Morlan assembled that County Attorney Nicholas and Judge Ezra Dean conspired to convict the defendants.[307]

This sketch of Joseph Gilbert was made during his trial in Jackson, Minnesota.

Morlan pointed to conclusions about the trial made by the *St. Paul Daily News* summarizing public reaction to the Jackson County decision:

"There has been left in the minds of a very large number of people an impression of a bitterly prejudiced court and a wide feeling that this trial—staged in an obscure and almost inaccessible spot, a year or more after the events concerned, before a judge who had previously admitted prejudice in declining to preside over a similar trial—savored more of persecution than of prosecution."

Ironically, the Gilbert and Townley relationship had dissolved before their trial in Jackson County was called. Gilbert led a mutiny of Nonpartisan League leaders, all challenging the charismatic Townley's belief that only one-man rule could keep the party ideologically pure. Townley believed he was that "one man." Now, Gilbert lobbied for a more democratically operated NPL. Townley crushed the revolt.

As NPL founder and leader, Arthur Townley maintained complete control of the League, including its treasury. He made no accounting of receipts flowing in through dues and investments. The two NPLers fell out after Gilbert's Red Wing conviction. Townley wondered if the League could afford the legal costs of Gilbert, Randall and Martin. An offended Gilbert challenged his chief with a signed statement, arguing "convictions, frame-ups and perjured testimony" [he referred to the Goodhue County trial] needed "a continuous and daring" defense. Townley exiled the rebel to North Dakota, handing him a less consequential assignment.[308]

NPL-paid attorneys did continue to represent the trio convicted at Red Wing, but Gilbert's transfer to North Dakota led him to write another letter, this one signed by 17 prominent League workers—N. S. Randall, Walter Liggett and J. Arthur Williams among them— that was sent to Townley. It protested the NPL president's autocratic management style. "We, workers…recognize your ability. We admire your qualities of leadership…. But if the League is to become national in fact, as well as name, it cannot continue as it now is, essentially a one-man movement." The Nonpartisan League king cleansed the Liggett-led publicity department of its boss and the many other employees who signed Gilbert's letter. Gilbert remained, for the time being, in North Dakota.[309]

In December 1919 the Minnesota Supreme Court weighed the appeals of Joseph Gilbert and Louis Martin, both convicted for interfering with enlistments during Kenyon speeches in 1917. The court decided that since "nearly all the questions raised [were] common to both [Gilbert and Martin] cases, they could be argued and submitted together." The court affirmed Gilbert's conviction and then turned to Martin.[310]

The Minnesota justices discovered questions in the Martin case that had been unanswered in the Gilbert decision. It was alleged during his original trial that Martin had told Kenyon citizens he "was pro-German" and that he knew the statements in the speeches made by Gilbert and Randall in Kenyon were true. One question for the court: Was Martin discouraging enlistment when, after hearing the Kenyon speeches, he told others who listened to the same talks that he, Martin, knew and accepted the content of those speeches to be true? The trial court had ruled the defendant's actions in hearing seditious statements and repeating those statements to others while asserting them to be true were just as unlawful as those by the men who actually made the statements.[311]

A second question centered on assertions made by Martin in the Kenyon barbershop incident. During that heated encounter, did Martin's support of the comments made by Gilbert and Randall in the first Kenyon speeches equate to teaching or advocating against enlisting in the military? The Supreme Court majority ruled that Martin had made seditious statements: "[Martin's] assertions were none the less a teaching and advocacy of the doctrine promulgated by Randall and Gilbert...."[312]

Andrew Holt dissented. He reasoned, Martin's "offensive and uncalled for remarks which started the brawl did not constitute a violation of the law." Martin's comments were a "mere affirmative answer" confirming he agreed with the sentiments made during the public addresses at Kenyon and thus did not violate the statute.

A majority of the Minnesota justices remained convinced that Martin's original conviction in Goodhue County was proper and denied him a new trial. In their finding, the justices pointed to U.S. Supreme Court decisions in *Schenck v. United States* (249 U.S. 47, 1919) and *Frohwerk v. United States* (249 U.S. 204, 1919) made after the Minnesota trial. The federal court ruling in *Frohwerk* noted: "When a nation is at war many things that might be said in time of peace are such a hinderance [sic] to its effort that their utterance will not be endured...and that no court would regard them as protected by any constitutional right."[313]

An earthquake of social change rumbled through the nation in 1920, making wartime loyalty trials yesterday's news. The Eighteenth Amendment of the Constitution outlawing the manufacture and sale of alcoholic beverages went into effect on January 1, and the Nineteenth Amendment giving women the right to vote was approved on August 18. The Great War, now being called the World War, was pushed onto newspapers' back pages. In Minnesota, sedition cases made against minor characters taken to court during the war had been dismissed. Prosecutors now typically refrained from calling for new trials for those who appealed their convictions and had been granted retrial.

A handful of prominent socialists and radicals, individuals involved in the more widely publicized wartime loyalty trials, remained on the minds of federal and state prosecutors. Most prominent was Eugene V. Debs, the nationally known leader of the American Socialist Party who received a ten-year sentence in March 1919 for committing seditious acts. Debs supporters viewed him as a martyr of the socialist cause, and did not desert their leader. In 1920, while locked up in Atlanta's federal penitentiary, he ran for president and received nearly a million votes, 3.4% of the popular vote.[314]

Nonpartisan League founder Arthur Townley did not possess the national renown of Gene Debs, but the successes of his socialist-leaning farmer group in seizing control of North Dakota's government in 1916 gained him considerable attention. After the war, the U.S. Department of Justice aggressively pursued the kind of radicalism they believed socialists such as Townley espoused. Republican Party regulars were among those closely following the progress of Townley and the NPL. Following years of infighting with progressive elements, GOP leaders were determined to return to a traditional conservative stance in the upcoming 1920 national elections. Political conservatives, particularly those in America's agricultural heartland, had no desire to see a potentially dangerous minor league leftist like Townley regain momentum.

Goodhue County's successful prosecution of Joe Gilbert, along with Jackson County's dual conviction of Townley and Gilbert, placed the League's most well known and politically dangerous personalities in the public spotlight; their continued legal appeals, doggedly pursued by a capable defense team, added to their notoriety.[315]

Although the Minnesota Supreme Court had refused to overturn Gilbert's Goodhue County sedition conviction, the United States U.S. Supreme Court agreed to consider his appeal.

☆   ☆   ☆

On November 10, 1920, Joseph Gilbert got his day before the U.S. Court. Gilbert's defense team was comprised of George Nordlin, assisted by Frederick A. Pike. James Markham and Minnesota Attorney General Clifford L. Hilton represented the state. Gilbert's attorneys claimed the Minnesota Sedition Law "is repugnant to the Constitution" since only Congress, and not the states, has the power to create law, and, secondly, the Minnesota statute "is obnoxious to the inherent right of free speech respecting the concerns, activities and interests of the United States of America and its government."[316]

An attorney himself, the defendant laid out the heart of his case

Clifford L. Hilton, Minnesota's attorney general, led or assisted in the prosecutions and appeals of Joseph Gilbert. The Gilbert case centered around 1917 speeches in Kenyon, which happened to be Hilton's birthplace.

in a court brief: "No state has the power to deprive citizens of the United States of a fundamental right." A biographer put it another way: "Gilbert did not say the things he was charged by the 'parrot chorus' with saying…in August, 1917, but even if he had said them, the Act under which he was convicted is unconstitutional because it poaches on the legislative power of the Federal Government."[317]

On December 13 the court issued its decision. A majority of the justices found the Minnesota Sedition Law proper and in line with a series of Supreme Court decisions regarding wartime governmental power. Justice Joseph McKenna, writing for the majority, explained the court's reasoning. A rough summary of the court's conclusions is included here:

1) "…this country is one composed of many and must on occasion be animated as one, and the constituted [government] must have power of co-operation against the enemies of all. Of such instance, we think is the statute of Minnesota and it goes no farther…[Minnesota] is not inhibited from making 'the national purposes its own purposes' to the extent of exerting its police power to prevent its own citizens from obstructing the accomplishment of such purposes."

2) "The [Minnesota] statute, indeed, may be supported as a simple exertion of police power to preserve the peace of the state…. As counsel for the state say…. It is simply a local police measure, aimed to suppress a species of seditious speech which the Legislature of the state has found objectionable."

3) "The First Amendment, while prohibiting legislation against free speech as such, cannot and obviously was not intended to give immunity to every possible use of language." Further, "[reasons for the American entry into the war were] known to Gilbert for he was informed in affairs and the operations of the government, and every word that he uttered in denunciation of the war was false…. He could have no purpose other than that of which he was charged." [Use of the state's police power was justified, thus did not violate the Fourteenth Amendment's due process clause regulating free speech.][318]

The justices upheld the lower court's decision by a 7 to 2 vote. Justice Louis D. Brandeis vigorously aligned himself with Gilbert's position, authoring a powerful dissent affirming the freedom of speech and indicting the Minnesota Sedition Law. That Minnesota law, he wrote, "…applies equally whether the United States is at peace or war. It abridges the freedom of speech and of the press, not in a particular emergency, in order to prevent a clear and present danger, but under all circumstances." Brandeis pointed out, "The state law affects rights, privileges, and immunities of one who is a citizen of the United States and it deprives him of an important part of his liberty. These are rights which are guaranteed protection by the federal Constitution; and they are invaded by the statute in question." Minnesota's law, Brandeis wrote, "aims to prevent not acts but beliefs."[319]

Justice Brandeis continued, "Congress, legislating for a people justly proud of liberties theretofore enjoyed and suspicious or resentful of any interference with them, might conclude that even in times of great danger, the most effective means of securing support from the great body of citizens is to accord to all full freedom to criticize the acts and administration of their country…." The justice also stated, "The right to speak freely concerning functions of the federal government is a privilege or immunity of every citizen of the United States which, even before the adoption of the Fourteenth Amendment, a state was powerless to curtail." The Brandeis dissent was, according to First Amendment scholar Zechariah Chafee, "the first time that any member of the court, in any kind of published opinion, squarely maintained that freedom of speech is protected against State action by the United States Constitution."[320]

United States Supreme Court Justice Louis Brandeis
Photo: Wikimedia Commons

Brandeis also cited a forceful rebuke of Minnesota's wartime Sedition Act and the rigorous manner in which it was enforced:

> "In the state of Minnesota because of what was claimed to be either inadequate federal law or inadequate federal administration, state laws of a sweeping character were passed and enforced with severity. Whether justified or not in adopting this policy of repression, the result of its adoption increased discontent, and the most serious cases of alleged interference with civil liberty were reported to the federal government from that state."[321]

Following the Supreme Court decision, Minnesota Attorney General Clifford Hilton forwarded the paperwork necessary to imprison Joe Gilbert. It ordered the NPL leader to report to Red Wing's Goodhue County Jail where he would pay a $500 fine and serve his one-year sentence.

"Gilbert Must Serve One Year in Prison," proclaimed a *Red Wing Daily Republican* banner headline following the Supreme Court's decision. Jens Grondahl, the *Republican*'s editor, had waited a long time to see Joe Gilbert in jail. Now one of the most dangerous and disloyal NPL leaders, in Grondahl's opinion, would be locked up just three blocks from his newspaper office. The newspaperman made no editorial comment on the decision, however. District Court Judge Albert Johnson, who presided over the trial that convicted Joseph Gilbert, said with some relief, "The last straw at which Gilbert had been grasping is gone." A pleased Goodhue County Attorney Thomas Mohn had pursued Gilbert from Kenyon to Red Wing to St. Paul and Washington D.C. He now commented matter-of-factly, "I felt confident that the United States Supreme Court would uphold the verdict."[322]

Weekly newspaper editors around the county published news of the Gilbert decision, sometimes using reprints from other sources and, like the *Daily Republican*, taking little editorial satisfaction from the Supreme Court ruling. Goodhue County newspapers had badgered Gilbert and the Nonpartisan League with unbending determination, at times combining half-truths, rumor and fearmongering. Why not celebrate now that their quarry—a person they proclaimed was a disloyal and dangerous seditionist—would be off the streets and was to be locked up? Had they tired of the chase and the story? Was there an element of guilt in their silence?[323]

Red Wing Daily Eagle, the only county newspaper showing sympathy for Joseph Gilbert and the NPL, printed a thorough review of Justice Louis Brandeis's dissent. With the war now behind them and ethnic tensions easing, editor N. P. Olson and his trio of news reporting sons were taking a more aggressive stance regarding the Minnesota Commission of Public Safety and its wartime exercise of power.

With the exception of the one-year term Joseph Gilbert had yet to serve, Goodhue County's sedition trials had been completed. While the county's 100-Percenters were gratified with the Nonpartisan Leaguer's pending incarceration, there were others, particularly local and state farmers affiliated with the NPL, who viewed it as rank injustice. The people of Goodhue County apparently had had enough of the loyalty trials and the divisions they propagated. The citizenry, newspaper editors included, put the divisive subject behind them.[324]

Red Wing Daily Republican editor Jens Grondahl reviews copy at his desk.

Gilbert remained free on $2,000 bail, paid by county farmers Arthur F. Johnson and Sam Thorstenson, until February 5, 1921, when friends drove him from St. Paul to Red Wing for incarceration. Three-and-a-half years had passed since the NPL organization manager uttered words during a speech in Kenyon that three courts found to be seditious. Shortly after 4:00 p.m., Gilbert arrived at the county jail and "chatted pleasantly" with County Sheriff John Anderson and a deputy sheriff, along with a *Red Wing Daily Eagle* reporter taking notes.[325]

The *Eagle* described Gilbert as being in a contented frame of mind and appearing "cheerful and optimistic" as he waited for his cell. Although 55, the prisoner looked "10 years younger." Gilbert declared, "There is really nothing to say now. If the State of Minnesota thinks it's right I be kept in jail for a year why that is all there is to it. I am inclined to take things philosophically, and, if the sheriff is willing, I am going to be well occupied with reading and writing during my stay here."

Gilbert admitted he was surprised by the Supreme Court ruling. He noted, that new trials were ordered for all Nonpartisan League speakers facing similar charges in Minnesota, although none had actually taken place. Gilbert said, "I am the only one who was denied a new trial and who has to go to jail."

"Gilbert was not at all resentful," commented the *Eagle* reporter. Yet the former Nonpartisan League leader continued to deny the statements attributed to him in Kenyon—the words that put him in jail. He stood for obeying laws passed in wartime, but, the prisoner said, "A citizen still had the right to criticize them."

Goodhue County's two-story lockup, located behind the courthouse, held ten cells, five on each level. Gilbert was grateful for his bathroom-library that had shelves for his books. He discovered that wearing prison clothes was a requirement. He was not allowed a watch or razor, but could shave twice weekly. Sheriff Anderson said Gilbert was permitted one bath each week. The prisoner asked for a daily wash and got it.[326]

Petitions requesting a pardon for Gilbert began circulating in Minnesota six weeks after his jailing. Gilbert's friends and supporters tried to convince him to bring a clemency plea to the state Board of Pardons. His old ally, James Manahan, drew up the application. But the prisoner wanted no part of such a deal. Writing to his attorney George Nordlin on March 28, 1921, Gilbert asserted that the board's function was to extend clemency to convicted persons to further the ends of justice, adding, "…in no circumstance would I demean myself by begging for pardon when I know I have not committed a wrong against my fellowman. If regaining my liberty depends upon stultifying myself, I prefer to remain a prisoner indefinitely…. I have long since disregarded what others think of my conduct. It is more important what I think of it. I know that nothing worthwhile is ever gained by compromising one's principles…."[327]

The *Minneapolis Daily Star* began its own campaign to free Gilbert, printing petition blanks and asking that they be signed and returned to the newspaper. Herbert Gaston of the *Star* wrote, "[Gilbert] is a man of irreproachable personal character… it is absurd to speak of any danger to the community in releasing him." Gaston and Thomas Van Lear, along with supportive Nonpartisan Leaguers, founded the *Star* in 1920 and thus, in this case, the newspaper was partisan.[328]

Surprising support for a Gilbert pardon came from Ambrose Tighe, counsel for the Minnesota Commission of Public Safety, the wartime nemesis of the NPL and Gilbert. Earlier, in February 1918, a rueful Tighe had shared second thoughts with former Governor John Lind about the commission and its autocratic ways. Lind was an original member of the commission who resigned his post in disgust.[329]

Two of the Board of Pardons' three members happened to have personal connections to Joseph Gilbert and his trials. Chief Justice Calvin L. Brown had led the Supreme Court of Minnesota that refused Gilbert's request for a new trial, and Minnesota Attorney General Clifford Hilton helped prosecute him in the state and before the United States Supreme Court. Despite Gilbert's opposition, the clemency appeal went to the board. Governor Jacob A. O. Preus agreed with the other members in rejecting the campaign to free the Goodhue County prisoner.

Gilbert later detailed his daily jail routine to his biographer, David Douthit. He slept in a hammock instead of the bed provided, and upon rising took a cold bath and ran naked up and down between the rows of cells. Mail arrived after breakfast.

The original 1859 Goodhue County Courthouse in Red Wing is pictured with the county jail—Joseph Gilbert's home for a year—to the rear, the last building in the complex.

Reading took up most of his time—newspapers, magazines, mail and also nonfiction books on science, history and philosophy, with fiction and poetry mixed in. A small table was provided for his portable typewriter. The inmate wrote frequently to his wife, Julie, and had many other correspondents, not counting fan mail. A talented writer, he wrote reviews of current books; some were published in Twin Cities newspapers.[330]

Sheriff Anderson allowed Gilbert to talk with visitors in the jail's office area. "We had company a lot. Our place was a regular hangout, and as many as twenty or thirty people would be here at a time." Wife Julie was his most frequent visitor, but his imprisonment was difficult for her. She suffered a nervous breakdown a few weeks before her husband's release, was placed under a physician's care, and received full time nursing assistance.

☆ ☆ ☆

On October 24, 1921, the United States Supreme Court ended more than two years of legal wrangling over the Jackson County case involving Gilbert and Arthur Townley. In July 1919 a jury had found that the two NPL leaders conspired to discourage enlistment in the armed forces. Federal authorities declined to take action, so the county draft board pursued the NPLers. Each man received a 90-day sentence, the maximum for conspiracy to commit a crime under Minnesota law. The U.S. Supreme Court had finally terminated the prolonged legal war, refusing a defense appeal to send the case back to the Minnesota High Court. Gilbert and Townley would have to serve their 90 days.[331]

Joseph Gilbert still had more than three months left to serve in Goodhue County Jail when news of the Townley conviction reached him. He took the information with composure, agreeing to surrender to Jackson County officials upon completing his sentence in Red Wing. Gilbert walked out of one jail on February 4 and reported to Jackson County Jail two days later.[332]

Upon his release in Red Wing, Gilbert declared to newspaper reporters, "I never felt better in my life." He added, "My imprisonment has given me time to do things I could not have found time to do otherwise. I have taken an extensive course in history, science and philosophy…. My imprisonment was the height of nonsense. It was so childish that I refused to become incensed about it and turned it into a period of study and rest."[333]

Joe and Julie Gilbert celebrate their Golden Wedding anniversary circa 1940. He never regretted standing on principle and going to jail, saying "There are no lost causes." Gilbert advocated for the cooperative movement in Minnesota until his death in 1956.

Summary: An Unenviable Record

In the days of expectation leading to the United States declaration of war, the Minnesota Legislature hurried to resolve matters relating to the coming conflict. Adjournment of the 40th regular session of that body neared, and the 41st session would not convene until January 7, 1919. Minnesota would be without a Legislature for a year and half. As part of their efforts to fill the governmental gap left by their absence, lawmakers created, by a nearly unanimous vote, a wartime agency they named the Minnesota Commission of Public Safety (MCPS).

Minnesota historians have written in wonderment about the wide-ranging scope of MCPS and its powers. William Watts Folwell commented, "a more liberal dictatorship could hardly have been conceded to the commission;" Steven Keillor considered the group "martial law in bureaucratic form;" William E. Lass called it "a virtual government in its own right, employing its own agents and constabulary;" while Theodore C. Blegen wrote that the commission was an "experiment in wartime with a local form of dictatorship." Historians would find truth in another Folwell comment, "The commission had no doubts about the range of powers conferred upon it and no scruples about employing them."[334]

Without condoning its excesses, Frederick C. Luebke provided needed context regarding the performance of the safety commission: "Instead one must understand that the MCPS was not itself a cause of the superpatriotic excess; it was a manifestation of a spirit found throughout the United States and among many public servants. The history of the Minnesota Commission of Public Safety readily demonstrates how easily intelligent men of good will can confuse personal and class interest with the public good, and how patriotic enthusiasms can distort commitment to democratic ideals."

Luebke's valid comments considered, the toxic influence of the Commission of Public Safety remained a principal cause of a political and societal environment that overwhelmed traditional civility in Goodhue County. A pervasive atmosphere of suspicion throughout the county, engendered by the commission and its abettors in the press, led to acts of violence and intimidation against German Americans and political opponents.

County 100-Percenters steadfastly endorsed government *not* of the people, but by the seven-man commission. They aligned, through their actions, with that body's strategy for dealing with Nonpartisan Leaguers and suspected pro-Germans. The Commission undertook, noted an MCPS postwar report, "To kindle the back fires of patriotism among the rank and file of this ilk…. [W]ith its leaders it used the mailed fist." That same report justified imprisoning opinion makers thought to be critical of the war effort: "Misinterpreting the constitutional guarantee of freedom of speech… these [opposition] leaders thought…that even in war times, they could properly oppose the government's policies in speech and writing." Nine Goodhue County residents found themselves indicted for such misinterpretation of their rights and charged with sedition.[335]

Loyal support of the United States as it advanced toward world war was deemed laudable by a majority of Americans—feelings that only grew stronger as the nation's involvement in the conflict deepened. Those considering themselves what former President Theodore Roosevelt called "100% Americans"—individuals holding unquestioning belief in all aspects of the government's wartime policies—viewed with suspicion citizens who had more nuanced ideas or even questions about the conduct of the war.

When did loyal patriotic love of country go too far and become the American antithesis, a vehicle for suppression of constitutional freedoms? It depended upon whom one asked and when they were asked. In Goodhue County, pro-Germans and socialist Nonpartisan Leaguers suspected of disloyalty—suspicions that needn't have proof attached—came in for particularly harsh treatment, most often at the hands of 100% Americans. During the war years, unlawful attacks against the allegedly disloyal were more likely to be approved or overlooked. Second thoughts regarding such excesses occurred, if they did occur, only after the restoration of peace.

In meaningful ways, Goodhue County accurately reflected the Commission of Public Safety's belief that in 1917–18 the state was under attack by homegrown subversives—an element that the commission pledged to eradicate by any means necessary. County officials and their influential 100% American allies earnestly adopted the commission's philosophy of repressive patriotism. In the process, Goodhue County became a Minnesota microcosm of the safety commission's wartime world.

President Woodrow Wilson pledged to win the Great War and make the world "safe for democracy." In this time of crisis, Minnesotans opted, through legislative action, to cede their own independence to the dictatorial power of the Commission of Public Safety. Perhaps a cadre of informed Minnesotans applying a cautious, thoughtful approach to wartime governance might have succeeded in protecting the state from subversion while safeguarding constitutional freedoms. But in the spring of 1917, this kind of enlightened leadership was not forthcoming.

The leading MCPS power broker proved to be Joseph Burnquist, who had become governor upon the death of his predecessor in December 1915. He deeply desired to remain in office. Supporting Burnquist, and sometimes leading him, was Minneapolis attorney John McGee, a man comfortably confident in his own capabilities and eager to pursue citizens he believed were not sufficiently patriotic. Burnquist and McGee agreed on the major challenges confronting their commission and threatening the state's political stability—possible pro-German sentiment among members of Minnesota's ethnic groups and political dissidents, particularly those suspected radicals who were to be found in organized farmer and labor groups.

Governor Burnquist, up for reelection in 1918, moved into the campaign season promising a continuance of his wartime policies. With the state Democratic Party in a weakened condition, his biggest challenge during the Republican Party primary election would come from the Nonpartisan League choice. In self-interest, the governor kept a sharp eye on the widening NPL farmer movement and maneuvered to put them at political disadvantage whenever and wherever he could. McGee saw the reelection of Burnquist as a top priority for keeping both men in power and Minnesota and the war effort safely on track.

Under the cloak of wartime sedition anxiety, county and community officials also used their positions to deny political opponents access to public halls and to outlaw political meetings of these rivals. Historian Carl Chrislock emphasized Goodhue County's place as a "valuable component" of the MCPS "anti-subversion network." Chrislock, a professor of history at Augsburg College, was a Goodhue County native. He described how Goodhue County's attorney, along with those of Jackson and Martin counties, advanced the goals of the Commission of Public Safety with their 1918 prosecutions of Arthur Townley and Joseph Gilbert. The actions of those county attorneys shackled the Nonpartisan League leaders to outstate courtrooms and hobbled the NPL campaign.[336]

The success of the Nonpartisan League in North Dakota justifiably unnerved Minnesota corporate interests. The League had taken political control of the neighboring state in 1916, then set about establishing state-owned milling and packing plants, and even banks. NPL leaders made it clear that Midwestern states were their next targets. A decision to move League headquarters to St. Paul in January 1917—renaming their organization the National Nonpartisan League in the process—appalled Minnesota industrialists and Main Street business operators. Those objecting to NPL goals joined the Commission of Public Safety in taking aim at the League.

Nowhere in Minnesota did the shortcomings of MCPS governance become more evident than Goodhue County. The commission promoted a crusade for patriotism and support for America's war effort that, while praiseworthy in its goals, became a guise for the intolerant. Occupied with matters of more consequence, the commission ignored the excesses of the 100% Americans who took it upon themselves to decide who was loyal and who was not, who was American and who was not.

Ambrose Tighe, the Commission of Public Safety's original counsel, grew introspective after the war ended and developed concerns about the commission and its work. Clearly, he harbored regrets. Tighe joined the movement supporting clemency for the Nonpartisan League's Joe Gilbert following the U.S. Supreme Court decision that jailed the Leaguer in Goodhue County. Gilbert had been a target of Burnquist allies throughout the war.

Tighe's analysis of the Minnesota Commission of Public Safety presents a lesson that hopefully will not have to be relearned. He wrote: "The ruthlessness of the commission's procedure shows, if further evidence was required, how dangerous it is to vest even good men with arbitrary power."[337]

☆ ☆ ☆

In a nation dependent on newspapers as the main source of news during the Great War years, the press possessed broad and largely unchecked power to influence readers and arouse broad pro-war emotions in the populace. Early in the war George Creel, President Wilson's director of the Committee on Public Information, wielding what a contemporary called "fertile ingenuity" and "prodigious energy," decided to get America's newspapers into the war effort. Creel advocated "unparalleled openness" about the war and self-censorship from journalists whom he expected to back the war out of loyalty. He called his plan "a plain proposition, a vast enterprise in salesmanship, the world's greatest adventure in advertising."[338]

Creel's ideas aligned with the natural inclinations of an active group of patriotic Goodhue County newspaper editors. Minnesota faced political and cultural dilemmas in 1917: the challenge of the socialistic pro-farmer Nonpartisan League and organized labor, along with public suspicion of German Americans. This encouraged the local press to enthusiastically enlist in the war against Germany and alleged Goodhue County radicalism as well.

Editors from Cannon Falls, Zumbrota, Pine Island, Kenyon, Wanamingo and Goodhue joined Jens Grondahl of the county's largest paper, the *Red Wing Daily Republican*, in becoming voluble superpatriots—100-Percenters who brooked no criticism of the national war effort. As Grondahl's Red Wing Printing Company book *Goodhue County in the World War* observed, "The newspaper men of Goodhue County…never failed to respond to the calls of their country and from the day we entered the great struggle…it may be said that the newspapers of this county *were wholly and solely in the service of the Government* [emphasis added]."[339]

Grondahl's words echoed in a Minnesota Commission of Public Safety-produced postwar self-evaluation. The MCPS pointed to the contributions and "splendid initiative and patriotism" of the people and volunteer groups. Which contributors stood out among the rest? "The most powerful," claimed the commission, "were the newspapers of the state, which with few exceptions struck and sustained a high tone of loyal agitation."[340]

From the war's onset, the Goodhue County press presumed the guilt of those charged with sedition, excused intimidation by mobs, belittled the seriousness of attacks on private property and individuals, printed distortions and rumors about political enemies, and endorsed the coercive measures used to compel citizens to pay amounts determined by Liberty Loan committees.

Political beliefs of the newspaper editors slipped from the editorial pages into news sections when they dealt with the Nonpartisan League. Although in 1917–18 ethical standards of journalism were still evolving, many readers believed that the local press could be counted on for reliable, accurate news coverage. Newspaper editors in Goodhue County nurtured their own prejudices, ignored their own conflicts of interest and granted favored treatment to those with whom they agreed.

The Nonpartisan League's 1917 recruiting campaign in the state's rural districts alarmed the Republican Party leadership, then dominant in Minnesota. With the exception of the N. P. Olson family, who ran *Red Wing Daily Eagle*, all Goodhue County newspaper editors and owners were Republican or, at least, leaned that way during the war. It was understandable that they supported that party's zealous resistance to the League. However, many went to the extreme of assuming the mantle of wartime superpatriots, surrendering their role as objective monitors of governmental affairs.

Newspapermen Jens Grondahl and Andrew Finstuen found themselves enmeshed in the stories they covered. Grondahl proved to be a whirlwind of activity as part of influential organizations—Liberty Bond committee member, editor of the *Red Wing Daily Republican*, and past president of both the city's Commercial Club and its Manufacturer's Association. He was called as a witness in one of the local sedition trials and reported on what took place. The Red Wing editor was the county's most recognized 100% American.

Kenyon's Finstuen became the lead witness in the three most important sedition trials in Goodhue County—those involving speeches made early in the war by Nonpartisan League speakers in that city. He chaired that controversial 1917 meeting and later claimed to have made a transcript of the speakers' words, an assertion hotly denied by the NPLers. Finstuen's testimony, backed by his notebook, was read into the record during the trials of Gilbert, Martin and Randall.

At a time when citizens subscribed to, read and relied on newspapers as their favored source of accurate information, Goodhue County editors rejected objectivity and failed their readers.

Goodhue County courtrooms were transformed into sites of wartime judicial partisanship. Following the Red Wing indictment of nine men on charges of sedition, Federal District Court Judge Albert Johnson publicly declared the county grand jury could soon be recalled for more such work. Johnson stated the jurors might "…go into secret session most any time because any person talking sedition or found in any way interfering with the prosecution of the war, should not have the comfort of waiting six months before he is brought to trial." He did this knowing his words would be published. Reasonable newspaper readers reviewing such a wide-ranging threat from a federal judge, especially comments made in the light of the indictments for treason in his courtroom, might well have questioned the existence of their First Amendment rights.

The very public kidnapping of Nonpartisan League organizer George Breidal from Red Wing's St. James Hotel led a deeply concerned Judge Willard Converse to act. Converse announced he would sequester a local jury which was involved in a county sedition trial of another NPL representative. He ordered the re-assembling of the grand jury to investigate the kidnapping incident. Judge Johnson, senior to Converse, as he was appointed to the federal bench in 1909, apparently overrode his colleague's announced decision. Johnson claimed no evidence regarding the kidnapping had been presented, hence no action was necessary. The judge failed to note whether any inquiry had been made by local police or the county sheriff. He put forth a single reason for dropping the Breidal case: It would cost too much to summon a grand jury.

Clearly, the citizens and officials of Red Wing knew far more about the Breidal abduction than they were willing to admit. Unmasked men seized a man from a hotel lobby, tossed him into a car and, with a parade of other vehicles trailing, raced down Main Street. The incident had to have been the talk of the town. With mistrust in the NPL at a high point in the city, there seemed to be little concern with the treatment Breidal received. It appears that an unspoken community consensus had emerged which protected the kidnappers from prosecution.

Johnson's disregard for the significance of Breidal's abduction made the jurist's decision all the more improper. Albert Johnson demonstrated to the people of Red Wing and Goodhue County, as well as those watching the NPL trials across the region, that he, a federal district court judge, would treat criminal behavior with a wink and a nod.

Another blow to judicial impartiality was the relationship between Johnson, who was the primary jurist in the county sedition trials, and Goodhue County Attorney Thomas Mohn, leader of the prosecution in those cases. Johnson and Mohn both were members of the Red Wing chapter of the Commercial Club, a partisan. anti-NPL association of businessmen with affiliates across the state. It is noteworthy that C. S. Dana, Clerk of Court, and court reporter L. M. Powers were or had been members of the club. Robert Putnam, a member of Joseph Gilbert's jury, was also enrolled, as was Putnam's father, William, who chaired the Goodhue County Commission of Public Safety.[341]

Judge Johnson injudiciously joined the ardently pro-war American First Association of Minnesota, a dedicated opponent of the Nonpartisan League and other allegedly disloyal groups and individuals; he also chaired Red Wing's AFA's Second Ward committee.

The judge's ambition for higher status—he had run unsuccessfully for election to the Minnesota Supreme Court in 1914—might have been nourished by the visibility he received while presiding over the highly publicized Goodhue County sedition trials. But Johnson's wartime work in pursuing the NPL likely appeared excessive to many after wartime intolerance waned. His attempts to win election as an associate justice in 1920 and chief justice in 1924 also failed.

Grand jury members, with Johnson's acquiescence, communicated a more extreme message than the judge. They issued unmistakable threats to county residents regarding less than 100% American behavior. The jurors released a unanimous and menacing edict titled "Upon the Loyalty of Goodhue County." The conclusion bears repeating: "It is a well-known fact that in a good many communities in this county there have been some pro-Germans and some fifty-fifty Americans.... [T]hese people are going to be very carefully watched...it is their duty to...come out in the open and commit themselves to the successful prosecution of the war. It is not enough for them to subscribe and do things when they are asked.... *In this way only can they remove from themselves the suspicions that have been raised in the last year. From now on we must all be boosters for the war and 100% American*" [emphasis added].[342]

Goodhue County residents might well have been even more alarmed by such courtroom intimidation if they had discovered that volunteer intelligence agents were secretly watching them. Each community and township in the county included members of the American Protective League, a secret, semi-official organization with keen-eyed operators on alert for instances of possibly seditious behavior. As *Goodhue County in the World War* reported, "Most people were unaware of the existence of [the APL], and it was largely through this secrecy that the work of the APL was so effectively performed." Only men of "proven loyalty" [by Minnesota Commission for Public Safety standards] were allowed to serve. The war history reported that Goodhue County APL agents stayed busy: "Slackers were rounded up, draft evaders apprehended and people spreading false reports" were discovered and stopped.[343]

Prejudicial actions taken by officers of the U.S. District Court in Red Wing and conflicts of interest found within the intertwined network of their like-minded associates during the Goodhue County sedition trials justify characterizing the resulting convictions as miscarriages of justice.

Wartime laws ceded immense power to the state Commission of Public Safety. Its considerable strength was only multiplied by county CPS organizations. Influential Red Wing banker William H. Putnam chaired Goodhue County's commission and dutifully followed state policy. A dedicated, hardworking servant of the war effort, Putnam sometimes led forays into the county in search of sedition or in support of Liberty Bond sales. His orders to terminate the June 1918 NPL Lindbergh-for-governor motorcade at the Red Wing city limits and mobilize the city's Home Guard to patrol city streets were legal under the Minnesota Sedition Act, but these actions exaggerated the danger. His decision to go over the heads of the city's elected leaders in deciding to act was another misstep.

Putnam's martial law declaration had the appearance of being politically motivated and an attempt to portray NPL farmers as dangerous radicals. His status as a lifelong Republican with three terms in the state Legislature to his credit [1903–1909] placed him in opposition to the Nonpartisan League's Charles Lindbergh Sr., the main challenger to the incumbent Republican governor. Outlawing the NPL political parade, and in the process signaling that League members were dangerous radicals, damaged

Lindbergh. The only threats to public safety in evidence during the NPL's extended journey through the county came from people harassing Lindbergh supporters. Red Wing residents who saw Home Guardsmen armed with rifles patrolling city streets must have been impressed by the power of the Goodhue County Commission of Public Safety and its chairman.

Goodhue County Nonpartisan Leaguers, organized labor and socialists in 1918 would have been challenged to find a better stereotype of a "Big Biz" insider than William Putnam. A wealthy, influential banker, investor and former legislator, he held unassailable power over the politically and economically disconnected. Putnam also chaired the county's Liberty Loan committee, likely the most widely feared and mistrusted of all wartime entities. Yet the former mayor of Red Wing, councilman and school board member was a natural choice for leadership in the county war effort. Civic leaders looked for local experience and maturity as the war began, and Putnam, who turned 70 in 1918, was a logical option.

Two major mistakes marred William Putnam's otherwise commendable efforts. He had dramatically overreacted by shutting down the city and calling out the Home Guard in the face of the NPL cross-county auto campaign. Citizens of Red Wing and participants in the convoy dealt with what Putnam viewed as a dangerous emergency with quiet calm. Instead of inciting the riots the chairman of the Goodhue County CPS predicted, the lengthy caravan of autos passed quietly through the city without incident.

Putnam also failed to rein in Goodhue County's Liberty Loan committee in spite of the bullying and coercive bond selling tactics it employed. After Goodhue County fell short of reaching its first two loan goals, he agreed to setting the amount citizens should pay and public shaming when they shirked. Although mostly figurehead, Putnam bore some responsibility for the excesses of the committee's escalating misdeeds.

In all, the Red Wing banker believed that it was his duty to serve and took his many responsibilities most seriously. More patriot than 100-Percenter, Putnam did his best.

Kenyon physician Joseph Gates, as dedicated to the war effort as any citizen in Goodhue County, was given to action first, contemplation later. Gates thrust himself into headlong confrontations against those equivocators who dared question the war in his presence. The former state legislator listened to the controversial Gilbert speech in Kenyon and became a star witness in three Goodhue County sedition trials. Gates also spoke at loyalty rallies, raised funds for the war effort, and threw NPL recruiter Breidal out of a Kenyon barbershop. But there was more than bravado in Gates and the family he led. His sons joined the armed forces, and his wife was a Red Cross volunteer. Joseph Gates was one of the county's 100% Americans whose beliefs, although sometimes misguided, were genuine. When Gates saw his country in peril, he took action and even enlisted.

German Americans often found themselves under suspicion in the anxiety-filled America of the Great War years. Often feeling the need to show their loyalty to the nation, and sometimes actually called upon to prove it, people with Germanic roots carefully maneuvered their way through the war. German Americans, Minnesota's largest immigrant group, endured months of mistrust, government spying, hostility and threats. They discovered that Goodhue County was not the place for half-hearted patriots, particularly those with German surnames. While not all became victims of overt intolerance, most discovered in tangible ways that some of their neighbors no longer considered them fully American.

George Creel's Committee of Public Information took a malignant interest in German Americans and their loyalties. His agency created the nationwide organization known as the Four Minute Men, volunteers who made brief speeches in support of wartime government policies. Goodhue County had at least 30 members. Among their goals: Instill in audiences suspicion of possible pro-German, anti-war elements. Creel advised orators that fear "was an important element to be bred in the civilian population." As author Daniel Okrent later observed, "When the fear was attached to all things German, it proceeded to breed like an out-of-control virus." That "virus" also spread to socialists, including those in the Nonpartisan League and labor union members.[344]

Joan Drenning Holmquist, editor of a 1981 study of Minnesota ethnic groups, decried this era of intolerance directed at German Americans. She characterized it "A blatant Minnesota example of legalized discrimination…a massive attack on immigrant groups launched during World War I by…the Minnesota Commission for Public Safety."[345]

It would take the end of war to bring the beginnings of a fresh start for Americans who found themselves in the No Man's Land of an ethnic divide.

In December 1920 the Supreme Court of the United States rejected Joseph Gilbert's contention that the Minnesota law under which he was convicted violated his guarantee of free speech. His attorneys claimed that legislation related to constitutional rights was reserved solely for Congress. States such as Minnesota had no legal standing in these matters. Writing a minority opinion, Justice Louis Brandeis agreed with Gilbert's defense, pointing to the Fourteenth Amendment text: "…nor shall any State deprive any person of life, liberty or property, without due process of law." Brandeis wrote, "I cannot believe that the liberty guaranteed by the Fourteenth Amendment includes only liberty to acquire and enjoy property."

Just five years later, the Supreme Court reversed course. With its unanimous ruling in *Gitlow v. New York*, the court concurred that Brandeis's dissent in *Gilbert*, based on Fourteenth Amendment protections of free speech, was essentially correct.

Although *Gitlow* was too late to keep Gilbert out of the Goodhue County jail, his constitutional rights had been confirmed.[346]

Joseph Gilbert's Goodhue County trial and the trials of his Nonpartisan League associates Louis Martin and N. S. Randall were largely political. While campaigning for NPL candidates and enlisting county farmers in their organization, the two men adhered to the League's position on the war as written by Gilbert. NPLers believed it was their right to criticize the government, even in wartime, and no doubt produced more colorful and controversial commentary than the words found in Gilbert's proclamation. The MCPS, employing its far-reaching 1917 mandate, asserted power over such free speech, and men like Joseph Gilbert went to jail.[347]

Erwin Chemerinsky, a prominent scholar in United States constitutional law, summarized what has too often happened when danger confronts the nation: "One of the worst aspects of American history is that at times of crisis we compromise our most basic constitutional rights, and only in hindsight do we recognize that it didn't make us safer."

Joseph Gilbert and his colleagues who were convicted during Goodhue County's loyalty trials of 1918 would no doubt endorse Chemerinsky's view. They would also have adhered to United States Supreme Court Justice Brandeis's observation at that time: *"Minnesota's [sedition] law aims to prevent not acts but beliefs"* [emphasis added].

Goodhue County citizens who took the law into their own hands in 1917–18 chose nationalism over patriotism. Operating under the assumption that German American citizens were suspect, zealots demanded that they prove their loyalty. Politicians, anxious about the 1918 elections, attacked rivals as subversives in hopes of making political gains. Newspaper editors endorsed attacks on individuals who failed their arbitrary 100% American test. Superpatriots dishonored anyone suspected of being "50–50 Americans," liberally splashing the stain of disloyalty on innocents.

The 100-percenters did not act in a vacuum. A rigid climate of repression created by state and county commissions of public safety nourished a culture of intolerance. Nativism, biased courts and press and insider politics flourished, while individual freedoms were suffocated.

As Chemerinsky suggests, times of anxiety and fear in America can produce a false patriotism that can be used to deprive Americans of their constitutional rights. This distressing and disheartening component of the American story repeats itself. In 1917–1918, it was replayed in Goodhue County.

134 ☆

Appendix

Departure of Red Wing's Company L August 27, 1917

Above: Troops assemble in front of the Red Wing Armory.

Left: The parade marched past the library, heading to Central Park.

Above: Marchers enter Central Park.

Left: The final leg was marching down Broadway to the train depot.

Crowds gather at the Milwaukee Road train depot and Levee Park.

The troop train departs.

THOMAS FRANKSON, LIEUTENANT GOVERNOR   GEO. W. PEACHEY, SECRETARY

State of Minnesota
SENATE CHAMBER

A. J. ROCKNE
ZUMBROTA, MINN.
SENATOR 19TH. DISTRICT

Zumbrota Minn Oct 12th 1917

Hon C.W. Henke Esq

St Paul Minn

    My Dear Sir; I have your letter and card sent therein. Replying will say that I am very busy in Court at present and it will be hard indeed for me to get away. I have been asked by many of the local committeemen here in this county to come to their meetings at their town halls and if I can do this I feel that I cannot very well spare any time to go other places in the state. I made ten talks when the last loan was placed and in nearly all of the towns that talks were had, the allotment was subscribed in full.

    I had however so much bad luck with my talks in the spring that I hardly know what to say to the people now. I urged all the boys to join the local militia companies at Red Wing and Zumbrota, arguing that they would be better taken care of and could be reached better from home if they were all in one or the other company. Since going the Camp Cody both companies have been disbanded and scattered more or less around. Then again I told the people here that if we could but fill up our companies the first draft would be very small from Goodhue county, not over fifty to fifty five men. I had the Congressional act before me when I made that statement and thought I was telling the people the truth. Later a ruling came down that only those who had enlisted prior to June 30 would be credited to the various counties on their quota. That ruling left this county with 80 men not credited on the first draft, and now these Non Partisan league men are around telling the farmers that I knew this all the time and that I delib ately went out and misrepresented matters to them, and many believe it. Then

Sen. A. J. Rockne's response to C. W. Henke of the Commission of Public Safety detailing problems with National Guard recruiting and the Nonpartisan League
National Nonpartisan League Papers, Speakers Bureau Records, MnHS

THOMAS FRANKSON, LIEUTENANT GOVERNOR   GEO. W. PEACHEY, SECRETARY

State of Minnesota
SENATE CHAMBER

A. J. ROCKNE
ZUMBROTA, MINN.
SENATOR 19TH. DISTRICT

there is considerable complaint here over the ~~act~~ fact that the first bonds
have not as yet been delivered to them. Have talked with several to-day
asking them to subscribe for the new loan and all have said that they
would like to have something to show for their first subscription before
they subscribed any more.

It is things like these that we have to contend with in the country
district and it would seem that some of these matters could be avoided
as well as not. In 1898 and again last year this county furnished more
soldiers than any county in the state in porportion to its population,
and it was rather a severe blow when the ruling of the department fixed
matters in a way that full credit was not given to all the men who had
enlised in the militia companies here and at Red Wing. I took the matter
up with Senator Nelson and others but was flatly told that no change would
be made. Friends of the boys at Camp Cody are coming to me more or less
every day complaining because the company has been disbanded and scattered in every direction, and it is hard indeed for me to explain to them
why this has been done when we were lead to believe that the boys would
be together.

We are going to make every effort to get the county to subscribe the
amount alloted to it on the second loan, and I feel that you people should
not call me away from here when work must de done here if we are to succeed.
However if you people think that some else could do better here and that
it would better for me to go into other counties I wil of course do all
that I can to help along wherever you ask me to go.

This letter is written confidentially and is not in any way for publication

Yours very truly *[signature]*

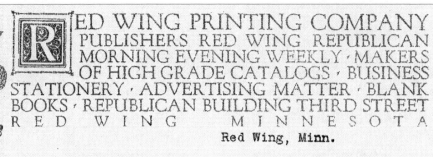

RED WING PRINTING COMPANY
PUBLISHERS RED WING REPUBLICAN
MORNING EVENING WEEKLY · MAKERS
OF HIGH GRADE CATALOGS · BUSINESS
STATIONERY · ADVERTISING MATTER · BLANK
BOOKS · REPUBLICAN BUILDING THIRD STREET
R E D   W I N G   M I N N E S O T A

Red Wing, Minn.

Oct. 26, 1917

Mrs. Thos. G. Winter,

2617 Dean Boulevard,

Minneapolis, Minn.

Dear Madame:

Pardon us for not having replied sooner to your kind
letter of recent date, asking for copies of the song "America,
My Country". The demand upon us has been exceedingly heavy. We
have sent many of the songs to France and we have contributed
many for the use at the cantonments by the entertainers provided
by the War Service Board. However, we feel that a vast number of
copies should be used in view of the extraordinary favor with
which this song has been received. We believe that some organization like yours should interest a number of philanthropic men
and women to obtain enough of this literature to supply army and
other patriotic needs. We are willing to sell them in large
quantities for non-commercial purposes at the cost of manufacture.
The schools are awakening to the value of this song and we have
received, perhaps, 250 unsolicited orders from High school and
county superintendents. We have received many lauditory letters
from governors of states, educators of high standing and patriots
of generally Extracts from these letters will soon be published
and they will show the nation wide interest in this song.

Jens Grondahl's letter to Mrs. Thomas (Alice Ames) Winter, head of the Women's Auxiliary of the MCPS, asking her assistance in promoting his national anthem
Minnesota Commission of Public Safety, Women's Auxiliary MCPS correspondence, MnHS

To show that we want to do our"bit", we are sending you with our compliments, one hundred copies of the song in A flat and five hundred copies of the postcard. Please use them as you deem best.

We received a letter from a man the other day, who said he wished he was rich so that he might give a copy of this song to every person in America,

Please let us hear from you again. Give us an idea, how many copies you could use to advantage provided the funds can be obtained.

It has been suggested by some that Supt. H. E. Griebenow of the South High School, Minneapolis, be invited to put this number on at the forth coming All-Minnesota Loyalty meeting, in St. Paul, November 9. Prof. Griebenow, I am informed, sings beautifully, and he has a glee club which sings the song. Also, it is possib4e that he would drill a large chorus, as large as possible, for that occasion. Would it not be well for you to take a interest in this right away. I am confident Prof. Griebenow would do this if asked.

Sincerely Yours,

[signature]

P.S. Also, the song should be sung at the educational convention in Minneapolis which begins Wednesday.

G.

(Bond of Officer)

Know all Men by these Presents,

That we *Fred J Seebach* as principal, and *Charles E Betcher* and *Robert W Putnam*

as sureties, are held and firmly bound to the State of Minnesota in the penal sum of one thousand dollars, ($1,000), lawful money of the United States, for which payment, well and truly to be made, we bind ourselves, our heirs, executors and administrators, jointly and severally, by these presents.

Given under our hands and seals this _____*16th*_____ day of *July* 191*7*

The conditions of the above obligation are such that, whereas the principal above named is now, or hereafter may be commissioned an officer of the Home Guard of Minnesota, and has in his possession or under his control, or has receipted for, or may hereafter receive or receipt for, or in his official capacity acquire, certain ordnance, ordnance stores, clothing, camp and garrison equipage, quartermaster's supplies and other public property, or either or all of said articles, and certain moneys or other public funds, turned over to him by his predecessor in command, or by the Governor of the State of Minnesota, or which may have come into his possession or under his control by virtue of his office, or may be retained by him upon his promotion, or received subsequent thereto. Now, if the said principal shall safely keep said property, and preserve the same in good and serviceable condition, and deliver the same to the Governor of the State of Minnesota, at the State Arsenal at St. Paul, Minnesota, or to any officer by him designated, whenever so ordered by the Governor, and faithfully account for any moneys so intrusted to him, and turn over to the Governor, or to any officer by him designated, whenever so required, the balance in his hands over and above all lawful disbursements allowed by competent authority, and comply with all rules, regulations and orders relating to accountability and care of property, then this obligation shall be null and void; otherwise to remain in full force and effect.

IN PRESENCE OF

L Meyer

J W Halliday

Fred J Seebach [SEAL]

Chas. E. Betcher [SEAL]

Robert W Putnam [SEAL]

State of Minnesota,

County of *Goodhue* } ss.

On this *16"* day of *July* 191*7*, personally came before me *Fred J Seebach, Charles E. Betcher, Robert W Putnam*

all of the County above named, to me well known to be the principal and sureties above named, and the persons who executed the foregoing bond, and they severally acknowledged that they executed the same as their free act and deed, and for the uses and purposes therein expressed.

NOTARIAL
SEAL

J W Halliday
Notary Public,
Goodhue County, Minnesota.

My commission expires *Sep 23* 191*7*

Officer's Bond of Capt. Fred Seebach, leader of Red Wing's Home Guard Company A, combined with its roster

Jan 22nd 1918

COMPANY "A", 5th BATTALION, MINNESOTA HOME GUARD, RED WING, MINN.

NAME and RANK	ADDRESS	NAME AND ADRESS OF NEAREST RELATIVE
Captain F.J.Seebach	815 Third Street	Kate Seebach,815 3rd St.
1st Lieut. C.J.Heglund	326 E 6th St.	AliceA.Heglund, 326E 6thSt
2nd Lieut. A.G.Rehder	912 Bush St.	Elsie Rehder-912 Bush St.
Sgt. C.I.Olson	866 Putnam Ave.	Margaret S.Olson-866 Putnam
" A.W.Zorn	Ahlers Flats	Agnes F.Zorn-Ahlers Flats
" C.J.Ahlers	" "	Sylvia Ahlers- " "
" R. M. Foot	928 Third St.	Olga Foot- 928 Third St.
" S.S.Lundquist	1321 Fourth St.	Mrs.S.S.Lundquist-1321 4th
" Charles E.Betcher	326 Pine St.	C.A.Betcher- 326 Pine St.
Corp. W.A.Jones	444 Fourth St.	Emma C.Jones- 444 Fourth
" D.J.Metzler	481 Seventh St.	Mathilda Metzler-481-7th
" R.W.Putnam	810 East Avenue	Winifred Putnam-810 East Ave
" C.B.Isaacson	239 E 4th St.	Josephine Isaacson,239 E4th
" E.J.H.Bredehorst	442 Seventh St.	Josephine Bredehorst,442 7th
" C.A.Josephson	820 Fifth St.	Mabel Josephson,820 5th St
Musc R.J.Koschitz	1911 West 5th	Mary Koschitz,1911 W 5th
" A.H.Andresen	Pleasant View Ave	Julia Andresen, Pl.View Ave
Cook J.T.Fulton	State TrainingSchool	Elizabeth Fulton, Same adrz
" E.P.Nordeen	417 East Ave.	Florence G.Nordeen,417 East
Artif. H.J.Vollmers	458 E 7th Street	Henry Vollmers,458 E 7th
Priv. C.H.F.Adler	208 Fulton St.	Edna E.Adler, 208 Fulton
" F.E.Andersen	916 West 3rd St.	Nell H. Andersen,916 W 3rdSt
" H.F.Anderson	533 Seventh St.	Almira Anderson,533 7thSt
" G.E.Aubrey	617 Potter Street	Margaret Aubrey,617 Potter
" W.L.Bakkela	219 Seventh St.	Louisa Bakkela, 219 7th St
" C.S.Barnhart	108 Fifth Street	Elfreda Barnhart,108 5th St
" J. M. Billo	216 Sixth Street	Anna P.Billo, 216-6th St.
" H.M.Bird	318 East 4th St.	Evlin Bird- 318 E. 4th St.
" E. C. Bryan	716 Central Ave.	Jessie Bryan,716 Cent.Ave
" W. W. Cary	448 Fourth St.	Mrs.W.W.Cary, 448-4th St.
" John Cebulski	621 Sixth Street	Matilda Cebulski,621-6th St
" P.H.Claydon	418 Ninth Street	Elizabeth Claydon-418 9thSt
" J.G.Dengler	725 West 4th St.	Mrs. John Dengler
" C. P. Diepenbrock	Red Wing,Minn.	Mrs.G.H.Diepenbrock-725 Rxkx Potter
" E. H. Dornfeld	1215 Bush St.	Othelia Dornfeld,1215 Bush
" A. W. Elder	1324 West 4th St.	Minnie Elder,1324 W 4th St
" B.Featherstone	720 Central Avenue	Edith Featherstone 720 Central Avenue
" C.W.Fenstermacher	302 East 7th St.	Estelle Fenstermacher 302 E. 7th St.
" J. G. Gerdes	234 East 3rd St.	Minnie Gerdes,234 E 3rd St
" D.R.Goldsmith	411 Dakota St.	Irmegarde Goldsmith,411 Dak.
" L. Hansen	816 Sturtevant St.	Hilma Hansen- 816 Sturtevant
" I. B. Harrison	110 Seventh St.	Lela Harrison,110- 7th St
" A. J. Hartman	428 Eight St.	Mary Hartman,428-8th St.
" A. M. Johnson	1219- 12th Street	M. Johnson, 1219-12th St.
" J. A. Johnson	461 East 7th St.	Mrs.J.A.Johnson,461 E.7th
" George Johnson	702 West 3rd St.	Etta Johnson, 702 W 3rd St

	R. E. Johnson	602 Plum Street	Fred Johnson,
"	V. W. Lamberg	220 East 4th	Gladys Lamberg, 220 E. 4th
"	R.H.Larson	1210 W. Main	Ida Larson, 1210 W. Main
"	A.H.Lidberg	711 McSorley St	Anna Lidberg, 711 McSorley
"	E. H. Lidberg	750 Central Ave.	Anna C. Lidberg, 750 Central
"	N. C. Lien	744 Central Ave.	Edna V.Lien, 744 Central
"	S. H. Lockin	914 West 3rd St.	Mrs.S.H.Lockin, 914-W3rd St
"	J. A. Loer	1471 Bush St.	Peter Loer, 1471 Bush
"	F.C.McCutcheon	903 W. 4th St.	Blanche McCutcheon 903 West 4th St.
"	F. W. McNeil	410 Seventh St.	Rose McNeil, 410-7th St.
"	M. A. McNiff	Ahlers Flats	Cora McNiff, Ahlers Flats
"	Geo. McPeek	740 Potter Street	Tillie McPeek, 740 Potter
"	L. C. Meyer	1011 Third Street	Florence Meyer, 1011-3rd St
"	W.S.Middlemass	529 Sixth Street	Mary Middlemass, 529-6th
"	P. A. Nelson	1117 West 4th St.	Mary Nelson, 1117 W.4th St
"	Axel Nielson	410½ Third St.	Mrs. A. Nielson, 410½-3rd
Priv.	Harry Olson	563 Bluff Street	Nettie Olson, 563 Bluff St.
"	A. A. Page	5th & West Ave.	Elvira Page, 5th& West Ave.
"	M. P. Paulsen	Prospect St.	Maude Paulson, Prospect St.
"	R. Perrott	1253 So.Park St.	Elizabeth Perrott, 1253 So.Park
"	A. E. Peterson	816 Bush St.	Mary Peterson, 816 Bush St.
"	S. P. Petersen	309 Plum St.	Bertha Peterson, 309 Plum St.
"	J. A. Prior	529 Buchanan St.	Alice Prior, 529 Buchanan St.
"	C. G. Sands	415 Dakota St.	Lanchen Sands, 415 Dakota St.
"	K. R. Seiler	622 Fourth St.	Ella Seiler, 622-4th St.
"	A. E. Seiz	807 Third St.	Harriet Seiz, 807-3rd St.
"	K. V. Smith	810 Fifth St.	Helen Smith, 810 Fifth St.
"	P. Sorensen	317 Third St.	Christina Sorensen, 317-3rd
"	H.F.VanBronkhorst	549 Ninth Street	Clara VanBronkhorst, 549-9th
"	J. F. Wagner	733 West Avenue	Elizabeth Wagner, 733 West Ave.

Entrance to the Red Wing Armory, built in 1901

The Nonpartisan League point of view

ANOTHER MOONEY CASE PROVIDED BY SUPREME COURT OF MINNESOTA

Frame-Up Case of Politicians Against Joseph Gilbert and L. W. Martin, Nonpartisan League Workers, Considered Only in Legal Aspects—Astounding Facts in First Trial Ignored.

BY A. B. GILBERT

With its decision, handed down on December 22 confirming the lower court sentence against Joseph Gilbert and L. W. Martin, the supreme court of Minnesota gives the country another Mooney case. Like Mooney's, these cases not only grew out of an attempt to "get" men prominent in championing the cause of the common people, but the supreme court did not go into the obvious evidence of an unfair trial in the lower court. Like the California court, the Minnesota court based its findings solely on the legal aspects of the lower court records and considered as facts the charges sustained by judge and jury under outrageous circumstances.

In April and May, 1918, the possibilities of League success loomed large in the minds of Minnesota politicians. Something had to be done to discredit the organization. One means at their disposal, as desperate men, was to use the legal power of the state for framing up the opposition leaders, and it was worked for all it was worth. Indictments came in thick and fast at League headquarters. At one time in this period Joseph Gilbert had no less than five indictments against him because he was organization manager of the League.

One of these came from Goodhue county, Minn., for alleged disloyal remarks made in August, 1917, or eight months previous. The men who brought the indictment had tried to get the federal government to take up the case, but federal agents had been at the meeting and found nothing wrong with it. Then after allowing one session of the grand jury to pass the gangsters brought an indictment under a state law when an indictment was badly needed for political effect.

Previous to and during the trial Goodhue county was terrorized by open and secret organizations opposing the League farmers, and from these people the jury had to be drawn. At the trial the judge ruled that Nonpartisan league members could not serve on the jury, although obviously the League should not have been on trial. Inasmuch as the League was so strong there that all were either for or against it, this ruling threw the defendant into the hands of the League opposition.

The proof of the alleged statements of Mr. Gilbert which met the approval of this one-sided jury and which the supreme court did not review, would be laughable if the case were not so serious. The opposition produced a parrot chorus who remembered 10 short sentences from his speech. All remembered the same sentences and the same words and practically nothing else, a most astonishing performance. The opposition also produced an editor who claimed to have taken notes in a little book during the speech with the book

Nonpartisan League circular explaining why the League believed two of its leaders were falsely convicted during their Goodhue County sedition trials claimed to have taken notes in a little book during the speech with the book on his knee in the open air. But the writing was in a fine, careful hand such as a man could write only at his desk with plenty of time. Furthermore, when asked to repeat the note-taking feat at another trial this editor failed miserably. Yet the judge admitted the doped-up book as evidence. Again, practically the same words were contained in an indictment against L. W. Martin in another case, and yet the judge would not allow this other indictment to be produced before the jury as evidence of a frame-up.

Mr. Gilbert declares that he did not make the statements attributed to him, that he confined himself to reading the League resolutions and to making brief comments in explanation. As a matter of fact only a political ass could have made the statements in the indictment, and no one who knows him would be able to think of Joseph Gilbert as an ass. Where the parrot chorus got the words, however, is evident. They are a crude parody on the League resolutions which the supreme court on another occasion declared to be proper.

When the jury brought in a verdict of guilty the defendant's lawyers asked for a stay of sentence, and the judge who had declared several times that the Nonpartisan league was not on trial forgot his pretense so far as to say that he would have to grant the stay on the condition that the League would cease work in Goodhue county. There was a tense moment in the court while everybody was recovering from the shock of this revelation, and then Mr. Gilbert reminded the judge that the Nonpartisan league was not on trial and that he could say that the League would not stop its work in that county.

L. W. Martin's case presents, if possible, an even more gross miscarriage of justice. At the time when the phrase "pro-German" was becoming current, Mr. Martin asked a barber friend of his at Kenyon, Minn.,

jokingly, if he could shave a pro-German. A patrioteer who happened to be present took this as an excuse for assault on Mr. Martin. Later a bunch of men gathered around him to continue the insulting and one of them hurled at him the questions, "Do you approve of Gilbert's and Randall's speeches? Do you approve of the La Follette speech?" Mr. Martin, of course, replied "yes."

Later, after he had brought an action for assault against the patrioteer who had choked him, Mr. Martin was indicted and convicted for "unlawfully and wilfully stating to certain named persons that he, the said Louis W. Martin, was a pro-German and that he, the said Louis W. Martin, knew that the aforesaid statements made by said Joseph Gilbert and N. S. Randall as hereinbefore set forth, were true, and that he, the said Louis W. Martin, affirmed and accepted said statements."

Mr. Martin, of course, accepted what these two men actually said and not what the parrot chorus alleged that they said. Moreover he had applied for admission to the army and had been rejected for poor eyesight. Later when the standards were lowered he was taken and is now a sergeant.

These cases will be carried further; if necessary, to the supreme court of the United States. But it is unfortunate for America that the country has to be disgraced by other cases of the Mooney kind. The Mooney case has created a stench not only in our own country but the whole world and this case must have the same result wherever the facts are known. The common people never ask anything but justice from the courts. They do, however, demand that our legal machinery and rigmarole of court practice shall not be used to railroad to prison those who are bold enough to champion their cause.

21

146 ☆ Patriot Hearts

E. H. NICHOLAS
COUNTY ATTORNEY OF JACKSON COUNTY
AT LEGAL, COURT HOUSE
JACKSON, MINNESOTA

March 27th. 1918.

Mr. F. A. Tiegen,
Minneapolis, Minnesota.

Dear Mr. Tiegen:

I met with a number of business men and bankers here last night, and went over the proposition of making a concerted effort in the state to bring the facts before the public in answer to the propaganda being preached by the Nonpartisan League. All the men present seemed to concur in the opinion that the plan is an admirable one, and are willing to do their share here in financing the movement.

The only adverse suggestions were by some of the merchants who feared that if they actively engaged in the fight or if it became known that they had paid money to assist in carrying on the fight that they would be boycotted by the members of the Nonpartisan League. It seems to me, however, that any business man has everything to gain, and nothing to lose by taking a stand in this matter.

I covered the ground very thoroughly with our men here, and they were very much astonished to learn the situation, and seemed very interest and anxious to render any assistance that they can in counter-acting this mammoth socialistic movement.

I am going to Lakefield this afternoon to talk with the business men up there, and will write you the result at an early date.

EHN-M.   Yours very truly,

                                          E. H. Nicholas

Shown here is another of the letters between Jackson County Attorney E. H. Nicholas and F. A. Teigen, a disaffected Nonpartisan League member. League attorneys believed Nicholas and Teigen were conspiring to frame Joseph Gilbert and A. C. Townley.

National Nonpartisan League Papers, Correspondence and Miscellaneous Papers, 1913–1927, Roll 4

F. A. Teigen's undated letter asking for money from a member of a Twin Cities politico-business group—historian William Folwell called it "the Patterson gang"— allegedly working to convict Gilbert and Townley
National Nonpartisan League Papers, Correspondence and Miscellaneous Papers, 1913–1927, Roll 4

UNITED STATES GOVERNMENT 3½% LIBERTY LOAN OF 1917

A Loan for Liberty & Democracy

"....That government of the people, by the people, for the people shall not perish from the earth...."

ABRAHAM LINCOLN

The Liberty Loan Is Your Loan

Probably never before in your life time has your country called on YOU for help! You have enjoyed the blessings of a Free People, your children have grown up in the proud and noble spirit of Democracy. Now your country calls YOU to turn your Savings into Soldiers—to do your share to save the principles for which the founders of this republic fought and bled and died.

Your Share Is A Liberal Subscription to the Liberty Loan

Accrued interest to be paid on date of final installment, credit being given at rate of 3½% for all prior installments paid. Payment in full may be made on and after allotment and before August 30, 1917, by giving two weeks' written notice. All payments to be made through your Bank or Trust Company or Postal Savings Bank, on notice from them.

Coupon Bonds: Coupon Bonds are payable to bearer and have coupons attached representing interest due. These coupons may be cashed at any bank on their due date without discount or charge of any kind. We recommend coupon bonds to subscribers as being the most convenient in case of resale.

Registered Bonds: Registered bonds are payable to your order and interest will be sent to your address twice a year by the Government. Smallest denominations of registered bond is $100.

Taxes: These bonds are free from all Income, State, County and City Taxes.

How to Buy Your Liberty Bonds

Below you will find the subscription blank prescribed by the Government for your use. Read it carefully before you fill it out and then be sure to write clearly and distinctly so that your subscription may be filled without fail.

After the blank has been filled in and signed place it in the enclosed envelope and mail to St. Paul Liberty Loan Committee, Old First National Bank Bldg.

Should you wish additional information before subscribing, call at the office of the Liberty Loan Committee, Fourth and Minnesota Streets, or ask your Bank or Trust Company or employer. Liberty Loan Headquarters telephone: N. W. Jackson 1672; T. C. 21-750.

Make No Payments to Solicitors or Agents of Any Kind

The Bank or Trust Company you indicate will notify you how and when to make payments to them, and you will receive your bonds from them when ready for delivery.

SUBSCRIPTION TO UNITED STATES GOVERNMENT LIBERTY LOAN BONDS

St. Paul, Minn. _____ 1917.

I wish to apply through _____ (Name of Bank or Trust Company or Employer.)

for _____ Dollars ($ _____) par value of United States Government "Liberty Loan" 3½% Coupon* bonds, subject to the official terms of subscription and allotment. I desire bonds in _____ Dollars denomination.

Remarks _____

Signed _____

Address _____

*It is understood coupon bonds are desired unless registered bonds are requested. See explanation above.

Authorized by Federal Reserve Bank. Issued by St. Paul Liberty Loan Committee.

St. Paul Liberty Loan Committee pamphlet explaining and promoting the U.S. Liberty Loan program

United States is recorded at the astounding figure of Two Hundred and Fifty Billion Dollars, which is nearly as much as the combined wealth of Great Britain, France, Germany and Austria Hungary, whereas the debt of the United States, including the present loan, is less than one-twentieth of the debt of those nations. There can be no doubt that a United States Government bond is the world's safest investment.

Bonds Good for Cash Any Time

These bonds will be broadly distributed and will be held by all the **banks and people of every class**, so that they will have at all times a ready market.
If for any reason, the owner of these bonds needs money he can immediately turn them into cash or make a loan on them at any of the banks.

Free from All Taxes

Our Government has made these bonds exempt from all State or Federal taxes (excepting, of course, estate and inheritance taxes) so that the income of 3½% is absolutely net to you regardless of the amount of your income.

How Uncle Sam Will Use Your Money

The entire proceeds of this loan will be kept in this country and will be used in the **payment of labor and the purchase of food and in the purchase of the products of our farms and factories.** The Northwest and St. Paul will benefit greatly from the money spent here to buy our products. A part of this first offering will be loaned by our Government to the Allies, but not a dollar will leave this country to pay for other than American products. **This money is loaned to the Allies, who give full security for repayment, so that they may continue to enter our markets and to pay us for our products. It all comes back to us** finally in payment for labor and material. It will broaden the market for our goods and increase demand for what we have to sell and make for **bigger, better business** not only throughout the Northwest, but also the entire country.

Description of Liberty Bonds

Price:	Par; that is, a $50 bond costs $50, a $100 bond $100, etc.
Interest:	3½%, payable one-half each six months; June 15th and December 15th.
Amounts:	$50, $100, $500, $1000 and larger.
Bonds Mature:	June 15th, 1947, but Government may redeem at any interest date on and after June 15, 1932, at par and interest.
Higher Interest Rate:	Should the Government issue bonds bearing a higher rate of interest during the war, these bonds are convertible without cost into the new bonds.
Allotments:	Bonds will be distributed as soon after June 15th as possible. The Government reserves the right to reject any subscriptions or to allot a smaller amount than is subscribed for, **except that $50 and $100 subscriptions will be allotted in full and may be paid for at once.**
Payments:	Bonds may be paid for in installments as follows:

2% on notice from Bank or Trust Company.
18% on June 28, 1917.
20% on July 30, 1917.
30% on August 15, 1917.
30% on August 30, 1917.

In Helping Your Government You Are Helping Yourself

When you buy a United States Government Bond you take advantage of the rare opportunity of:
First, doing your patriotic Duty, and,
Second, of Benefiting Yourself Financially!
Others are called to lay down their lives—you are only asked to buy the safest investment known and receive a good rate of interest in return.
The bonds pay 3½% interest now—½% more than the Government has paid for 40 years.
If the war lasts a long time and additional war bonds bearing a higher rate of interest become necessary, your 3½% bond will be changed to one bearing the increased interest rate without cost. (This assures you the highest interest the Government will pay.)
If the war does not last long, history shows that a United States Government Bond paying 3½% will in all probability sell for much more after the war than you pay for it now.
3% Spanish War Bonds sold at 110.
In 1898 this country borrowed money to finance the Spanish War. Bonds were sold at par. They bore 3% interest—½% less than the present bonds bear—and within a few months after the close of the war their market price was 110—every man, woman and child who bought those war bonds at issuance made, besides the interest, a **net profit of 10% on the principal sum invested.**

Subscriptions will be received only up to June 15th next

Come to the Front—Subscribe Now

United States Government Bonds Are the World's Safest Investment

---

The Country Is Watching the Citizens of St. Paul

Let us show the rest of the country where St. Paul stands. St. Paul's quota of the Liberty Loan is six million dollars—and St. Paul will make good.
Take what you can for yourself—take some for your wife, your sister, your brother, father or mother—and above all for **your children.** What finer thing for any one than to be able to say, "I loaned Uncle Sam money to help carry on the war for humanity!" What other single thing can so accentuate to our people the sacredness of our Government, the oneness of its people in devotion to the flag and all that the flag means?
Send in your own subscription—and those of your family. You are loaning **direct to your government.** The ordinary "brokerage" and other charges do not exist in this transaction. Banks, Trust Companies and Bond Houses are handling the bonds free of charge. All are acting for love of country and out of devotion to the country in its endeavor to do a big thing in a big way—a way worthy of the United States of America.

Safest Investment in the World

When you invest in a Liberty Bond, you get a signed "Promise to pay" backed by the total resources of the richest nation on the face of the globe. The annual income of the United States is estimated to be Fifty Billion Dollars, or enough to pay off the present loan twenty-five times every year. The wealth of the

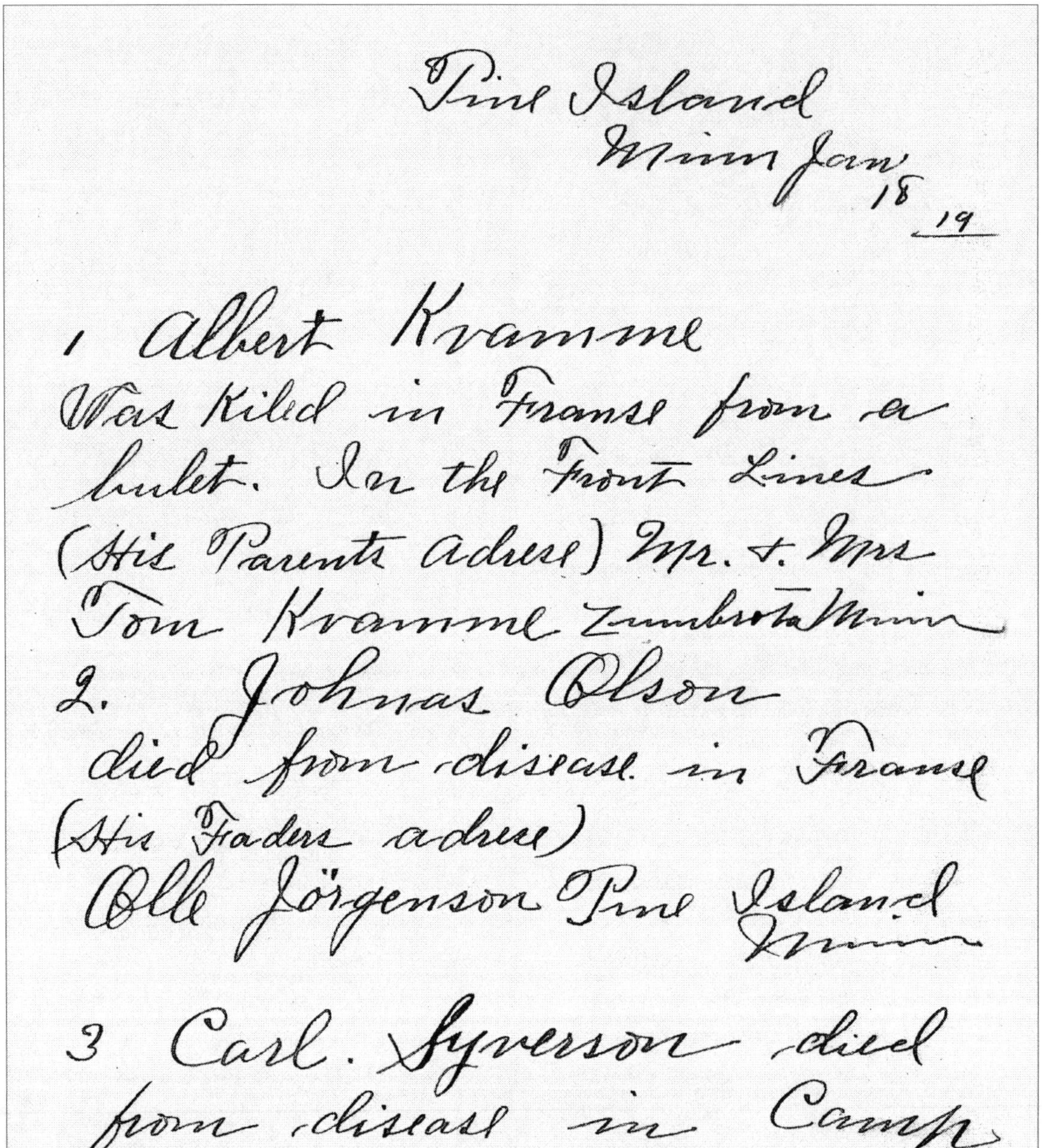

Pine Island
Minn Jan
18
19

1 Albert Kvamme
Was Kiled in Franse from a
bulet. In the Front Lines
(His Parents adress) Mr. & Mrs
Tom Kvamme Zumbrota Minn
2. Johnas Olson
died from disease in Franse
(His Faders adrese)
Olle Jörgenson Pine Island
Minn

3 Carl. Syverson died
from diseass in Camp

This is all the Information I
can giv about this 3 boys.
Mr. Lewis J. Trelstad Pine Island Minn

Two Goodhue County responses to the MCPS request for information regarding war dead

Lone Pine Grain and Stock Farm
M. O. FLOAN, PROPRIETOR

Zumbrota, Minnesota, Jan 16th 1919
R. F. D. NO. 4

Chas. W. Henke St. Paul

Dear Sir your letter of
Jan 4 received and contents
noted. I send you a list
of the boys from the
township of Wanamingo
where I reside.

Gilbert Olstad Zumbrota
nearest relative Mrs. John Olstad "

Alfred Westerube Kenyon
Nearest relative Mr. & Mrs. Martin Westerube
Kenyon Minn

Chester Tongen Zumbrota
Nearest relative Andrew Tongen "

Alfred Fladhammer "
Nearest relative O. K. Fladhammer "

This is all I have heard of
so far. yours truly
M. O. Floan Zumbrota
Minn

Sources and Acknowledgements

A host of knowledgeable scholars has diligently researched and documented Minnesota's divisive Great War years, a time when the home front seethed with uncertainty and fear. Confronted but not confounded by the era's complex issues and alarming events, these historians crafted ably researched narratives that enabled readers to comprehend the dangers facing the state and nation in 1917–18. I know the work of these historians. Their collected works provided the background necessary to begin this project.

William Watts Folwell, first president of the University of Minnesota and author of a still-respected history of the state, was present during those turbulent days. He later documented, in some astonishment, how Minnesota governance was conceded to a "dictatorship" known as the Minnesota Commission of Public Safety. While the MCPS played a lead role in a state inundated by ethnic, political and nationalist unrest, there was a fascinating supporting cast of angry farmers, radical labor groups, superpatriots, monopolists, secret agents, socialists, profiteers and provocateurs.

Folwell led the way for the growing contingent of researchers upon whom I relied. Carl H. Chrislock's *Watchdog of Loyalty: the Minnesota Commission of Public Safety During World War I,* a comprehensive, primary-sourced study, was particularly useful. So, too, were Robert L. Morlan's published works on the Nonpartisan League, specifically *Political Prairie Fire*, Millard L. Gieske's *Minnesota-Farmer Laborism: The Third Party Alternative*, and Carol E. Jenson's "Loyalty as a Political Weapon: The 1918 Campaign in Minnesota," *Minnesota History* (Summer 1972). Books, articles and commentaries by Frederick C. Luebke, John E. Haynes, La Vern J. Rippley, Bruce L. Larson and D. Jerome Tweton were among many that proved valuable.

It appeared to me, a Goodhue County native who has written extensively of its history, that the county might well serve as a Minnesota microcosm of those turbulent Great War days. After all, county officials held acknowledged leadership roles in disturbing statewide political and cultural conflicts, particularly the nativist superpatriotism and persistent anti-German sentiment bedeviling local residents and other Minnesotans. In Goodhue County, indictments and convictions for sedition, prejudice in courtrooms, biased newspaper reporting, coercive war loan campaigns and neighbor-against-neighbor violence became part of the wartime environment.

Researching Goodhue County's daily and weekly newspapers provided an information base, general news and, of equal importance, editorial comment. I read all the 1917–1918 issues of the *Cannon Falls Beacon, Zumbrota News, Kenyon News* and *Pine Island Record,* and editions of other weeklies selected by date. A thorough reading of the *Red Wing Daily Republican* and its rival *Daily Eagle* was also conducted, with a focus on sedition trials and follow-ups from incidents published in the county weekly papers. Important county stories with statewide applications were cross-checked in Twin Cities daily newspapers, particularly the *St. Paul Pioneer Press* and *Minneapolis Tribune*.

The Minnesota Historical Society houses Minnesota Commission of Public Safety (MCPS) Papers in the Minnesota State Archives. Helpful letters, documents and reports regarding individual Goodhue County residents produced insights into issues of the day. Among subgroups producing material for this book were Speakers Bureau Records, Agents Reports to T. G. Winter, Casualty Lists and Related Materials, Women's Committee Records and Correspondence with Counties. The National Nonpartisan League papers and its Correspondence, including Miscellaneous Papers in particular, produced insights into the internal goings-on of an NPL on the march and under fire.

MnHS Manuscript Collections provided access to the Joseph Gilbert Papers, Joseph A. A. Burnquist Papers, James A. Manahan and Family Papers, John Lind Papers, Susie Stageberg Papers, Arthur Le Sueur Papers and Knute Nelson Papers. Also located at the Minnesota Historical Society and used in this project: Goodhue County District Court Indictment Records, Minnesota War Records Commission Correspondence, America First Association Papers and Adjutant General: Home Guard Records unit reports.

My appreciation goes to archivist and Jean Chesley Library manager Afton Esson for facilitating research at the Goodhue County Historical Society. He helped make that organization's excellent photograph collection accessible. I am grateful to GCHS Executive Director Dustin Heckman for his support of this book project.

David Schmidtke, Deputy Director of the state Legislative Reference Library, and Ted Hathaway, Manager, Special Collections, Hennepin County Library, were generous with their time and expertise. Staff members at the Minnesota Historical Society proved, as always, knowledgeable and efficient, as did the professionals at Minneapolis Central Library and St. Paul's George Latimer Central Library.

It takes special talent and editorial skill to read the writings of another and then undertake to constructively evaluate their work. My wife, Diane Johnson, and our friend Rita Thofern both possess the knowledge, talent and patience for the job along with an unhesitating determination to challenge the author when needed. They hold the combined skills of a insightful critical reader and an able editor. Ruth Nerhaugen is another such reader-editor on this project. She possesses the added title of professional writer as a longtime member of the Red Wing *Republican Eagle* staff. Nerhaugen's lifelong interest in local history is particularly helpful with a book such as *Patriot Hearts*. My thanks are extended to each of these skilled, competent women.

A sincere thank you is offered to Carol Duff, a longtime friend of Red Wing and its history and creator of the Philip S. Duff, Jr. Endowment. She assures that the fund achieves its missions, among them encouraging residents to "educate themselves on the role of Red Wing…as part of the rest of the world." The Duff Endowment sponsored this book.

Image Credits

Goodhue County Historical Society—cover, vii, 3 bottom, 5 bottom, 8, 10, 13, 16 bottom, 17 left, 27, 29, 30, 32, 35, 37, 40, 42–43, 51, 62, 64, 69, 74, 76, 77, 80 right, 82, 84, 92, 94, 100, 103, 104, 105, 107 top left and bottom, 109, 112 bottom, 120, 122, 134–135, back cover left

Elizabeth Williams Gomoll collection—31

Minnesota Historical Society—1, 2, 36, 39, 60, 63, 88, 90, 96, 123, 154, back cover right

Minnesota Legislative Reference Library—5 top and right, 14, 16 middle, 17 right, 18

Hennepin County Library—16 top, 49, 50, 56, 80 left, 81, 107 top right, 117

A man who appears to be a Nonpartisan League organizer poses next to his auto. The image shown on the car door is the cover of *The Nonpartisan Leader*, June 28, 1917.

Notes

Choosing Sides

1 "Lindbergh is Hung in Effigy in Street Here during Night," *Red Wing Daily Republican*, June 15, 1918, 1. *Cannon Falls Beacon*, June 14, 1918, Meridel Le Sueur, *Crusaders: The Radical Legacy of Marian and Arthur Le Sueur* (St. Paul: Minnesota Historical Society Press, [hereafter MHS Press] 1984) xvii. Goodhue County had been reliably Republican since the party first appeared on the Minnesota ballot in 1859. Voters backed the Republican in every election for president, governor, U.S. senator and U.S. House of Representatives between 1859 and 1916 with one exception. They chose Theodore Roosevelt, the Bull Moose party candidate in 1912, Bruce M. White, et al., *Minnesota Votes: Election Returns by County for Presidents, Senators, Congressmen, and Governors, 1857–1977*, (St. Paul: Minnesota Historical Society, 1977) 18.

2 Carol Jenson, "Loyalty As a Political Weapon: The 1918 Campaign in Minnesota," *Minnesota History*, 43/2 (Summer 1972): 44–46.

3 William Watts Folwell, *A History of Minnesota* (St. Paul: MHS, 1926, 1969) 3: 557. Folwell provides a concise history of the Minnesota Commission of Public Safety in Appendix 19, 3: 556–575.

4 House File No. 270, 765.

5 Here and below, Robert L. Morlan, *Political Prairie Fire: The Nonpartisan League, 1915–1922* (St. Paul: MHS Press, 1955) 136–137. See *Nonpartisan Leader*, June 14, 1917, for a copy of Gilbert's position paper on the "war question." Dwight Riley Jessup, "Joseph Gilbert and the Minnesota Sedition Law: a Case Study in American Constitutional History," M. A. Thesis, University of Minnesota, 1965, 67.

6 For a Goodhue County view on 100-Percent loyalty see "To Make Old Goodhue 100 Percent American," *Red Wing Daily Republican*, March 15, 1918, 4, by Jens K. Grondahl, the newspaper's editor. Mark Sullivan, *Our Times: America and the Birth of the Twentieth Century*, Dan Rather, editor, (New York: Scribner, 1996) 477. Sullivan, an acclaimed magazine writer at the twentieth century's turn, originally wrote this six volume series in 1926. Rather edited and reduced the series to one book in 1996. The Roosevelt quote is found on page 477.

7 Here and below, Carl H. Chrislock, *Watchdog of Loyalty: The Minnesota Commission of Public Safety During World War I*, (St. Paul: MHS Press, 1991) 68–79. Chrislock points out the primary election contest between Burnquist and Neill on page 69.

8 Jenson, "Loyalty As a Political Weapon," 44–46. William Milliken, "Defenders of Business: The Minneapolis Civic and Commerce Association," *Minnesota History*, 50/2 (Spring 1986): 4. Had Red Wing businessman David M. Neill defeated Burnquist in their 1912 Republican battle to be the party's lieutenant governor candidate, Neill, not Burnquist, would have likely become governor.

9 Jenson, "Loyalty As a Political Weapon," 44–46. Morlan, *Political Prairie Fire*, 74–75, 90. National Nonpartisan League, *Memorial to the President of the United States Concerning Conditions in Minnesota, 1918*, 95, a copy dated April 1918 is found in MnHS Collections.

10 Bruce L. Larson, *Lindbergh of Minnesota: A Political Biography*, (New York: Harcourt Brace Jovanovich, Inc., 1973) 215–218. Lynn and Dora Haines, *The Lindberghs* (New York: Vanguard Press, 1931) 281.

11 "Loyalty Resolution," *Red Wing Daily Republican*, March 14, 1918, 4.

12 Gilbert v. State of Minnesota," 254 U.S. 325, 41 S. Ct. 125.

Seeds of Discord

13 George E. Akerson, "'War Measures' Due for Final Action in Legislature Monday," *Minneapolis Tribune*, April 6, 1917, 9; "Hot Words in Alien Bill Debate," St. Paul *Daily News*, April 5, 1917, 1, 5. Minnesota *House Journal*, 1917, 1468–69. In February 1918, the Commission of Public Safety passed an Alien Registration Act, ordering all unnaturalized aliens to register themselves and immediate family. These records are open to the public at the MnHS Gale Family Library in St. Paul.

14 Minnesota Legislative Reference Library, "Legislators Past & Present," Oscar Seebach, District 19, 1917–1918 and Anton V. "A. V." Anderson, District 19, 1915–1918. www.leg.state.mn.us. Franklyn Curtiss-

Wedge, *History of Goodhue County, Minnesota* (Chicago: H. C. Cooper and Co., 1909) 963–64. St. Paul *Daily News*, April 5, 1917, 5 [quote].

15 George F. Authier, "Minnesota Poet Honored by Having Poem Read into Records by Congressman," *Minneapolis Tribune*, April 8, 1917, 8.

16 Bernard S. Parker, *World War I Sheet Music Collection*, "Sheet Music (Filed Alphabetically by Song Title)" George A. Smathers Libraries, University of Florida, Gainesville.

17 "Singing of New Anthem is Heard 50 Miles Away," *Minneapolis Tribune*, October 13, 1917, 2. Madeline Angell, Red Wing, Minnesota, *Saga of a River Town* (Minneapolis: Dillon Press) 274. Parker, *World War I Sheet Music Collection*, A–13.

18 Here and below, Jens K. Grondahl to Mrs. Thos. G. Winter, October 26, 1917, see copy of letter in Appendix, page 138. The *Progressive Teacher*, 24/1 (January 1918): 40, *Virginia Journal of Education*, 12/1 (September 1918): 16, and *The Historical Outlook* 10 (January–December 1919): 206–207 were among periodicals receiving and printing copies of *America, My Country*. Other Grondahl poems printed in his newspaper during the war included "We Go to Get the Kaiser," "The Message from France," and "The Madness of Monarchs." Some around Goodhue County could still recall his 1898 Spanish-American War poem "Fighting for Cuba."

19 Here and below, for a sense of the Goodhue County economic environment about 1917, see Frederick L. Johnson, "The Growing Economic Base," and "The March of Progress" in *Goodhue County, Minnesota: A Narrative History* (Red Wing: Goodhue County Historical Society [hereafter GCHS], 2000) 149–160, 185–198. For background on the wheat boom, see Merrill E. Jarchow, "King Wheat." *Minnesota History* 29/1 (March 1948): 1–35 and Henrietta M. Larson, *The Wheat Market and the Farmer in Minnesota, 1858–1900*, (Ph.D. diss., New York: Columbia University, 1926) 68.

20 Among the prominent accumulating great wealth were Theodore Sheldon, who sold his Main Street mercantile business to enter the grain trade, later going into banking, and Lucius Hubbard, a newspaper owner who invested first in grain milling and later in railroads before becoming governor of Minnesota in 1881, see Johnson, *Goodhue County, Minnesota* 149–160, 185–198.

21 James J. Hill, "History of Agriculture in Minnesota," *Minnesota Collections* 8 (February 1918): 282–283.

22 Here and below, total value of implements and machinery, thanks to advances in mechanization, would jump from $631,000 in 1900, moving to $4 million in 1920, with livestock valuation advancing from $2 million to $7 million during the same period. The number of farms in the county was holding steady in the early 1900s—3,210 in 1900, 3,040 a decade later, and back up to 3,128 in 1920. Goodhue County farm values are found in Bureau of Census, Fourteenth Census of the United States, 1920, *Agriculture*, "Farms and Farm Property," (Washington: Government Printing Office, 1925) 498, and number of farms in county is from Bureau of Census, United States Census of Agriculture, *Number of Farms by States and Counties, 1925, 1920, 1910, and 1900* (Washington: Government Printing Office, 1925) 16.

23 Johnson, *Goodhue County, Minnesota*, 39–42. Theodore C. Nydahl, "The Early Norwegian Settlement of Goodhue County, Minnesota," Master's Thesis, University of Minnesota, 1929, 36–37. See Carleton C. Qualey, "Pioneer Norwegian Settlement," *Minnesota History* 12/3 (September 1931): 270 for 1874 visitor's quote. He added that in Wanamingo Township there were only two persons who were not Norwegian.

24 G. J. "Dick" Kunau, "Ethnic Settlement Patterns in Goodhue County," ca. 1975. Kunau was Goodhue County Agricultural Agent and a University of Minnesota professor who conducted a study of the county's nineteenth century ethnic settlements.

25 Ann Reagan, "The Irish," in June Drenning Holmquist, editor, *They Chose Minnesota: A Survey of the State's Ethnic Groups*, (St. Paul: MHS, 1981) 130. Richard Heaney, "Belle Creek Irish Settlement," unpublished, undated paper, GCHS biography files.

26 Holmquist, *They Chose Minnesota*, 159, 223–234, 251–252.

27 Theodore Roosevelt, "Hyphenated Americans," an October 12, 1915, New York City speech, http://unhyphenatedamerica.org/2014/05/05/teddy-roosevelt-unhyphenated-america-speech/.

28 Mark Sullivan, *Our Times: America a the Birth of the Twentieth Century*, edited by Dan Rather (New York: Scribner, 1966) 477.

29 Christian M. Dallavis, "Extending Theories of Culturally Responsive Pedagogy: An Ethnographic Examination of Catholic Schooling in an Immigrant Community in Chicago," PhD dissertation, University

of Michigan, 2008, 53, 65–67. "The Pope Against "Cahensleyism," *Chicago Tribune*, December 4, 1898, 34.

30 George L. Hicks and Philip E. Leis, "Ethnic Encounters: Identities and Contexts," in Holmquist, *They Chose Minnesota*, 12.

31 LaVern J. Rippley, "Conflict in the Classroom: Anti-Germanism in Minnesota Schools," *Minnesota History* 47/5 (Spring 1981): 170–183; quotation comes from a front page headline in Commission of Public Safety's weekly newspaper, *Minnesota in the War*, December 1, 1917, 1.

32 Here and below, Carl H. Chrislock, *Ethnicity Challenged: The Upper Midwest Norwegian–American Experience in World War I*, (Northfield: Norwegian-American Historical Association, 1981). Johnson, *Goodhue County: A Narrative History*, 201–203, 173–177. Centennial Book Committee, *Zumbrota: The First 100 Years* (Zumbrota: The Committee, 1956) 209–210. *Goodhue County in the World War*, 160–161. "May Organize Rural Guards," *Duluth Herald*, June 25, 1917, 7. "Auxiliary Denied Use of U.S. Uniform," *Cook County News Herald*, July 7, 1917, 3. Franklin F. Holbrook, *Minnesota in the Spanish-American War and the Philippine Insurrection*, (St. Paul: Minnesota War Records Commission, 1923) 1–8, 52–53, 309–314. Oscar Seebach to Jens [Grondahl] May 22, 1898, in GCHS Oscar Seebach biography file. After the Great War, Seebach, by then a Lieutenant Colonel, served in Germany as part of the army of occupation.

33 Here and two paragraphs below, Frederick L. Johnson, "Goodhue County's Battle with Booze and the Rest Island Experiment," *History Center News*, 50/1 (Winter 2016) 1–6. White, et al., *Minnesota Votes*, 184. Jack S. Blocker, Jr., *American Temperance Movement: Cycles of Reform* (Boston: Twayne Publishers, 1989) 67. Johnson, *Goodhue County Minnesota*, 133–138, 219.

34 *Legislators Past & Present*, Anton Julius Rockne, https://www.leg.state.mn.us/legdb/fulldetail?ID=13680 Frederick L. Johnson, "Anton Julius Rockne (1886–1950)" *MNopedia*, http://www.mnopedia.org/person/rockne-anton-julius-1868–1950.

35 Marilyn Albrecht, "Early Newspapers and Editors: The *Republican Eagle* and Its Predecessors," *Goodhue County Historical News*, 13/3 (November 1979): 1–3. "John Stone Pardee," Archives and Special Collections, Kathryn A. Martin Library, University of Minnesota, Duluth, https://libarchive.d.umn.edu/?p=creators/creator&id=656 Pardee was co-editor of *History of Duluth and St. Louis County*, 1910.

36 Here and below, Curtiss-Wedge, *History of Goodhue County*, 673–674. "William H. Putnam," Legislators Past & Present, Minnesota Reference Library, https://www.leg.state.mn.us/legdb/fulldetail?ID=14445. America's big move in banking, the creation of the Federal Reserve System as the central bank of the United States, resulted in a more stable national financial system. Twelve Federal Reserve Districts were organized, including District 9, based in Minneapolis. That district encompassed Minnesota, North and South Dakota and Montana.

37 Here and below, Martin J. Anderson, "The Development of the Dairy Products Industry in Minnesota," *Minnesota Dairy and Food Department Bulletin 52* (1914): 30–37. Frederick L. Johnson, "Arthur W. Parkin," (1872–1963) *MNopedia*, http://www.mnopedia.org/person/parkin-arthur-w-1872–1963. The state agriculture department endorsed Pine Island's importance in dairying by appointing town residents John J. Roch and John B. Baumgartner as Parkin's immediate successors. Johnson, *Goodhue County Minnesota*, 152–154. Mrs. C. T. (Ruth) Mondale, "Pine Island Cheese Industry: A. W. Parkin, 1873–1963," *Goodhue County Historical News*, 2/2 (November 1968): 1, 3.

38 John D. Hicks, "The People's Party in Minnesota," *Minnesota History* 5/5 (November 1924): 555–556. George M. Stephenson, *John Lind of Minnesota* (Minneapolis: University of Minnesota Press, 1935) 335. Frederick L. Johnson, "Professor Anderson's 'Food Shot from Guns'," *Minnesota History* 59/1 (Spring 2004): 7–15.

39 Julia Wiech Lief, "A Woman of Purpose, Julia B. Nelson," *Minnesota History* 47/8 (Winter 1981): 309–313.

40 Frederick L. Johnson, "Susie Williamson Stageberg, 1877–1961," *MNopedia*, http://www.mnopedia.org/person/stageberg-susie-williamson-1877–1961. Millard L. Gieske, *Minnesota Farmer–Laborism: The Third Party Alternative* (Minneapolis: University of Minnesota Press, 1979) 187–192. Elmer A. Benson, "Politics in My Lifetime," *Minnesota History* 47/4 (Winter 1980): 154–157.

41 Curtiss-Wedge, *History of Goodhue County*, 1033–1034. *Legislators Past & Present*, Frederick A. Scherf, https://www.leg.state.mn.us/legdb/fulldetail?ID=14673. Scherf's parents, Anton and Elizabeth, came to Goodhue County in 1860, claiming 160 acres in the midst of Hay Creek's German immigrant community. The couple later owned and operated a 593-acre farm. Fred Scherf to Knute Nelson, January 6 and February 1, 1916, Knute Nelson Papers, MnHS.

42 Frederick L. Johnson, "The Thirteenth Minnesota and the Battle for Manila," *MNopedia*,

http://www.mnopedia.org/event/thirteenth-minnesota-and-battle-manila. Franklin F. Holbrook, *Minnesota in the Spanish–American War and the Philippine Insurrection* (St. Paul: Minnesota War Records Commission, 1923). *Legislators Past & Present*, Oscar Seebach, https://www.leg.state.mn.us/legdb/fulldetail?ID=14720.

43 Here and below, "Dr. J. A. Gates," *Red Wing Daily Republican*, June 10, 1916, 4. Grondahl quoted Lynn Haines and his book *The Minnesota Legislature of 1909*, adding the appraisal by Haines, "has not been questioned publicly by Dr. Gates nor retracted by Mr. Haines." "Jens Kristian Grondahl," in Marion Shutter, ed. *Progressive Men of Minnesota* (Minneapolis: Minneapolis Journal, 1897) 88. *Legislators Past & Present*, Jens Kristian Grondahl, https://www.leg.state.mn.us/legdb/fulldetail?ID=13111. Final vote totals in Lieutenant Governor primary were Thomas Frankson, 23,831, James A. Peterson, 20,781, and Joseph Gates, 13,376.

44 "Recall Dr. Gates' Wanamingo Speech," *Red Wing Daily Republican*, June 17, 1916, 1, although this article is not attributed, Grondahl surely authored it. The article theorizes Dr. Gates was angry with Red Wing voters for not being supportive enough in earlier elections. Davis's comments are found in *Zumbrota News*, June 16, 1916, 2.

45 "Summary of North Dakota History–Nonpartisan League," www.history.nd.gov provides a helpful overview of the NPL in North Dakota. Charles R. Lamb, "The Nonpartisan League and Its Expansion into Minnesota," *North Dakota Quarterly* 49/3 (Summer 1981) 108–143. Larry Remele, "Things as They Should Be, Jeffersonian Idealism and Rural Rebellion in Minnesota and North Dakota," *Minnesota History* 51/1 (Spring 1988): 15–18. Morlan, *Political Prairie Fire*, 20–26. James A. Manahan, *Trials of a Lawyer* (Minneapolis: Farnham Printing & Stationery Co., 1933) 206–210. Charles E. Russell, *The Story of the Nonpartisan League; a Chapter in American Evolution*, (New York and London, 1920) 207–208, 212–213. On 232 Russell writes, "For years the minds of NPLers had concentrated on one question: "…whether North Dakota was to be ruled from the Great Northern Railroad Office in St. Paul or by its own people." Willis H. Raff, "Civil Liberties in Minnesota, World War I Period," M.A. Thesis, University of Minnesota, 1950, 100–102. Folwell, *History of Minnesota*, 3:546.

46 Herbert E. Gaston, *The Nonpartisan League* (New York: Harcourt, Brace and Howe, 1920) 60–61, Gaston worked as an NPL editor. Morlan, *Political Prairie Fire*, 20–26, 87. The NPL reported a membership of 40,000 in late 1916. The recruiters moved into Minnesota the following spring. Davis Douthit, *Nobody Owns Us: The Story of Joe Gilbert, Midwestern Rebel*, (Chicago: Cooperative League of the U.S.A., 1948) 98. Some $50,000 in income from enrollees had been spent on "Tin Henrys" driven by organizers in search of more initiates. Theodore Saloutos, "The Rise of the Nonpartisan League in North Dakota, 1915–1917," *Agricultural History* 20/1 (January 1946): 43–61. "Nonpartisan League," Summary of North Dakota History, State Historical Society of North Dakota website, http://history.nd.gov/ndhistory/npl.html, accessed January 17, 2014. Karen Starr, "Fighting for a Future: Farm Women of the Nonpartisan League," *Minnesota History* 48/6 (Summer 1983): 257.

47 Morlan, *Political Prairie Fire: The Nonpartisan League*, 20–26, 87. Carl H. Chrislock, *The Progressive Era in Minnesota, 1899–1918*, (St. Paul: MHS, 1971) 109–113, 145–147. *Story of the Non-Partisan League of North Dakota* (Aberdeen, SD: Aberdeen Daily American, 1916). Gaston, *The Nonpartisan League* 41–52. Tweton, "The Nonpartisan League's Rise to Power." Manahan, *Trials of a Lawyer*, 219–220 carries the first Townley quotation. For a thoughtful discussion on farmer discontent, see John D. Hicks, *The Populist Revolt: A History of the Farmers' Alliance and the People's Party* (Minneapolis: University of Minnesota Press, 1931). Remele,"Things as They Should Be," 15–22, adds perspective to the growing farmer unrest in Minnesota and North Dakota and the roots of the Nonpartisan League. Gaston, *The Nonpartisan League*, 5 is the source of the second Townley quote.

48 Morlan, *Political Prairie Fire*, 123, 126. Transcription of an interview with Joseph Gilbert, January 27, 1954, 3–4, Joseph Gilbert Papers, MnHS, Gilbert quotation found on page six. Douthit, *Nobody Owns Us*, 3–36, 45–58, the story of Gilbert's activism as a socialist begins on page 45, see page 91 for the account of his meeting with Townley. White, et al. *Minnesota Votes*, 16, 18–19.

49 Here and below, interview with Joseph Gilbert, 2–3, Gilbert said, "I was always socialist." White, et al. *Minnesota Votes*, 19, 182–183, support for the socialist candidate in 1916 was greatest in less populated northern counties: Lake led the way with 28 percent of 1,327 voters, followed by Roseau (19 percent), Beltrami (18 percent), Carlton and Aitkin (16 percent). Nick Salvatore, *Eugene V. Debs, Citizen and Socialist*, (Chicago: University of Illinois Press, 1983). *Minneapolis Tribune*, March 12, 1918, 1, 4. Two leading experts

on the League agreed the NPL was socialist; Robert L. Morlan noted, "Most of the League's organizers throughout the years were Socialists," and John D. Hicks, called the League's program essentially an experiment in state socialism. Morlan, *Political Prairie Fire*, 31. Theodore C. Blegen, *Minnesota: A History of the State* (St. Paul: MHS, 1975) 468.

50 Iric Nathanson, "Thomas Van Lear: City Hall's Working-Class Champion" *Minnesota History* 64/ 6 (Summer 2015): 225–228. William Millikan, "The Minneapolis Civic and Commerce Association Versus Labor During W. W. I," *Minnesota History* 50/1 (Spring 1986): 3–6. Peter Rachleff, "Turning Points in the Labor Movement: Three Key Conflicts," Clifford E. Clark, Jr. editor, *Minnesota in a Century of Change* (St. Paul: MHS, 1989) 204. David Paul Nord, "Minneapolis and the Pragmatic Socialism of Thomas Van Lear," *Minnesota History* 45/1 (Spring 1976): 3–10, Van Lear and many in the Minneapolis organized labor movement left the Socialist Party because of that group's failure to support the war effort. They organized the Municipal Nonpartisan League, later enlarged into the Working People's Nonpartisan Political League.

51 Doris Kearns Goodwin, *The Bully Pulpit: Theodore Roosevelt, William Howard Taft, and the Golden Age of Journalism* (New York: Simon & Schuster, 2013), see Chapter Twenty-Eight, "Bosom Friends, Bitter Enemies," for a description of the Roosevelt-Taft break and the 1912 Republican convention. Roger E. Wyman, "Insurgency in Minnesota: The Defeat of James A. Tawney in 1910," *Minnesota History* 40/7 (Fall 1967): 317–329 considers the 1910 primary election contest in the first district race for Congress between the progressive Sydney Anderson and the Old Guard's James Tawney. Anderson won in all but two counties in the district, taking 55.8% of the Republican vote. It was the kind of split vote that worried Republican leaders.

52 Here and below, White, et al., *Minnesota Votes*, 18, 170–180. Chrislock, *The Progressive Era in Minnesota*, 54–58.

53 Gilbert Papers, "Interview with Joseph Gilbert, January 27, 1954," 6–7. Burnquist made the statement in a widely publicized letter to the Nonpartisan League's March 1918 political convention in St. Paul. See Chrislock, *Watchdog of Loyalty*, 294.

54 Gilbert Papers, "Interview with Joseph Gilbert, January 27, 1954," 6–7. White, et al., *Minnesota Votes*, 19.

55 Nord, "Minneapolis and the Pragmatic Socialism of Thomas Van Lear," 3–10. Chrislock, *Watchdog of Loyalty*, 63. Gaston, *The Nonpartisan League*, 158–172.

56 Martin Gilbert, *A History of the Twentieth Century, Volume One: 1900–1933*, (New York: William Morrow and Co., 1997) 70–73, 474–477, provides an overview of the rise of the Bolshevik communists in Russia and the first stages of their revolution. Anthony Read, *The World On Fire: 1919 and the Battle with Bolshevism* (New York: W. & W. Norton and Co., 2008), see "Prologue: The Spark," 3–11. "Socialism's Offensive," *New York Times*, Dec. 13, 1917, 12. A sampling from *New York Times* editions from late 1917 note the Bolshevik brutality: "Petrograd Battle Is Still In Doubt," Nov. 14, 1917, 1, "Rebels Destroy Shrines Of Moscow," Nov. 19, 2, "Outside The Pale," Nov. 25, 1917, E2, "The Bolshevist Mind," Dec. 10, 1917, 14, "Anarchists," Dec. 27, 1917, 10. Headlines in 1918 became more alarming.

57 Morlan, *Political Prairie* Fire, 136–137. William Millikan, "Defenders of Business," 4.

58 *Are You Ready to Hand Over Your Farm to a Bunch of Socialist Adventurers: That's What Townleyism Means, Mr. Farmer*, 1918, National Nonpartisan League, "Printed Materials, Pamphlets: Anti-League, Anti-Socialist, and Loyalty Publications, undated and 1910–1924," Roll 2, Frame 76, M182A, MnHS.

59 Charles R. Lamb, "The Nonpartisan League and Its Expansion into Minnesota," *North Dakota Quarterly* 49/3 (Summer 1981): 130–134.

60 Thomas Fleming, *The Illusion of Victory* (New York: Basic Books, 2003) 60–62.

61 Here and below, Robert L. Morlan, "The Nonpartisan League and the Minnesota Campaign of 1918," *Minnesota History* 34/6 (Summer 1955): 221. Interview with Joseph Gilbert, January 27, 1954, 4, Joseph Gilbert papers, MnHS.

62 James Manahan and Family papers, *Autobiography* [first draft] Chapter 11–12. The draft is handwritten in pencil and not paginated.

63 Gilbert interview, 4. Minnesota Historic Farms Study, *Developmental Periods in the Historic Context "Euro-American Farms in Minnesota, 1820–1960*," www.dot.state.mn, 3.43–3, 46. Lamb, "The Nonpartisan League and Its Expansion into Minnesota," 118.

64 "An Interview Henry Hinrichs, the history of the Featherstone prairie and farming in his lifetime, July 26, 1978," GCHS Oral History Collection, 1.5.74, File 74, 32–33, 35–37, 54.

65 Gilbert's United States passport provides descriptive physical detail, Gilbert Papers, MnHS.

66 Douthit, *Nobody Owns Us*, 4–16. Hjalmar Bjornson, "Bitter Free Speech Fight Recalled in Biography of Minnesota Rebel," unattributed, undated newspaper clipping in the Joseph Gilbert Papers, MnHS.

67 Gilbert interview, 6. Morlan, *Political Prairie Fire*, 36, 123, 126–127, 136. Douthit, *Nobody Owns Us*, 98, 102, 105. A description of the contentious Federation of Labor convention is carried in Chrislock, *Watchdog of Loyalty*, 184–185.

68 Here and two paragraphs below, Marilyn Albrecht, "Early Newspapers and Editors," *Goodhue County Historical News*, 13/3 (November 1979): 2–3. National Newspaper Association, "NNA: The Early Years," https://www.nnaweb.org/about-nna?articleTitle=nna-the-early-years--1316122170--54--about-nna. The plaque honoring Briggs and the founding of the NEA remains on the building to this day.

69 *Goodhue County in the World War* (Red Wing: Red Wing Printing, 1919) 179–180.

70 Odd S. Lovoll, "Gaa Paa: A Scandinavian Voice of Dissent," *Minnesota History* 52/3 (Fall 1990): 88–99. Lovoll considers other radical newspapers of the era in this study.

71 Chrislock, *Watchdog of Loyalty*, 28–29.

72 Here and three paragraphs below, a summary of the legislative service of Grondahl, Finstuen and Rockne is found in the Minnesota Legislative Reference Library: Legislators Past & Present, www.leg.state.mn.us. W. F. Toensing, *Minnesotan Congressmen, Legislators, and Other Elected Officials*, (St. Paul: MHS, 1971) 37, 46, 102. "Goodhue County Editors," [photo page] *Goodhue County in the World War*, 184–185. Albert Marshall, "A Brief History of Red Wing Newspapers," manuscript, GCHS collections, Red Wing. Marilyn Albrecht, "Early Newspapers and Editors," and Jeannette S. Burch, "The Cannon Falls Weeklies," *Goodhue County Historical News*, 13/3 (November 1979): 1–4. 5. Accounts of other Goodhue County newspapers—Frank Callister "Kenyon Papers Survived Many Publishers," Howard Bailey, "Zumbrota Newspapers," Leah Nell Peterson, "*Goodhue County Tribune*," and Loraine M. Vettel, "History of Pine Island Newspapers"—are in *Goodhue County Historical News*, 14/1 (February 1980): 1–4. A photo of Sandstad in his Spanish-American War uniform is in *Goodhue County in the World War*, 33A. Curtiss-Wedge, *History of Goodhue County, Minnesota*, 649–661. Frederick L. Johnson, "Anton Julius Rockne (1868–1950)" *MNopedia*, December 11, 2013, http://www.mnopedia.org/person/rockne-anton-julius-1868-1950.

73 Here and below, "Jens K. Grondahl," Curtiss-Wedge, *History of Goodhue County*, 658–660, profile of Grondahl includes a photograph. George F. Authier, "Minnesota Poet Honored by Having Poem Read into Records by Congressman," *Minneapolis Tribune*, April 8, 1917, 8.

74 The quotation source regarding Grondahl's "imbibing" is Albert Marshall, the newspaperman who took over the *Republican Eagle* in 1940. See Marshall, "A Brief History of Red Wing Newspapers," manuscript, GCHS; Johnson, *Goodhue County: A Narrative History* 238, 348, n5; Angell, *Red Wing: Saga of a River Town*, 210–211, 241.

75 Frank Callister, "Early Newspapers and Editors," *Goodhue County Historical News*, 14/1 (February 1980) 2–3. Cole and Finstuen bought out Anton Rockne (co-owner of the *Zumbrota News*), Dr. Joseph A. Gates, and Adolf Knutson, who had combined to save the weakening *Leader* at the century's turn.

America, Goodhue County, and the Onset of War

76 "Registration Proceeding Quietly Throughout U.S.," *Red Wing Daily Republican*, June 5, 1917, 1. "2567 Men in County Register," *Red Wing Daily Republican*, June 5, 1917, 1.

77 March, *History of the World War* 469–470. Matthew J. Davenport, *First Over There: The Attack on Cantigny, America's First Battle of World War I* (New York: St. Martin's Press, 2015) 40–48.

78 Here and below, A. J. Rockne to C. W. Henke, October 12, 1917, Minnesota Commission of Public Safety, *Speaker Bureau Records*, Goodhue County, MnHS. Henke headed the state Speakers Bureau, a Commission of Public Safety organization.

79 Ibid. Rockne also cited Goodhue County's tradition of sending men into federal military service, "In 1898 and again last year [1916 Mexican border deployment], this county furnished more soldiers than any county in the state in proportion of its population."

80 Mark Sullivan, *Our Times: America at the Birth of the Twentieth Century* [condensed version, Dan Rather, editor] (New York: Scribner, 1996) 491–492. Francis A. March, *History of the World War* (Philadelphia: United Publishers of the United States and Canada, 1919) 464–467.

81 Here and below, Centennial Book Committee, *Zumbrota: The First 100 Years* (Zumbrota: 1956) 209. Angell, *Saga of a River Town*, 252, 254, 307. *Zumbrota News*, August 13, 1917.

82 "Ordered to Mobilize," *Zumbrota News*, June 23, 1916, 2. *Zumbrota: The First 100 Years*, 207–209. "National Guard is Called Out by Wilson as a Result of Mexican Crisis," *Red Wing Daily Republican*, June 19, 1916, 1, 7. "Off to War," *Zumbrota News*, June 30, 1916, 2. "Thousands Bid Goodbye to the Departing Soldiers," *Red Wing Daily Republican*, June 26, 1916, 1. Folwell, *History of Minnesota*, 3: 529–530. U.S. Department of State Archive, "Punitive Expedition in Mexico, 1916–1917" http://2001-2009.state.gov/r/pa/ho/time/wwi/108653.htm. Max Boot, *The Savage Wars of Peace* (New York: Basic Books, 2002), see chapter 8, "The Dusty Trail: The Pancho Villa Punitive Expedition, 1916–1917," 182–204 for an overview this expedition. After two failed attempts to welcome the Zumbrota unit back with a formal banquet—uncertain troop train connections resulted in confusion—Company D soldiers arrived in Zumbrota a half-hour after midnight on December 20. They then enjoyed the long-delayed home-cooked meal.

83 Here and below, "Hundreds Picnic with 'L' Soldiers," and "Thousands Say Farewell to Patriots," *Red Wing Daily Republican*, August 27, 1917, 1. *Zumbrota: The First 100 Years*, 209–212. *Goodhue County in the World War*, 185–186.

84 *Goodhue County in the World War*, 160–161, 183–186. Adjutant General, National Guard, Home Guard Records, "Enlistment Papers and Oaths of Office, 1917–1919," 5th Battalion, Company A, MnHS. Lieut. Harvey Johnson, "Company L," *Goodhue County in the World War*, 183–185. *Zumbrota: The First 100 Years*, 209–210. "Company D," *Goodhue County in the World War*, 185–186.

85 Lewis's poems from 1917 are found in the April 27, May 25 and July 20 *Cannon Falls Beacon* editions.

86 The Lewis quotations come from the *Cannon Falls Beacon*, "Local Happenings," June 1, 1917, 4 and June 22, 4.

87 See "County Correspondence," *Cannon Falls Beacon*, June 22, 1917, 4; August 24, 1918, 2.

88 Here and below, "New Items," *Zumbrota News*, August 10, 1917, 7. Douthit, *Nobody Owns Us*, 106–107. Morlan, *Political Prairie Fire*, 126, notes N. S. Randall's high NPL ranking.

89 "State v. N. S. Randall," *Minnesota Reports: Cases Argued and Determined in the Supreme Court of Minnesota*, Vol. 143, (St. Paul: Keefe-Davidson Co., 1920) 203. Randall was also accused of saying, "The rot that is being pulled off nowadays by our government with reference to this war is something so disgraceful that you have no idea of it…. We must save food for the allies they say; we must save food for them whether we get anything for ourselves."

90 Douthit, *Nobody Owns Us*, 106–108, Finstuen reported Gilbert's mention that the U.S. government was shipping a lot of coffins to Europe, hoping that "they won't be used for our boys." *Minnesota Reports*, Vol. 143, 204. "Townley Case Heard by Supreme Court," *Minneapolis Tribune*, April 29, 1919, 9.

91 *Minnesota Reports: Cases Argued and Determined in the Supreme Court of Minnesota*, Vol. 142, (St. Paul: Keefe and Davidson Co., 1920) 484–486. Justice Andrew Holt, in his dissent, used the term "brawl" to describe the Kenyon barbershop incident. "Kenyon Doctor Takes Stand Against Martin," *Minneapolis Tribune*, June 30, 1918, 9. There are small differences between the *Minnesota Reports* account and that of the newspaper.

92 *Minnesota Reports*, Vol. 143, 204. "Nonpartisan League Organizer, Called Traitor, Ejected from Barbershop, Wants $50,000," *Minneapolis Tribune*, September 27, 1917, 5. "The State News in Brief," *Zumbrota News*, October 5, 1917, 6, mentioned "coat of tar and feathers" in reference to the August 18 incident in Kenyon.

93 "Local Happenings," *Cannon Falls Beacon*, October 5, 1917, 5.

94 *Goodhue County in the World War*, 178. Among the news stories about Gates's defeat: "Kellogg has Big Lead for Senator in Early Returns," *St. Paul Pioneer Press*, June 20, 1916, 4 and "Frankson Nominated Over J. A. Peterson," *Minneapolis Journal*, June 20, 1916, 6. Final vote totals in the Lieutenant Governor primary were Thomas Frankson, 23,831, James A. Peterson, 20,781, and Joseph Gates, 13,376. In November 1917 the Minnesota Republican Party added the Kenyon doctor to its Central Committee.

95 *Goodhue County in the World War*, 92–93. "Doings in Kenyon and the Vicinity," *Kenyon News*, June 6, 1918, 1. "Farewell to Dr. Gates," *Kenyon News*, August 1, 1918, 1. "Gates family tree has deep Kenyon roots," Rochester *Post Bulletin*, July 26, 1990, http://www.postbulletin.com/gates-family-tree-has-deep-kenyon-roots-cutline-joe-gates/article_f877ad51-0b0b-5941-b9e4-77d411e33099.html. "Foes of Burnquist Name New Member of State Committee," *Minneapolis Tribune*, November 16, 1917, 11. *Kenyon News*, June 22, 1922. "American Legion Post Still Active in Kenyon," *Kenyon Leader*, March 23, 2105.

96 John S. Pardee to T. G. Winter, August 7, 1917, Minnesota Commission of Public Safety, Agents' Reports to

T. G. Winter, 1917–1919. "John Stone Pardee," Archives and Special Collections, Kathryn A. Martin Library, University of Minnesota, Duluth, https://libarchive.d.umn.edu/?p=creators/creator&id=656.

97 National Nonpartisan League Papers Undated and 1913–1927, Roll 4 has a series of documents following the title page "Anarchy in Minnesota" which contains a transcription of Sheriff Boehlk's letter to Townley. The NPL report noted that a fire hose "had been laid from a hydrant with the apparent purpose of turning it upon the crowd assembled to hear the address."

98 National and State Executive Committee of the National Nonpartisan League, *Memorial to the President of the United States Concerning Conditions in Minnesota* (St. Paul: National Nonpartisan League, April 1918) 40–42. Jenson, "Loyalty As a Political Weapon," 49.

99 "Alleged Nopartisan (sic) Organizer Silenced," *Minneapolis Tribune*, October 26, 1917, 13. W. H. Putnam to H. W. Libby, secretary of the Minnesota Commission of Public Safety Commission, October 25, 1917, State Archives, Minnesota Commission of Public Safety, "Correspondence with Counties," Goodhue County, Box 1.

100 "Farmers Aroused: Good. County Farmers' Association Protest Barring of Speaker," *Zumbrota News*, November 16, 1917, 2.

101 W. H. Putnam to H. W. Libby, October 25, 1917. "Farmers Aroused," *Zumbrota News*, November 16, 1917, 2.

102 Ibid. State Senator Rockne had become chairman of the Senate Finance Committee in 1915 and exerted considerable power at the state level. See "Rockne, Anton Julius," *MNopedia* entry by author http://www.mnopedia.org/person/rockne-anton-julius-1868-1950.

103 Quotation is from the *Nonpartisan Leader* of October 4, 1917, 5–6, 15 and found in Jessup, *Joseph Gilbert and the Minnesota Sedition Law*, 71.

104 "Up Hader Way," *Zumbrota News*, December 14, 1917, 3. Gjemse ran a farm in Hader that included apples and berries. A letter from Gjemse is found in "Your Corner," *The Minnesota Horticulturist* 26 (1896): 307. *Catalogue of Carleton College, 1890–91*, 50, shows Lars Johnson Gjemse was a junior in the English Academy at the Northfield, Minnesota, school.

105 "Nonpartisans Ask State Protection," *St. Paul Pioneer Press*, October 11, 1917, 5. Douthit, *Nobody Owns Us*, 114–117.

106 Douthit, *Nobody Owns Us*, 116.

107 "Meeting Largely Attended," *Zumbrota News*, November 16, 1917, 4. The Barnes-authored pamphlets were titled, "Why Burnquist Cannot Run on His Record," and "What Will You Do About This," National Nonpartisan League Papers, Undated and 1913–1927, MnHS Primary Resources, Pamphlets.

108 "Big Loyalty Meeting," *Zumbrota News*, November 16, 1917, 2.

109 "Local News," *Zumbrota News*, December 7, 1917, 2. Elwyn B. Robinson, *History of North Dakota* (Lincoln: University of Nebraska Press, 1966) 332, 340. Baer got his start with the NPL as political cartoonist for *Nonpartisan Leader*, at that time published in Fargo. "Non-Partisan Meeting," *Zumbrota News*, December 14, 1917, 3.

110 Jens Grondahl, "To Make Old Goodhue 100 Percent American," *Red Wing Daily Republican*, March 15, 1918, 4.

111 Franklin F. Holbrook and Livia Appel, *Minnesota in the War with Germany* (St. Paul: MHS, 1932) 2: 226–228. Peter Rachleff, "Turning Points in the Labor Movement: Three Key Conflicts," in *Minnesota in a Century of Change*, Clifford E. Clark Jr., editor (St. Paul: MnHS Press, 1989) 204–205. Chrislock, *Watchdog of Loyalty*, 194. *Report of the Minnesota Commission of Public Safety* (St. Paul: L. F. Dow Co., 1919) 12. Brig. Gen. W. F. Rhinow, *Adjutant General of the State of Minnesota, Thirtieth Biennial Period Ending, December 31, 1918* (Minneapolis: 1919), 1: 253–259.

112 Mark Sullivan, *Our Times*, 518–521. "The Home Guards," *Goodhue County in the World War*, 160–161. March, *History of the World War*, 469.

113 Here and below, "The Home Guards," *Goodhue County in the World War*, 160.

114 Here and below, William Millikan, "Defenders of Business: The Minneapolis Civic and Commerce Association," *Minnesota History* 50/1 (Spring 1986): 13–17, quotation found on page 10.

115 Chrislock, *Watchdog of Loyalty*, 200. Millikan, "Defenders of Business," 14–17.

116 George M. Stephenson, *John Lind of Minnesota* (Minneapolis: University of Minnesota Press, 1935) 335. Chrislock, *Watchdog of Loyalty*, 200.

117 Douthit, *Nobody Owns Us*, 5–7. Chrislock, *Watchdog of Loyalty*, 183–187.

118 Gieske, *Minnesota Farmer-Laborism: The Third-party Alternative*, 34–35. William Millikan, "Maintaining 'Law and Order': The Minneapolis Citizen's Alliance in the 1920s," *Minnesota History* 51/6 (Summer 1989) 220, 228–229 discusses APL operations in Minneapolis. *The Gas Age*, 41 (January to June 1918): 509 notes "Fred E. Schornstein has assumed his new position at manager of Red Wing Gas, Light and Power Co." Horace C. Peterson and Gilbert E. Fite, *Opponents of the War, 1917–1918* (Madison: University of Wisconsin Press) 18 ff. *Goodhue County in the World War*, 177.

119 Emerson Hough, *The Web* (Chicago: American Protective League, 1919) offers a spirited defense of the APL and its war against sedition. It attacks groups the APL considered anti-war and even treasonous. See page 76 for its critique of the Nonpartisan League and its "…socialistic schemes." *Goodhue County in the World War*, 177. Chrislock, *Watchdog of Loyalty*, 271. Operative No. 71, *A Story of War Service Rendered by the Minneapolis Division of the American Protective League* (Minneapolis? 1919?).

120 "Loyalty of Towns Throughout the State Pledged at Meetings," *Minneapolis Tribune*, December 20, 1917, 8, counties holding Loyalty meetings included Martin, Rock, Pipestone, Cottonwood, Lincoln, Lyon, Jackson, Douglas and Traverse. "Former German Nobleman Coming," *Red Wing Republican Eagle*, March 13, 1918, 1, notes Neill arranged for F. Osten-Sachen, a German nobleman with three sons in the U.S. military, as featured speaker for the America First Goodhue County tour. Chrislock, *The Progressive Era in Minnesota*, 161–163.

121 "Memo: Pine Island Interference, League Meeting, January 19, 1918," *National Nonpartisan League Papers*, Roll 4, Undated and 1913–1927, MnHS. Mayor Parkin later told Williams that he would not permit the soliciting of members for the League that day. Williams again agreed. J. Arthur Williams made anti-NPL author Aloysius Anthony Vissers's list [*The Nonpartisan League vs. the Home* (Milwaukee: Burdick-Allen Co., 1922)] page 34, of "Paid Organizers and Leaders of the National Non-Partisan League." Vissers wrote Williams was a former Socialist candidate for mayor of Grand Forks, ND.

122 Jenson, "Loyalty As a Political Weapon," 50–51. *Anarchy in Minnesota*, pamphlet in National Nonpartisan League Papers, MnHS Manuscript Collection.

123 James Manahan's handwritten autobiography, first draft, not paginated, chapters 11 and 12, James Manahan and Family Papers, MnHS.

124 State v. A. C. Townley and Another [Joseph Gilbert], May 2, 1919, No. 21,266, in Henry Burleigh Wenzell, *Minnesota Reports*, Vol. 142, "Cases Argued and Determined in the Supreme Court of Minnesota, February 7–May 29, 1919" (St. Paul: 1920) 326–333. "Townley's Arrest Ordered," *Minneapolis Tribune*, February 12, 1918, 1, Townley's arrest for conspiring to discourage enlistments was tied to Gilbert's earlier actions and ensuing trial at Lakeville. Prosecutors asserted Gilbert was acting as "an agent of Townley."

125 Here and below, Douthit, *Nobody Owns Us*, 122–123. Douthit uses Gilbert's colorful account of the Jackson County incidents on page 117. Manahan, *Trials of a Lawyer*, 235–236 provides his version of the auction of Kaiser Bill, the parrot.

126 Manahan, *Trials of a Lawyer*, 237–238. "Mob Threatens James Manahan," *Red Wing Daily Republican*, February 12, 1918, 1. "Nonpartisan Body Manager Sent to Jail 3 Months," *Minneapolis Tribune*, February 13, 1918, 1.

127 "Nonparty League is Barred From Martin County," *Minneapolis Tribune*, February 14, 1918, 1. "Action of Deputy Prevents Gathering at Town Far From Train," *Minneapolis Tribune*, February 19, 1918, 1.

128 Douthit, *Nobody Owns Us*, 127–133. "Townley Arrested Together With Aide as Draft Hinderer," *Minneapolis Tribune*, March 1, 1918, 13.

129 "Held Caucus and Drove Out Breidal," *Kenyon News*, March 7, 1918, 1. *Red Wing Daily Republican*, May 1, 1918, 3 gave the number in the Kenyon crowd.

130 Here and below, "Local News," *Zumbrota News*, March 15, 1918, 6. "Nonparty Agent is Deported by Village Caucus," *St. Paul Pioneer Press*, March 8, 1918, 1.

131 George Brobeck to O. G. Sandstad, editor, *Kenyon News*, February 28, 1918, 1.

 57 The Cannon Falls report is carried, along with other news items, in column four next to the Breidal article, see *Kenyon News*, March 7, 1918, 1. Johnson, *Goodhue County*, 159.

132 *Faribault News* item is found in *Kenyon News* March 14, 1918, 4, in an untitled paragraph at the bottom of page 4. "Resolution," *Kenyon News*, March 8, 1918, 5.

134 Mrs. Fred Kingsley to State Safety Commission, March 1, 1918, Minnesota Commission of Public Safety, "Correspondence with Counties," Box 1, MnHS collections.

135 *Indictment Record 2, 1897–1922*, 188–199, Minnesota District Court (Goodhue County) Indictment Records, MnHS, State Archives. "Strong Arm of the Law to Stop Sedition, Local Residents Charged with Seditious Acts," *Red Wing Daily Republican*, March 14, 1918, 1.

136 Jens Grondahl, "A Patriotic Classic," *Red Wing Daily Republican*, March 12, 1918, 2.

137 Here and one paragraph below, *State of Minnesota, First Judicial District, District Court, Goodhue County, Indictment Record 2, 1897–1922*, File 909, March 14, 1918, 185–193, 196, 201. The handwritten indictments prepared in this District Court ledger by clerk C. S. Dana are found in the collections of MnHS. Don and May Seebach, *The Ancestors and Descendants of Ehrenfried Seebach (1808–1897) and His Wife Maria Kruz (1815–1887)*, 229, 239, 247–248.

138 *Indictment Record 2, 1897–1922*, 193. "Eight Charged with Sedition; Released on Bail," *Red Wing Daily Republican*, March 18, 1918, 1, 4.

139 Ibid. 196, 201–202. There were two Goodhue men, father and son, by the name of Herman Zemke living in Goodhue at the time of the indictment, March 14, 1918. The elder Zemke's brother, Frederick, was married to Maria Seebach, a sister of the indicted John Seebach. This information comes from Brad Hernlem who has studied Seebach family records and believes the elder Zemke was the person indicted on the 14th.

140 *State of Minnesota, First Judicial District, District Court, Goodhue County, Indictment Record 2, 1897–1922*, Files 894 (Gilbert), 895 (Randall) 899 (Martin). Gilbert A. Flom, John A. Bradley, Thomas A. Tosa, and Charles Lindholm, who claimed to be in attendance at the Kenyon meeting and supported the testimony against Gilbert and Randall, did not testify. "Strong Arm of the Law to Stop Sedition," *Red Wing Daily Republican*, March 14, 1918, 1.

141 *Indictment Record 2, 1897–1922*, file 894, page 194.

142 "Indicted Men Arraigned in District Court: Eight Charged with Sedition; Released on Bail," *Red Wing Daily Republican*, March 18, 1918, 1–2. Ibid. 203. *Indictment Record 2, 1897–1922*, file 894, page 194. "Nonpartisan Leaguers Plead Not Guilty to Disloyal Utterances," *Minneapolis Tribune*, March 19, 1918, 7.

143 Here and below, Jens Grondahl, "The Mark of Cain," *Red Wing Daily Republican*, March 14, 1918, 4.

144 "Strong Arm of the Law to Stop Sedition," *Red Wing Daily Republican*, March 14, 1918, 1. *Goodhue County in the World War*, 178 lists "Judge Albert Johnson" as a ward chairman of the America First Association.

145 Douglas A. Hedin, *Results of Elections of Justices to the Minnesota Supreme Court, 1857–2010*, www.minnesotalegalhistoryproject, October 20, 2010, 41, 44, 47–48 [revised thereafter]. Johnson failed to make it through the June 21, 1920, primary for associate justice. He placed second in the eight-person September 16, 1924, primary for chief justice but lost to incumbent Samuel B. Wilson in the November general election.

146 "Loyalty Resolution," *Red Wing Daily Republican*, March 14, 1918, 4. Members of the Grand Jury were H. P. Hulebak, foreman, Robert W. Putnam, John Bremer, H. G. Husbyn, N. F. Nelson, J. C. Brunkhorst, August Klug, W. F. Deline, Oscar Holm, O. K. Severson, Hjalmar Olson, John P. Mark, Ed M. Schenach, John Davidson, Samuel Kraft, Anders Mosberg, H. G. Tiedemann, J. H. Bradley, H. U. Pattridge, Martin Vomhof, Otto Andrist, W. D. Hayward, H. W. Nelson. State of Minnesota, *First Judicial District, District Court, Goodhue County, Minutes, 1854–1982*, March 14, 1918, 57.

147 Charles R. Lamb, "The Nonpartisan League and Its Expansion into Minnesota," *North Dakota Quarterly* 40/ 3 (Summer 1918): 118, 130-133. See Table 6, "Nationality and Date of Joining the NPL." Lamb, in evaluating Table 5 "Nationality" concludes, "From this general description it would seem that the most telling explanation of NPL membership is *ethnic background* [emphasis added], not economic or type of farming variables." See also Ralph Lee Kloske, "Nonpartisan Leaguers in Minnesota: A Consideration of Organizers, Members and Voters" (Master's thesis, University of Wisconsin–Madison, 1976) 186–189. Folwell. *A History of Minnesota*, 3: 558. Barbara Stuhler, *Ten Men of Minnesota and American Foreign Policy, 1898–1968* (St. Paul: MnHS, 1973) 38, Stuhler points out nearly forty percent of the new Minnesotans were ethnically Scandinavian (Swedish, Norwegian, Danish), and five percent Irish.

148 *Report of the Minnesota Commission of Public Safety* (St. Paul: L. F. Dow Co., 1919) 81.

A Deepening Divide

149 Russell, *The Story of the Nonpartisan League*, 212.

150 "Joseph Gilbert speech, St. Paul, December 5, 1917," 10–11, National Nonpartisan League Papers undated and 1913–1914, Roll 4, has a transcription of Gilbert's speech to streetcars workers.

151 Here and below, "Governor Refuses to Talk at St. Paul Convention; Disloyalty Charged," *Minneapolis Tribune*, March 12, 1918, 1. Gov. Burnquist specifically singled out Joseph Gilbert for his "disloyalty." Among the many newspapers carrying the full version of Gov. Burnquist's letter to the NPL was *Kenyon News*, March 14, 1918, 2. Crislock, *The Progressive Era in Minnesota*, 164–165. "Governor Refuses to Talk at St. Paul Convention," *Minneapolis Tribune*, March 12, 1918, 1. Jenson, "Loyalty as a Political Weapon," *Minnesota History* 43/ 2 (Summer 1972): 52. For copies of the NPL invitation to Burnquist and his reponse, see Arthur Le Sueur Papers, Box 2, Correspondence Jan.–Dec. 1918, MnHS, Manuscript Notebooks.

152 A circular with a copy of the Burnquist letter is found in Minnesota Commission of Public Safety, Main Files, Nonpartisan League Folder 1, MnHS collections.

153 Here and below, "A. C. Townley is Arrested Second Time," *Minneapolis Tribune*, March 12, 1918, 1. "Prosecutor Puts Treason Brand on Nonpartisans," *Minneapolis Tribune*, March 15, 1918, 1. Crislock, *The Progressive Era in Minnesota*, 164–165. "Gilbert, Martin and Randall Indicted," *Minneapolis Tribune*, March 15, 1918, 5.

154 Nathanson, "Thomas Van Lear: City Hall's Working-Class Champion" 225–228. Millikan, "The Minneapolis Civic and Commerce Association Versus Labor During W. W. I," 3–6.

155 White, *Minnesota Votes*, 8, 101–102. Congress members who voted against the war with Germany were Charles R. Davis (Third District), Harold Knutson (Sixth), and Carl Van Dyke, (Fourth, St. Paul). Ernest Lundeen of Minneapolis and the Fifth Congressional District also voted against the war resolution. Chrislock, *Watchdog of Loyalty*, 48.

156 Larson, *Lindbergh of Minnesota*, 216–218.

157 White, *Minnesota Votes*, 92–98 details Lindbergh's Sixth District support as he won election to Congress five consecutive times, 1906–1914. Larson, *Lindbergh of Minnesota*, 179–190, 211–213, notes the ethnic makeup of the Sixth District. Morlan, *Political Prairie Fire*, 192–193. Lynn and Dora Haines, *The Lindberghs*. 281. A. Scott Berg, *Lindbergh* (New York: G. P. Putnam's Sons, 1998) 48–49, Berg's biography of Charles Sr.'s internationally famous aviator son notes the former congressman's slide "into political ignomity."

158 Chislock, *Watchdog of Loyalty*, 43–44.

159 Larson, *Lindbergh of Minnesota*, 229–230, describes Lindbergh's congressional stance and the publication of *Why Your Country is at War*. "Invariably," writes Larson in this biography, "the principal message [of the book's critics] was that Lindbergh was disloyal."

160 *Lindbergh of Minnesota*, 222–223. Martin Gilbert, *The First World War, A Complete History*, 411, provides information on the buildup of the American Expeditionary Forces in France.

161 Curtiss-Wedge, *History of Goodhue County*, 1033–1034, Scherf's parents preempted 160 acres of Hay Creek land in 1860. Minnesota Legislative Reference Library, Legislators Past & Present, "Scherf, Frederick A." http://www.leg.state.mn.us/legdb/fulldetail.aspx?ID=14673. Johnson, *Goodhue County*, 204. GCHS Oral History Collection, #218, "German Men and Women." Mildred Scherf, "Reminiscing—Hectic Days During World War I," GCHS Scherf biography file. On June 24, 1987, the author and Jean Chesley of GCHS interviewed Scherf regarding NPL and F-L Politics. She discussed the visits of the Lindberghs, father and son.

162 F. A. Scherf to Knute Nelson, January 6 and February 1, 1916, Knute Nelson Papers, MnHS. Theodore C. Blegen, *Minnesota: A History of the State* (Minneapolis: University of Minnesota Press, 1963) 471.

163 Larson, *Lindbergh of Minnesota*, 223.

164 Chrislock, *The Progressive Era in Minnesota*, 169–171.

165 Morlan, *Political Prairie Fire*, 165. Chrislock, *Watchdog of Loyalty*, 298–300, Burnquist made his comments regarding McGee to Minneapolis City Council representatives. Some council members had demanded McGee's resignation. George M. Stephenson, "The John Lind Papers," *Minnesota History*, 17/2 (June 1936): 160–161. Johnson, *Goodhue County Minnesota*, 178. John Lind gave financial assistance for college to his cousin, Alexander P. Anderson, another Goodhue County Swedish American. A. P. Anderson eventually invented the puffing process for cereal grains. Anderson returned to Burnside Township, later annexed by Red Wing, and continued his research on Tower View farm. See also *John Lind*, MNopedia, http://www.mnopedia.org/person/lind-john-1854-1930.

166 George M. Stephenson, *John Lind of Minnesota* (Minneapolis: University of Minnesota Press, 1935) 335.

167 Here and below, "I'm Pro-German Martin Said, Is First Testimony," *Minneapolis Tribune*, April 4, 1918, 1.

168 "Witness Testimony Charging Martin with Disloyalty Unshaken," *Minneapolis Tribune*, April 5, 1918, 4. Chrislock points out the *Tribune's* strong support of the Burnquist campaign and Commission of Public Safety and editorial hostility toward the NPL, Chrislock, *Watchdog of Loyalty*, 312, 328, as does Larson, *Lindbergh of Minnesota*, 218, 244–245.

169 Morlan, *Political Prairie Fire*, 167. "Martin Acquitted," *Zumbrota News*, May 2, 1918, 1.

170 Nonpartisan League, "Martin Cleared of Disloyalty Charge, Nonpartisan League Organizer is Acquitted by District Court Jury on First Ballot," May 1918 pamphlet, Minnesota Commission of Public Safety, Main Files, Nonpartisan League Folders.

171 "Martin Acquitted," and "Another Mess of Falsehoods," *Kenyon News*, May 2, 1918, 1; *Zumbrota News*, April 12, 1918, 1.

172 S. S. Lewis editorial, *Cannon Falls Beacon*, April 19, 1918, 4.

173 "Warsaw Voters are Loyal to the Core," *Kenyon News*, March 21, 1918, 1.

174 "News Note," *Kenyon News*, March 28, 1918, 4.

175 Here and below, *Goodhue County in the World War*, 153. William Putnam, 70 in 1918, was director of the Goodhue County Public Safety Commission and treasurer of the county's Red Cross Chapter. Putnam ran the Pierce, Simmons & Co. bank, a leading financial institution in Red Wing and Goodhue County. He had served three terms in the state Legislature and was a two-time mayor of Red Wing, Curtiss-Wedge, *History of Goodhue County*, 673–674.

176 A. J. Rockne to C. W. Henke, October 12, 1917, Minnesota Commission of Public Safety, *Speaker Bureau Records*, Goodhue County, MnHS. Rockne was responding to a request from Henke, head of the state Speakers Bureau, to decline a request that he make a speech outside Goodhue County.

177 "Another Mess of Falsehoods," *Kenyon News*, May 2, 1918, 1, makes note of the bond drive shortfall and its details. *Zumbrota News*, April 12, 1918. Johnson, *Goodhue County*, 206–207.

178 Zechariah Chafee, Jr., *Free Speech in the United States* (Cambridge: Harvard University Press, 1941) 248. Chafee examined state laws affecting freedom of speech in war and peace. Douthit, *Nobody Owns Us*, 138. Chrislock, *Watchdog of Loyalty*, 225.

179 Here and below, Phil Davies, "Federal Reserve's Role During WWI," in *Federal Reserve History*, November 2013, www.federalreservehistory.org//Events/DetailView/17. *Goodhue County in the World War*, 153.

180 Johnson, *Goodhue County, Minnesota*, 210. *Goodhue County in the World War*, 153–154. *Indictment Record 2, 1897–1922*, 203.

181 Hildegard Binder Johnson, "The Germans," in *They Chose Minnesota: A Survey of the State's Ethnic Groups* (St. Paul: MnHS, 1981) 153–159, quote 158, 175–177. See also Binder's Table 8.1, 158, "Germans in Minnesota by County, 1860–1970." David Lanegran, "Hildegard Binder Johnson, 1908–1993," *Journal of Geography*, 93/2 (1994).

182 "Loan Drive Planned," *Zumbrota News*, March 29, 1918, 2. Information on the card system is found on the same page under the heading "Card Index To Track Bond Giving." Zumbrota men chosen to make Liberty Loan sales calls were Ira D. Warren, A. S. Baken, Albert Severson, August Perry and Anton Johnson. Among those meeting to decide upon the county's Third Liberty Loan strategy were Leo Schafer and J. D. Grover, Zumbrota, Ole Sauness, Zumbrota Township, A. C. Ylvisaker, Pine Island, William McWaters, Minneola, Frank Freeman, John Berg and Olaf Horen, Roscoe.

183 Ibid.

184 "Over 1900 Subscribers to Third Liberty Loan in City," *Red Wing Daily Republican*, April 24, 1918, 1. "Nearly a Million and a Half for Old Goodhue," *Red Wing Daily Republican*, April 19, 1918, 1. The *Daily Republican* printed the names and amounts given of each Red Wing resident—businesses and industries as well—in a series of front page articles "Subscriptions to Third Liberty Loan." The series, with jumps to later pages, carried more names, began on April 17 and continued for a week. *Goodhue County in the World War*, 153.

185 Here and below, *Goodhue County in the World War*, 154. Chrislock, *Watchdog of Loyalty*, 287–289.

186 "Liberty Loan Day, Saturday Sept. 28," September 13, 1918, *Cannon Falls Beacon*. "To Everybody in Goodhue County," *Red Wing Daily Republican*, September 13, 1918, 1. The *Beacon* and *Daily Republican* were among newspapers that printed an advertisement for the special loan day. They listed specific bond

drive locations to which county residents should report. Town Halls served townships, while village halls of Kenyon, Zumbrota, Goodhue, Wanamingo and Pine Island were bond operation centers. Those from Cannon Falls were to report to the Commercial Club; Red Wing residents would go to the armory. In some cases, schools and stores became bond selling headquarters.

187 Johnson, *Goodhue County*, 210–211. *Report of the Minnesota Commission of Public Safety*, 9 (St. Paul: L. F. Dow Co. 1919) 125–126 carries the text of Order Number 44. The full report of the MCPS is online, HathiTrust Digital Library, http://babel.hathitrust.org/cgi/pt?id=loc.ark:/13960/t9960710g;view=1up;seq=132. Chrislock, *Watchdog of Loyalty*, 289. *Red Wing Daily Republican*, October 14, 1918.

188 "Happenings Around Goodhue County," *Kenyon News*, October 3, 1918, 1. "Cannon Falls Goes Way over the Top," *Cannon Falls Beacon*, October 4, 1918, 1. "Great Response in Fourth Liberty Loan Campaign, Goodhue County Completes Allotment on First Day," *Red Wing Daily Republican*, September 28, 1918, 1.

189 "Subscriptions to Loan Pouring in at Headquarters, $300,000 in Early P.M." *Red Wing Daily Republican*, September 28, 1918, 1. Grondahl's comments are in a page two editorial, "A Remarkable Accomplishment."

190 "Over $21,000 of Non-Subscribers," *Red Wing Daily Republican*, October 11, 1918, 1.

191 Frederick L. Johnson, *Red Wing: A Portable History* (Red Wing: City of Red Wing Heritage Preservation Commission, 2007) 24–27. A year prior to the formation of the Commercial Club, members of the Red Wing Civic League involved their community in the nationwide City Beautiful Movement. League members were already at work creating Levee, Colvill, and John Rich parks.

192 *Officers, Members, Articles of Incorporation, By-Laws and House Rules of the Red Wing Commercial Club of the City of Red Wing, Minnesota* (Red Wing: Red Wing Printing Co., 1909–1910) 6 7, 17. In 1919 the Commercial Club took the name Chamber of Commerce.

193 Here and below, "Members of the Red Wing Commercial Club," *Officers, Members, Articles of Incorporation, By-Laws and House Rules of the Red Wing Commercial Club of the City of Red Wing, Minnesota*, 8–15. Two Red Wing Commercial Club handbooks are known to exist, 1907–1908 and 1909–1910. Both are found in CGHS collections. It is possible, but unlikely, that Commercial Club members referred to in the text were no longer members during the 1917–1918 war years. All were still alive and living in Red Wing during and after the war.

194 "Over $21,000 of Non-Subscribers," *Red Wing Daily Republican*, October 11, 1918, 1.

195 Johnson, *Goodhue County*, 210–211. "Bond Slackers in District Court," *Red Wing Daily Republican*, October 14, 1918, 1. "Over $21,000 of Non-Subscribers," *Red Wing Daily Republican*, October 11, 1918, 1. Chrislock, *Watchdog of Loyalty*, 224, quotes Thomas E. Cashman, a future member of the state Commission of Public Safety, who ran Steele County's Second Liberty Loan drive. Cashman's explanation of the bond campaign's coercive power notes, "This Liberty Bond Campaign has done wonders towards making seditious people loyal in this county."

196 *Goodhue County in the World War*, 154. Arthur R. Rogers described the goals of the Third Liberty Loan in an article in the Federal Reserve District's weekly newspaper, "We Will Because It is Right," *The Liberty Bell*, March 20, 1918, 1, 3. John H. Rich, a leading and versatile Red Wing banker and businessman, served as first Chairman of the Board and reserve agent of the Ninth District during the First World War.

197 *Goodhue County in the World War*, 154–158.

Goodhue County's Sedition Trials

198 Here and below, "Nonpartisan League Organizer Kidnapped and Driven from the City, Taken by Force from Hotel," *Red Wing Daily Republican*, May 1, 1918, 1, 3. The newspaper reported the Kenyon crowd reached 300. "Kidnaping (sic) Charge to be Sifted for Bearing on Randall's Trial," *Minneapolis Tribune*, May 2, 1918, 5.

199 Here and below, "Nonpartisan League Organizer Kidnapped…" 1, 3. "Local News," *Zumbrota News* May 3, 1918, 3.

200 "Investigation of Kidnaping (sic) Stopped," *Red Wing Daily Eagle*, June 18, 1918. Randall's jury was sequestered in the Goodhue County Courthouse and guarded by sheriff's deputies.

201 Here and below, "State Testimony Against Randall Very Damaging," *Red Wing Daily Republican*, 1, 3. "Gilbert Guilty," *Zumbrota News*, May 17, 1918, 2, reports date for convening the grand jury.

202 Here and below, "Defense Inning in Randall Case Nearly Over, League Organizer (sic) Give Their Own Opinion," *Red Wing Daily Republican*, May 2, 1918, 1. "Jury Finds Randall Guilty of Sedition," *Red Wing Daily Republican*, May 4, 1918, 1. "Randall Guilty Jury Decides," *Minneapolis Tribune*, May 4, 1918, 1. "Defense Inning in Randall Case…," 1, 7. Members of the Randall jury were Adolph Berg, Red Wing, foreman; Peter Tri, Pine Island; Fred Altmeyer, Red Wing; J. H. Lothrop, Roscoe; M. J. Bolum, Red Wing; William Larson, Burnside; Joseph Persig, Hay Creek; Edward Hunecke, Frontenac; S. B. Whitney, Cannon Falls; Charles Widholm, Stanton; C. G. Ernst, Vasa. Jury praised Sheriff John A. Anderson for making their stay in the courthouse while under sequestration "most pleasant."

203 *Minnesota Reports*, Vol. 143, "State v. N. S. Randall, 204–210. Justice Holt wrote for the court in ordering a new trial. "Randall Disloyalty Verdict is Reversed, *Minneapolis Tribune*, July 4, 1919, 8. This report provides the specific reasons the Minnesota Supreme Court gave for its decision to order a new trial for Randall.

204 "Randall Guilty, Jury Decides in Court," *Minneapolis Tribune*, May 4, 1918, 1. "Four Months in Jail for N. S. Randall," *Red Wing Daily Republican*, May 7, 1918, 1. "County Correspondence," *Cannon Falls Beacon*, May 31, 1918, 5.

205 "Cited to Appear in Court," *Red Wing Daily Republican*, May 4, 1918, 1. Johnson, *Goodhue County*, 208. "Action Against Scherf Dismissed," *Red Wing Daily Republican*, May 7, 1918, 1.

206 Committee on Public Information, *Four Minute Men Bulletin*, May 22, 1917, n.p. "Four Minute Men," *Goodhue County in the World War*, 170. Creel supplied his Four Minute Men with advice on organizing their talks. He also advised searching newspapers for editorials and speeches that might provide talking points. Following the war's end, the Committee on Public Information reported its speakers bureau made more than 7.5 million talks to about 314 million people.

207 "Four Minute Men," *Goodhue County in the World War*, 170.

208 *State of Minnesota, First Judicial District, District Court, Goodhue County, Minutes, 1854–1982*, 56, lists members of the county grand jury, including R[obert] W. Putnam, chosen on March 11, 1918. H. P. Hulebak was appointed foreman.

209 Cyrus A. Field, "Proceedings in Memory of Associate Justice Clifford L. Hilton," *Minnesota Reports*, Vol. 246, (St. Paul: 1956) 2–3. Hilton, coincidentally, had been born in 1866 in Kenyon, site of the alleged sedition. Douthit, *Nobody Owns Us*, 139, notes Gilbert's legal team included George Nordlin, Thomas V. Sullivan, Frederick A. Pike and Arthur Le Sueur.

210 "Selecting Jury to Try Gilbert," *Red Wing Daily Republican*, May 7, 1918, 1. Morlan, *Political Prairie Fire*, 171–172.

211 *Gilbert v. State of Minnesota*, 254 U.S. 325. Jessup, "Joseph Gilbert and the Minnesota Sedition Law," 114–116. *Red Wing Daily Republican*, May 7, 1; May 10, 1918, 1, 4, 8.

212 *Nonpartisan Leader*, May 27, 1918, 6. *Red Wing Daily Republican*, May 10, 1, 4, 1918. "Gilbert Kenyon Talk Burned, Says Witness," *Minneapolis Tribune*, May 10, 1918, 8. Joseph Gates underwent extensive questioning while on the witness stand. He stated the words from Gilbert's talk were "burned" into his memory. A[rthur] B. Gilbert, "Another Mooney Case Provided by Supreme Court of Minnesota: Frame-up Case of Politicians Against Joseph Gilbert and L. W. Martin, Nonpartisan League Workers, Considered Only in Legal Aspects—Astounding Facts in First Trial Ignored." (St. Paul: December 1918?]. Gilbert, no relation to the defendant, wrote this defiant objection after the Minnesota Supreme Court reviewed the Joseph Gilbert trial and let his conviction stand. A. B. Gilbert worked as associate editor of *Nonpartisan Leader* at the time. He used the NPL deprecatory phrase "parrot chorus" twice in this article.

213 Dwight Wiley Jessup, *Joseph Gilbert and the Minnesota Sedition Law: A Case Study in American Constitutional History*, M.A. Thesis, University of Minnesota, 1965, 114–115. *Nonpartisan Leader*, May 27, 1918, 1. Morlan, *Political Prairie Fire*, 171.

214 "About Our Yellow Neighbor," *Kenyon News*, June 6, 1918, 1. *Red Wing Daily Republican*, May 10, 1918, 1, 4. Johnson, *Goodhue County*, 208.

215 Joseph Gilbert papers, MnHS. For a copy of Gilbert's testimony, see Midland Cooperative, Inc. files; he founded and then ran the *Midland Cooperative* newspaper from 1933 to 1953. Gilbert quotation is from "Nonpartisan State Chief Found Guilty," *Minneapolis Tribune*, May 11, 1918, 1.

216 Grondahl's comments are in May 15, 1918, *Daily Republican*. For Lewis's statement, see "County Correspondence," *Cannon Falls Beacon*, May 10, 1918, 2.

217 Ibid.

218 "A Fleeting Victory for the Conspirators," *Nonpartisan Leader*, May 27, 1917, 6.

219 "Gilbert Guilty, 1ˢᵗ Ballot," [May 10] and "Gilbert Guilty, Gets Year in Jail, Also Fined $500," *Red Wing Daily Republican*, May 11, 1918, 1. Jessup, *Joseph Gilbert and the Minnesota Sedition Law*, 119. Gilbert's quoted words are from Douthit, *Nobody Owns Us*, 142–143.

220 A[rthur] B. Gilbert, "Another Mooney Case Provided by Supreme Court of Minnesota." Arthur Gilbert became an NPL turncoat in 1924.

221 "Kenyon and Vicinity," *Kenyon News*, April 25, 4.

222 The news story cited was originally published in *Goodhue News* and reprinted in *Zumbrota News* on April 26, 1918, 3, under heading "Goodhue News."

223 "Respectfully Submitted," *Goodhue Enterprise*, May 9, 1918, 2.

224 "Superintendent Beito's Annual Report," *Cannon Falls Beacon*, May 10, 1918, 1. "Banish German from High School," *Red Wing Daily Republican*, June 8, 1918, 3. See also, Minnesota Commission of Public Safety's *Report of Special Committee on German Text Books use in Public Schools of Minnesota*, (St. Paul: December 1917) 4–5; The report notes 270 suspect books were examined, provides the list, and notes 47 of them had "a distinct German atmosphere."

225 "Yellow Daubs for O. F. Henkel's Home," *Red Wing Daily Republican*, June 11, 1918, 2. The Red Wing newspaper used Henkel's account that appeared in *Minnesota Leader*.

226 "Let's be Reasonable," *Zumbrota News*, May 24, 1918, 2.

227 "County Correspondence," *Cannon Falls Beacon*, May 31, 1918, 5. On May 23, NPL leader Arthur Townley visits a farmers' picnic at Oscar Ranstad's place near Wanamingo. Townley had been convicted of sedition but continued to fight for the Nonpartisan League cause while his legal appeals were considered. "Kenyon and Vicinity Happenings," *Kenyon News*, May 23, 1918, 4.

228 "About Our Yellow Neighbor," *Kenyon News*, June 6, 1918, 1.

229 "Declare League to be Disloyal," *Red Wing Daily Republican*, June 6, 1, and June 7, 1, 7. Allen and Nicholas had addressed audiences in St. Peter and Rochester prior to the Red Wing visit, see "Allen and Nicholas Ask Democrats Help Nominate Burnquist," *Minneapolis Tribune*, May 29, 1918, 6. "Nonparty is Scored by E. H. Nicholas," *Red Wing Daily Eagle*, June 7, 1918, 7.

230 *Cannon Falls Beacon*, June 7, 1918, 4.

231 "A Communication," *Zumbrota News*, June 14, 1918, 3 carries the report of the Pine Island mass meeting.

232 "Loyal Men Compel Council to Deny Park to League; Nonpartisan League Leaders Will Not be Permitted to Speak in City, Council Rescinds Original Permit," *Red Wing Daily Republican*, June 11, 1918, 1, 5. Jens Grondahl, "Don't Thwart Patriotism," *Red Wing Daily Republican*, June 11, 1918, 2.

233 "Man has Stroke After Attack," *Red Wing Daily Republican*, June 13, 1918, 1, 2.

234 O[liver] M. Thomason, *The Beginning and the End of the Nonpartisan League* (St. Paul: Self-published, 1920) 120–121.

235 "Non-Partisan Parades Forbidden in City," and "Nonpartisan Meet Barred from City," *Red Wing Daily Eagle*, June 11, 1918, 1.

236 Chrislock, *Watchdog of Loyalty*, 307. "No-Party League Barred From City," *Red Wing Daily Republican*, June 11, 1918, 1, 5.

237 Here and below, "No-Party League Barred From City," *Red Wing Daily Republican*, June 11, 1918, 1, 5. "The Non-Partisan Parade," *Kenyon News*, June 13, 1918, 1. "Didn't Recognize Them," *Red Wing Daily Republican*, June 12, 1918, 1. The Red Wing newspaper differed with *Kenyon News* account of the trip, writing that a group of young Kenyon men had prepared to ambush the motorcade with a shower of bad eggs, but the autos took a different route.

238 Here and below, "Non-Partisan Parades Forbidden in City," *Red Wing Daily Eagle*, June 11, 1918, 1. "No-Party League Barred From City," *Red Wing Daily Republican*, June 11, 1918, 1, 5. "Happenings," *Cannon Falls Beacon*, June 14, 1918, 6.

239 "No-Party League Barred From City," *Red Wing Daily Republican*, June 11, 1918, 1, 5.

240 W. H. Putnam and Thomas Mohn, "Order Forbidding Nonpartisan League Parade in Red Wing," *Red Wing Daily Republican*, June 11, 1918, 1. The order's specific language regarding possible riots noted "a great many loyal citizens…who are doing their utmost in supporting our Government in this hour of peril,

consider and brandish the banners and symbols of said League as badges of disloyalty and treason; and… it is the firm belief and opinion of the undersigned that such a parade and the flaunting of the banners and symbols of said League would incite and cause breaches of the peace and riots."

241 County Attorney Thomas Mohn added to Putnam's comments and explained why Company A had been activated. "No-Party League Barred From City," *Red Wing Daily Republican*, June 11, 1918, 5. "Non-Partisan Parades Forbidden in City," *Red Wing Daily Eagle*, June 11, 1918, 1.

242 Ibid.

243 "Hon. A. V. Anderson Makes Statement," *Red Wing Daily Republican*, June 15, 1918, 2. Anderson met with *Daily Republican* editor Jens Grondahl to correct "erroneous statements" in the *Republican* in regard to the June 11 parade. He followed up with a letter to the newspaper.

244 "Non-Partisan Parades Forbidden in City," *Red Wing Daily Eagle*, June 11, 1918, 1.

245 "Yellow Paint For Paraders in Goodhue Village," *Red Wing Daily Republican*, June 12, 1918, 1, 5.

246 Here and below, "Hon. A. V. Anderson Makes Statement," *Red Wing Daily Republican*, June 15, 1918, 2. For biographical information about Anderson, see Minnesota Legislature's website, http://www.leg.state.mn.us/legdb/fulldetail?ID=10956. "Happenings," *Cannon Falls Beacon*, June 14, 1918, 6. "Yellow Paint for Paraders in Goodhue Village," *Red Wing Daily Republican*, June 12, 1918, 1, 5. Anderson asserted NPL organizer George Breidal had been a passenger in the car but had not, as the *Republican* reported, been carrying any liquor.

247 "Happenings," *Cannon Falls Beacon*, June 14, 1918, 6.

248 S. S. Lewis, editorial, *Cannon Falls Beacon*, June 14, 1918, 4. Beneath this piece, Lewis informed readers that Nonpartisan and Republican candidate names appeared on the same ballot. He warned, "The Nonpartisans stole the livery of the Republican Party to serve the Kaiser in."

249 Chrislock, *Watchdog of Loyalty*, 273.

250 A. Scott Berg, *Lindbergh* (New York: G. P. Putnam's Sons, 1998) 48. Morlan, "The Nonpartisan League and the Minnesota Campaign of 1918," 228–230.

251 *Red Wing Daily Eagle*, June 11, 1918, 8. "Loyalty Talks at Factories," *Red Wing Daily Republican*, June 13, 1918, 2. *Goodhue County in the World War*, 177.

252 Editorial, June 13, 1918, 4, *Red Wing Daily Republican*, 4.

253 "Loyalty to be Tested," *Goodhue Enterprise*, June 13, 1918, 1.

254 "The Political Pot," *Zumbrota News*, June 14, 1918, 2.

255 "Lindbergh is Hung in Effigy in Street Here During the Night," *Red Wing Daily Republican*, June 15, 1918, 1.

256 Mildred Scherf, "Reminiscing—Hectic Days During World War I," GCHS Scherf biography file. Mildred Scherf was Fred Scherf's daughter. The author interviewed Ms. Scherf on June 24, 1987, regarding Farmer-Labor politics. She told of the yellow paint incident.

257 "Speaker Failed to Appear at Meeting, Nonpartisan Gathering on Sargent Farm Missed the Expected Program," *Red Wing Daily Eagle*, June 17, 1918, 1.

258 Ibid. Hall, a Red Wing native, had been city attorney in 1910 and would be elected judge for the First Judicial District in 1928.

259 Lynn and Dora B. Haines, *The Lindberghs* (New York: Vanguard Press, 1931) 282, 284, 292. Robert L. Morlan, "The Nonpartisan League and the Minnesota Campaign of 1918," *Minnesota History* 34/6 (Summer 1955): 221–232. Morlan provides an overview of Lindbergh's campaign activity throughout the state.

260 Morlan, *Political Prairie Fire*, 200–201. Chrislock, *Watchdog of Loyalty*, 308, records St. Paul *Daily News* view of the Burnquist win.

261 "The Treason of the Press," *Nonpartisan Leader,* July 8, 1918, 7. The *Leader* also took on the "damnable charge made by the newspapers of the state that the activities of the organized farmers have been disloyal and unpatriotic."

262 "Empty Burnquist Victory," *Red Wing Daily Eagle*, June 18, 1918, 4.

263 "Goodhue County Goes For Burnquist By a 2 to 1 Vote," *Red Wing Daily Eagle*, June 18, 1918, 1. "Goodhue County Gives Burnquist a Majority of Two Thousand," *Red Wing Daily Republican*, June 18, 1918, 1, see also, *Official Returns for Goodhue County: Primary Election, June 17, 1918*, 4.

264 "Kenyon and Vicinity News," *Kenyon News*, June 20, 1918, 4.

265 *Official Returns for Goodhue County: Primary Election, June 17, 1918. Red Wing Daily Republican*, June 18, 1918.

266 "Seebach On Trial In U.S. Court," *Red Wing Daily Eagle*, June 25, 1918, 1. "Proceedings At Seebach Trial," *Red Wing Daily Republican*, June 26, 1918, 1, 8. "Seebach Tells Court He Favored England As Against Germany," *Red Wing Daily Eagle*, June 26, 1918, 1. "Seebach Case in Jury's Hands Late Today," *Red Wing Daily Republican*, June 26, 1918, 1, 8. Eight character witnesses supported Seebach's testimony: Bernard Gerlach, Axel Johnson, Andreas F. Anderson, M. T. Nilan, Henry Schroer, Nicholas Staiger, Gustav Beckmark and Robert Utes.

267 "Seebach Found Guilty in U.S. District Court," *Red Wing Daily Republican*, June 27, 1918, 1, 2.

268 Seebach defense team's request for a new trial was made on October 8, see "Seebach Denied New Trial," *Minneapolis Tribune*, October 9, 1918, 8. The June 28, 1918 *Minneapolis Daily News* censured the defendant. See Johnson, *Goodhue County Minnesota*, 209.

269 "Pick Martin Jury in Quick Time," *Red Wing Daily Republican*, June 28, 1918, 1, 4. "Martin Case to Jury on Monday," *Red Wing Daily Republican*, June 29, 1918, 1.

270 "State v. Louis W. Martin," in *Minnesota Reports: Cases Argued and Determined in the Supreme the Supreme Court of Minnesota*, Vol. 142, 484–487. "Martin Case to Jury on Monday," *Red Wing Daily Republican*, June 29, 1918, 1.

271 Here and two paragraphs below, Chrislock, *Watchdog of Loyalty*, 289–291.

272 Ibid. 290–291.

273 Haines, *The Lindberghs*, 279.

274 *Goodhue County in the World War*, 145.

275 Minnesota National Guard, "History of the 34th Infantry Division," http://www.minnesotanationalguard.org/units/34id/history.php. Johnson, "Company L," *Goodhue County in the World War*, 184, notes eagerness of Red Wing men to volunteer for combat.

276 *Goodhue County in the World War*, see "Kenyon Village" section. "Doings in Kenyon and the Vicinity," *Kenyon News*, June 6, 1918, 1 and "Farewell to Dr. Gates," August 1, 1918, 1.

277 War Records Commission, Box 6, "Killed and Wounded by County," MnHS. Johnson, *Goodhue County, Minnesota*, 213. *Goodhue County in the World War*, See "The Honored Dead," 143–151, "Path of Fire: The Meuse-Argonne Offensive of 1918, http://www.firstworldwar.com/features/pathoffire.htm.

278 "Citizens in Long Line of Autos Escorted Drafted Boys," *Zumbrota News*, June 28, 1918, 1. "Thousands to Bid Troops Farewell," and "Thousands Cheer Troops Leaving for Camp Grant," *Red Wing Daily Republican*, June 24 and June 25, 1918, 1.

279 "Thousands Cheer Troops Leaving for Camp Grant," *Red Wing Daily Republican*, June 25, 1918, 1. This account, along with words quoted, from *Daily Republican*.

War Ends, Trials Continue

280 Johnson, *Goodhue County, Minnesota*, 212–213. *Goodhue County in the World War*, 145, 150.

281 S. S. Lewis, editorial, *Cannon Falls Beacon*, April 19, 1918, 4. Lewis quotations are from *Cannon Falls Beacon*, "Local Happenings," June 1, 1917, 4 and June 22, 4. Johnson, *Goodhue County, Minnesota*, 209. See also GCHS Oral History Collection #74 (interview with Henry C. Hinrichs), 36, 44. Hinrichs reported about Featherstone houses and buildings splashed with yellow paint.

282 S. S. Lewis's comments calling for more civility in Goodhue County are found in *Cannon Falls Beacon*, June 14, 4; July 19, 4; August 2, 4, 1918. For Grondahl's words, see Editorial, June 13, 1918, 4, Red Wing *Daily Republican*, 4.

283 Peter J. DcCarlo, "Minnesota Motor Corps," *MNopedia* http://www.mnopedia.org/group/minnesota-motor-corps. Captain Leonard Cary, *How Minnesota Gave to the United States the First Military Motor Corps* (Minneapolis: Bancroft Printing, 1919) 8–14. *Goodhue County in the World War*, 161–165. Folwell, *A History of Minnesota*, 3:319.

284 Paul Nelson, "Cloquet, Duluth and Moose Lake Fires, 1918," *MNopedia*, http://www.mnopedia.org/event/cloquet-duluth-and-moose-lake-fires-1918.

285 Here and below, for Goodhue County newspaper reports on influenza issues noted, see *Red Wing Daily Republican*, October 4, 7, 10 and 12, 1918; Zumbrota *News*, October 11 and 18, 1918. *Red Wing Hospital*

Minute Book, 1914–1922, GCHS. United States Department of Health and Human Services, "The Great Pandemic: The United States in 1918–1919, Minnesota," http://www.flu.gov/pandemic/history/1918/your_state/midwest/minnesota/. See also "The Influenza Pandemic of 1918, https://virus.stanford.edu/uda/.

286 White, et al., *Minnesota Votes*, 183–184. "General Election Returns For Minnesota, Held on Tuesday, November 5, 1918," *Minnesota Legislative Manual*, 1919, has complete results for each county.

287 N. S. Randall to H. G. Teigan, November 5, 1918, National Nonpartisan League Papers, Undated and 1913–1927, Roll 14, MnHS.

288 Here and below, Gieske, *Minnesota Farmer-Laborism: The Third-party Alternative*, 33. Morlan, "The Nonpartisan League and the Minnesota Campaign of 1918," *Minnesota History* 34/6 (Summer 1955): 232. *Minnesota Legislative Manual*, 1919, see 556–557 for Goodhue County votes, at http://www.leg.state.mn.us/archive/sessions/electionresults/1918-11-06-g-man.pdf. Chrislock, *The Progressive Era in Minnesota*, 171. Another former Joseph Gilbert attorney caused problems for the 1918 Farmer-Labor candidates. A letter written by LeSueur to William Haywood and taken from confiscated IWW files showed the attorney believed America's entry into the Great War would make their "radical work" much more difficult. Chrislock, *Progressive Era in Minnesota*, 172–173.

289 Larson, *Lindbergh of Minnesota*, 252–253. For biographical information on Rich and his service at the Federal Reserve Bank of Minneapolis, see "John H. Rich, Former President" https://www.minneapolisfed.org/about/more-about-the-fed/presidents-of-the-minneapolis-fed/johnhrich and "Historical Overview: Federal Reserve Bank of Minneapolis," https://www.minneapolisfed.org/about/more-about-the-fed/history-of-the-fed/historical-overview-federal-reserve-bank-of-minneapolis.

290 Here and below, Johnson, *Goodhue County, Minnesota*, 212. *Minnesota Legislative Manual*, 1919, 678. David Neill ran the Red Wing telephone company and had been president of Red Wing Manufacturing Company as well president of the city's Commercial Club.

291 Here and below, Johnson, *Goodhue County, Minnesota*, 217–218.

292 N. S. Randall to H. G. Teigan, November 21, 1918, and December 15, 1918, and Teigan to Randall, December 24, 1918, National Nonpartisan League Papers, Undated and 1913–1927, Roll 14, MnHS.

293 N. P. Olson, "Autocracy in Minnesota," Red Wing *Daily Eagle*, November 21, 1918, 4. Chrislock, *Watchdog of Loyalty*, 314–323.

294 Here and below, *Inaugural Message of Gov. J. A. A. Burnquist to the Legislature of Minnesota, 1919* [St. Paul, 1919] 4, (quotation on 6). Chrislock, *Watchdog of Loyalty*, 315–316.

295 Chrislock, *Watchdog of Loyalty*, 315–318, quote on page 323, see Chrislock's cogent summary of Minnesota political developments in the immediate aftermath of the Great War that weakened the Burnquist administration and empowered the nascent NPL-Labor alliance.

296 Frederick L. Johnson, "Susie Williamson Stageberg," *MNopedia*, April 15, 2013, http://www.mnopedia.org/person/stageberg-susie-williamson-1877-1961. Stageberg was the F-L's unsuccessful candidate for Secretary of State in 1922, 1924 and 1928. She resisted vigorously in 1944 when discussions to create a new political coalition that would unite the Farmer-Labor and Democratic parties commenced. Stageberg believed such a merger would weaken the F-L's socialist faction. The DFL came into being in April 1944 and continues to this day. The Red Wing radical resigned from that party in 1950, observing, "We were called 'Red Bolsheviks' and 'Free Lovers' in the twenties. We must dare to be called 'Communists' now."

297 Scherf's *The Organized Farmer* had a 13-year run, June 12, 1919, to July 15, 1932. Minnesota Historical Society has original issues and microfilm copies of the weekly.

298 Henry Burleigh Wenzell, State v. N. S. Randall, July 3, 1919, No. 21,284 in *Minnesota Reports*, Vol. 143. "Cases Argued and Determined in the Supreme Court of Minnesota, June 6–October 17, 1919," (St. Paul: 1920) 203–207, 210. "Randall Disloyalty Verdict is Reversed," *Minneapolis Tribune*, July 4, 1919, 8.

299 Ibid.

300 For more details leading up the trial and the Townley and Gilbert appeal, see Henry Burleigh Wenzell, State v. A. C. Townley and Another," *Minnesota Reports*: *Cases Argued and Determined in the Supreme Court of Minnesota*, Vol. 149, April 22–July 15, 1921, (St. Paul: The Pioneer Company, 1922) 7–24. Nicholas provided details of Townley's speeches in St. Paul, New Ulm, Glencoe and Cambridge.

301 Folwell, *History of Minnesota*, 3: 571–574. This information comes from Folwell's Appendix 19, "The Minnesota Commission of Public Safety."

302 "The Non-partisan League, Townleyism and Lindbergh Plainly Discussed," *Red Wing Daily Eagle*, June 6, 1918, 5. "Nonparty is Scored by E. H. Nicholas," *Red Wing Daily Eagle*, June 7, 1918, 7.

303 Here and below, Morlan, *Political Prairie Fire*, 255–261, Morlan presents details of the Jackson County trial of Townley and Gilbert. "The History of the Jackson County 'Frame Up,'" July 28, 1919, 1. Folwell, *History of Minnesota*, 3:573, [n73].

304 Here and below, Folwell, *History of Minnesota*, 572, the pamphlets were titled *National Nonpartisan League War Program and Statement of Principles* and *Resolutions Adopted by the Nonpartisan League Conference Held at St. Paul, Sept. 18–19–20, 1917*. Morlan, *Political Prairie Fire*, 256–259. E. H. Nicholas to F. A. Teigen, June 13, 1918, National Nonpartisan League Papers, "Correspondence and Miscellaneous Papers, 1913–1927," Roll 4. National Nonpartisan League Papers, "Correspondence and Miscellaneous Papers, 1913–1927," Roll 4, MnHS, contains, "Data Relating to the Nonpartisan Leader's expose of Ferdinand A. Teigen and E. H. Nichols," two letters, a Teigen, note and the Albert Allen telegram.

305 H. C. Peterson and Gilbert C. Fite, *Opponents of War, 1917–1918* (Madison: University of Wisconsin Press, 1957) 156.

306 Here and below, W[alter]. W. Liggett, "The History of the Jackson County 'Frame Up,'" *Nonpartisan Leader*, July 28, 1919, 1. Liggett, the author of this story, would be murdered in 1935, a sensational crime that fascinated Minnesotans. The muckraking journalist was gunned down in Minneapolis in a murder that was never solved. For an overview on Liggett, see his daughter's account: Marda Liggett Woodbury, *Stopping the Presses: The Murder of Walter W. Liggett*, (Minneapolis: University of Minnesota Press, 1995).

307 Morlan, *Political Prairie Fire*, 261.

308 Douthit, *Nobody Owns Us*, 146–147. Douhit provides Gilbert's detailed accounts of the break up, including quotations used here and below.

309 Names of NPL rebels on the list were Joseph Gilbert, Arthur B. Gilbert, Walter W. Liggett, N. S. Randall, Murray King, J. E. M. Jauncey, W. G. Roylance, George D. Brewer, Carl Beck, Charles R. Barnes, O. J. Nelson, W. S. Shoemaker, W. H. Quist, Alfred Knutson, L. J. Duncan, Arthur Williams, O. M. Thomason and David Paquin, Douthit, *Nobody Owns Us*, 147 [n7].

310 *Minnesota v. Gilbert*, 141 Minn. 263, 169 N. W. 790, December 22, 1919. Chrislock, *Watchdog of Loyalty*, 166–168. Henry Burleigh Wenzell, "State v. Louis W. Martin," *Minnesota Reports, Cases Argued and Determined in the Supreme Court of Minnesota*, Vol. 142 (St. Paul: Keefe–Davidson Co. 1920) 484–487. Johnson, *Goodhue County*, 208. Morlan, *Political Prairie Fire*, 136–137. Representing the defendants were George Nordlin, Thomas V. Sullivan, Frederick A. Pike and Arthur Le Sueur. Clifford L. Hilton, state attorney general, and Thomas A. Mohn, Goodhue County Attorney, argued for the respondent.

311 "State v. Louis W. Martin," 484. A. B. Gilbert, "Another Mooney Case Provided by Supreme Court of Minnesota," this pro-Nonpartisan League broadside is from late 1918 or early 1919 and is located in MnHS collections.

312 Here and below, State v. Louis Martin, 484–487.

313 Frohwerk v. United States 249 U.S. 204 (1919).

314 Paul S. Boyer, editor, *The Oxford Companion to United States History* (New York: 2001) 176. Socialist Party members ran Debs for president in November 1920 while their candidate was in prison. He received over 920,000 votes.

315 Morlan, *Political Prairie Fire*, 336–337. Joseph Gilbert interview, January 27, 1954, 6.

316 Douthit, *Nobody Owns Us*, 172–173. "Gilbert v. State of Minnesota," 254 U.S. 325, 41 S. Ct. 125. Justice Joseph McKenna delivered the opinion of the Court. For an online version of the decision in the Gilbert case, see https://www.law.cornell.edu/supremecourt/text/254/325.

317 Ibid.

318 Ibid.

319 Ibid.

320 "Gilbert v. State of Minnesota," 254 U.S. 325, 41 S. Ct. 125. Morlan, *Political Prairie Fire* quotes Chafee, 172–173.

321 Ibid. Brandeis cited Report of New York Bar Association, vol. 42, 296.

322 "Gilbert Must Serve One Year in Prison," *Red Wing Daily Republican*, December 13, 1920. "Mohn Pleased with Sentence," *Kenyon News*, December 16, 1920, 8.

323 "Gilbert to Jail," *Zumbrota News*, December 17, 1920, 6. The *News* reprinted a *St. Paul Pioneer Press* story on the conviction. "Gilbert Convicted," *Kenyon News*, December 16, 1920, 8, credited *Red Wing Daily Republican* as the article's source. "U.S. Court Affirms Gilbert Conviction," *Red Wing Daily Eagle*, December 13, 1920, 1. "Goodhue County Jail to be Home of Jos. Gilbert," *Red Wing Daily Eagle*, December 14, 1920, 1, 5. "Opposite Opinions of Supreme Court Judges" and "Justice Brandeis Opinion," *Red Wing Daily Eagle*, December 15, 1920, 4.

324 County newspapers, with the exception of the *Red Wing Daily Eagle* which sent a reporter to the county jail, gave brief coverage or none at all of Joseph Gilbert's arrival in Red Wing.

325 Here and three paragraphs below, "Joseph Gilbert Arrives to Begin 1 Year Sentence," *Red Wing Daily Eagle*, February 5, 1921, 1. Editorially, the *Eagle* had cautiously supported the Nonpartisan League during the war, so it was not surprising it had a reporter on hand for Gilbert's arrival. N. P. Olson edited the *Eagle*, but it is likely one of his sons, Ted, Elmer or August, who assisted him, conducted the interview. Douthit, *Nobody Owns Us*, 179. "Gilbert Begins Year's Sentence," *Red Wing Daily Republican*, February 6, 1921.

326 Douthit, *Nobody Owns Us*, 180.

327 Ibid. 181–182.

328 "League Worker Denied Pardon," *Minneapolis Tribune*, April 27, 1921, 1. Douthit, *Nobody Owns Us*, 181–182.

329 Tighe to Lind, February 13, 1918, John and Norman Lind Papers, MnHS.

330 Here and two paragraphs below, Douthit, *Nobody Owns Us*, 181–187.

331 Folwell, *A History of Minnesota*, 3: 572–575.

332 "Townley's Last Plea, Lost, Goes to Jail in Week," *Minneapolis Tribune*, October 25, 1921, 1. "Gilbert's Term in Goodhue Jail Expires Today," Red Wing *Daily Republican*, February 4, 1922, 2. Folwell, *History of Minnesota* 3: 575, incorrectly notes Gilbert's release was February 7.

333 Douthit, *Nobody Owns Us*, 188.

Summary: An Unenviable Record

334 Folwell, *A History of Minnesota*, 3: 556–557, 570, Appendix 19. Folwell wrote his study of the MCPS, "The Minnesota Commission of Public Safety," according to Russell W. Fridley's Introduction written in 1969, [3: ix] "while some of the heat and hysteria of the World War I era still prevailed." Fridley was then director of the MnHS. Chrislock, *Watchdog of Loyalty*, 52–60. Steven J. Keillor, *Hjalmar Petersen of Minnesota: The Politics of Provincial Independence* (St. Paul: MnHS Press, 1987) 43. *William E. Lass, Minnesota: A Bicentennial History* (New York: W. W. Norton, 1977) 179. Theodore C. Blegen, *Minnesota: A History of the State* (Minneapolis: University of Minnesota Press, 1963) 473.

335 Minnesota Commission of Public Safety, *Report*, 44.

336 Chrislock, *Watchdog of Loyalty*, 273.

337 Ambrose Tighe to John Lind, February 13, 1918, John and Norman Lind Papers, MnHS.

338 Sullivan, *Our Times: American at the Birth of the Twentieth Century*, abridged 1966 edition, 550–551.

339 *Goodhue County in the World War* (Red Wing: Red Wing Printing, 1919) 179–180.

340 Minnesota Commission of Public Safety, *Report*, 42.

341 See Red Wing Commercial Club membership lists in the 1907–08 and 1909–1910 club handbooks in the collections of Goodhue County Historical Society.

342 "Loyalty Resolution," *Red Wing Daily Republican*, March 14, 1918, 4. Members of the Grand Jury were: H. Pulebak, foreman, Robert W. Putnam, John Bremer, H. G. Husbyn, N. F. Nelson, J. C. Brunkhorst, August Klug, W. F. Deline, Oscar Holm, O. K. Severson, Hjalmar Olson, John P. Mark, Ed M. Schenach, John Davidson, Samuel Kraft, Anders Mosberg, H. G. Tiedemann, J. H. Bradley, H. U. Pattridge, Martin Vomhof, Otto Andrist, W. D. Hayward, H. W. Nelson. The full title of the resolution was "Upon the Loyalty of Goodhue County in Matters Pertaining to the War with Germany;" see *State of Minnesota, First Judicial District, District Court, Goodhue County, Minutes, 1854–1982*, 57.

343 *Goodhue County in the World War*, 177. Chrislock, *Watchdog of Loyalty*, 159. For a broader view of APL

activity, see Operative 71, *A Story of War Service Rendered by the Minneapolis Division of the American Protective League* (Minneapolis: 1919).

344 Daniel Okrent, *Last Call: The Rise and Fall of Prohibition* (New York: Scribner) quotation, 101. *Goodhue County in the World War*, 170.

345 Holmquist, ed., *They Chose Minnesota*, 10. H. W. Libby, Secretary, *Report of Minnesota Commission of Public Safety*, Order Number 25, "Providing for Registration of Aliens," 100–103. A listing of the 35 questions asked on "Alien Registration and Declaration of Holdings" form is found on pages 101–103.

346 See http://darrow.law.umn.edu/documents/Gitlow%20Supreme%20Ct.pdf. for a copy of the Gitlow decision. Editors of Encyclopaedia Britannica, *Gitlow v. New York*, http://www.britannica.com/event/Gitlow-v-New-York. Benjamin Gitlow, a former state assemblyman and Communist Party member from New York City, was arrested by city police in November 1919 and charged with criminal anarchy, a crime under state law. Gitlow lost his appeal, but the Court ruled both state and federal governments were required to apply the Fourteenth Amendment's due process clause in regulating speech.

347 Morlan, *Political Prairie Fire*, 136–137. See *Nonpartisan Leader*, June 14, 1917, for a copy of Gilbert's position paper on the "war question." Jessup, "Joseph Gilbert and the Minnesota Sedition Law," 67.

Index

MCPS, 126; on dissolution of MCPS, 110; view on NPL prosecutions, 93-94; *Tribune*'s support of Burnquist, 166n168

City Hospital (Red Wing), *76*

Civic League, and City Beautiful Movement, 167n192

Civic and Commerce Association (CCA), 20-21; created CA, 45; evolved from Commercial Club, 21

Civic Improvement Club, deny NPL request, 52

Civilian Auxiliary (CA), organized labor upset about, 45; supported by MCPS, 45

Claydon, L. E. (doctor), statement about Carl Seebach's stance, 54

Clarkfield, NPL picnic, *90*

Cloquet-Duluth Fire, 104

Cole, O. Clark, co-owner of *Kenyon Leader*, 29

Commercial Club (Red Wing), 74-75, 128, 129; against NPL, 74-75; become Chamber of Commerce, 167n192; meeting place for Liberty Loan committee and township officials, 72; standing committees, 74; NPL against, 74. *See also* Red Wing Commercial Club.

Commercial Hotel, 51, *51*

Commission of Public Safety. *See* Minnesota Commission of Public Safety.

Committee on Public Information (CPI), 67, create Four Minute Men, 132; interest in German-Americans, 132; number of talks given, 168n206; war bond campaign, 67. *See also* Creel Committee.

Communist Party (Russia), 22

Company A, Fifth Battalion, Minnesota Home Guard, *42-43, 104*; base of operations, 44; escort draftees, 102; makeup of membership, 44; mobilized, 91, 170n241; organized labor upset about, 43; patrol Red Wing streets, 91; roster, *141-2*; sent to St. Paul to restore order, 43-44

Company D, *32*; called up, 33; deployment to Europe, 34; deployment to Mexican border, 34; sendoff to Europe, 34; return, 161n82; Spanish-American War, 33

Company G, Spanish-American War, 33-34

Company L, *31*; called up, 33-34; deployment to Europe, 34, *134, 135*; deployment to Mexican border, 34; sendoff to Europe, 34, *35*

Congress, establishes Selective Service System, 44

Converse, Willard L. (judge), announce jury sequestration, 128; has grand jury investigate Breidal case, 78; limit number of defense witnesses, 79; prejudicial error, 111; preside over Randall trial, 77, 78, 79

Cornwell, Leon L., interrogate bond slackers, 75; member of Liberty Loan executive committee, 68, *69*

Creel, George, 132; CPI member, 79; get newspapers into war effort, 127; idea for Four Minute Man concept, 79

Creel Committee, 67. *See also* Committee on Public Information.

–D–

Dana, C. S. (clerk of court), member of Commercial Club, 129

Davis, E. F. (Edgar F.), *30*; active in NPL, 30; advise voting for printed list of candidates, 95; editorial on Gates's actions, 64; 127; editorial regarding Breidal's removal from Kenyon, 51; links bond drive failure and NPL, 68; newspaper editor, 18, 30; views on pro-German remarks, 37

Davis, Thomas, 64; Farmer-Labor candidate, 106; NPL choice for lieutenant governor, 106; part of Gilbert's defense team, 106

Dean, Ezra C. (judge), *112*; conspiracy, 114; opposition to NPL, 112; prejudicial rulings, 114

Debs, Eugene V., in prison, 117; leader of American Socialist Party, 117; socialist candidate for president, 20, 21, 117

Degner, Carl, treasurer of Farmers Association, 40, 47; protest takeover of meeting, 40

Democratic Farmer Labor Party, 17; Stageberg resistance to merger, 172n296

Democratic Party, weakness of, 94, 126

Dennison (village), *x*, Lindbergh and Townley effigies in, 88

Department of Justice (U. S.), pursue radicalism, 117

Doely, Owen (doctor), Four Minute Men member, 79